You Don't Have To Be Gay

*Hope and freedom for males struggling
with homosexuality or for those who
know of someone who is*

Jeff Konrad

Pacific Publishing House
Hilo, Hawaii

Library of Congress Cataloging-in-Publication Data

Konrad, J. A., 1955-
    You don't have to be gay : hope and freedom for males struggling
with homosexuality, or for those who know of someone who is / Jeff
Konrad. -- Rev. ed.
        p.   cm.
    Includes bibliographical references and index.
     ISBN 0-942817-08-7 (pbk. : alk. paper) : $14.95
     1. Konrad, J. A., 1955---Correspondence.   2. Gay men--United
States--Correspondence. 3. Homosexuality, Male--United States.
4. Masculinity (Psychology)--United States.   I. Title.
HQ76.K65 1992
305.38'9664--dc20   92-17351
                                                                   CIP

ISBN 0-942817-08-7

FOR THE RECORD

This book is not an attack against those who have embraced homosexuality. If you are happy with your homosexual identity, *You Don't Have To Be Gay* is not for you.

The sole purpose of this book is to educate people about the root causes of homosexuality, to offer sound counsel on how a person struggling with homosexual feelings and desires can overcome them, and to help those who are not happy as homosexual to change their identity.

Extreme care was taken in considering the title for this book. It is not meant to be accusatory in any way. *You Don't Have To Be Gay* is a straightforward statement concerning homosexuality. It isn't, "You *shouldn't be* gay," but rather, if you really don't want to, "You *don't have to be* gay."

DEDICATION

*This book is dedicated
to my father for his inspiration,
encouragement, and support.*

*My deepest, most heartfelt love and
thanks goes to Maureen Dunn
for loving me through the
darkest days of my life.*

ACKNOWLEDGEMENTS

Special thanks and appreciation to:

Dr. Elizabeth Moberly for giving me a cognitive understanding of my feelings and the drive behind them;

Vernon W. Hunt III and *Robert E. Smith* for pulling me back from the edge and going beyond the call of friendship;

Larry and Faith Shelton for reaching out to me when I needed it most;

David E. Steege for loving me unconditionally into my new identity;

Anway Jones, *Brad Sargent* and *Rick Pettit* for volunteering their time in the editing of this revision, and for their encouragement and support of this work;

Vernon W. Hunt Jr., for making this book a reality;

To all my friends for loving and supporting me throughout this project...I love you all!

Do you wish you didn't have homosexual thoughts and desires? Driven to do things you never dreamed of doing? Dreading someone finding out your secret? Are you frustrated by your homosexual relationships? Tired of your lifestyle? Experiencing anxiety over being alone, or perhaps teetering on the edge of suicide?

I want you to know that I understand—I've been there. I know the pain, the loneliness and despair. I feel your hurt.

Because I've experienced both the "light" and "dark" sides of the gay life, I understand the ambivalent feelings you may have toward homosexuality. Speaking for myself, entering the gay community was the first time I ever experienced any form of acceptance or approval from other men. I finally believed that I fit in somewhere. I found people who shared and understood my feelings.

These underlying desires for acceptance and a sense of connection with other men are legitimate and should be fulfilled. However, homosexual behavior does not satisfy this inner drive. Indeed, involvement in the gay life, for most, brings only *momentary* gratification. The feelings of acceptance are short-lived. But understanding same-sex needs and fulfilling them in appropriate and healthy ways brings about *long-term* satisfaction.

You Don't Have To Be Gay comes out of my own prior struggles with homosexuality. It is my desire to help you understand the root causes of homosexuality and how to overcome a homosexual orientation. Despite what we hear from the media and the world at large, *your homosexual orientation can be changed*. I want you to know there is hope!

This book is based on a series of letters I wrote to a friend of mine named Mike. In an informal and personal way these letters clearly and simply explain what factors lead a man to view himself as homosexual, and what issues must be dealt with in overcoming it.

Homosexuality. What is it? Are people born this way? If not, how does a homosexual identity develop? How can a homosexual orientation be changed? These are just a few of the questions which will be addressed in the following pages. You will discover that a man of any age really doesn't have to be gay if he doesn't want to be.

"You don't have to be gay! Really!" Believe me, I understand your probable skepticism. I struggled with same-sex attraction for over 25 years. If I had discovered a book that stated change was possible, I probably would have dismissed it as being unrealistic, wishful thinking or just a book full of religious rhetoric.

Most homosexuals believe they have no say in their sexual orientation, that in fact they were born gay, because the roots to a homosexual identity originate in early childhood. Since some know they were "different" as far back as they can remember, it is understandable how they think they were born "that way."

I felt different for most of my childhood. As an adolescent I began to suspect I had homosexual tendencies. Whenever I would read books on psychology or sociology, I would immediately check the index to see if there was a heading for homosexuality. I was constantly on the lookout for possible clues into my feelings and attraction toward other guys, which I feared might be homosexual in nature. Most, if not all, of the books I read in my youth offered no answers or solutions.

Eventually, I acted out on those feelings and acquired a homosexual identity. I had a gay lover for approximately four years and experienced love for the first time ever in this relationship. We were truly in love, but something was still missing. The relationship wasn't enough for me. I continued searching for another man to satisfy my deepest needs and desires. I was looking for the perfect "Mr. Right."

I didn't seek help for some time because I thought it was impossible to change. I believed the myth "Once gay, always gay." Severe depression and dissatisfaction with my homosexual lifestyle— particularly my inherent insecurities and jealousies—brought me to an exhaustive study of homosexuality, more specifically, a study in the formation of gender identity.

I immersed myself in books, seminars and counseling. Then I sifted through all this information and discerned what was true and practical from what was purely theoretical and technical. As I applied this new understanding, I found the freedom I so desperately sought. It began with understanding the *root causes* and gaining insight into the *real problem.*

Through healthy introspection, I was able to pinpoint these root issues in order to deal with them one at a time. I discovered the barriers in my life that blocked proper fulfillment of legitimate same-sex needs. For instance, I was overly sensitive. I felt unlovable, inadequate, insecure and inhibited. My self-image, on a scale from one to ten, was on the negative side of zero! I also was lazy. I lacked any motivation to change and was afraid of trying.

Bringing these root issues to the surface, I began working through past hurts, misconceptions and my wrong responses. I no longer felt I was a helpless victim of past circumstances.

In the pages to follow you will not only discover that homosexuals are not born gay, but you will also begin to experience the tremendous freedom in knowing you have a choice.

I realize the word *choice* upsets a lot of individuals, so let me explain. First, I'm not saying you woke up one day and chose to be sexually attracted to other men. With the discrimination and pain that so often accompanies the homosexual, who in his right mind would choose to be gay?

What I am saying is that being gay is an acquired identity, an identity brought about through the misinterpretation of events and its subsequent responses. Many of my childhood experiences were beyond my control, but my responses were my own choices. An inappropriate response to a situation here, another one there— eventually they all added up to a distorted image of myself...and, for me, a homosexual identity.

Since homosexuality is an acquired identity, it makes sense that you can choose to change your identity. As adults we can choose to respond to things in a healthy and mature manner rather than reacting in childish and foolish ways. This book will show you that you do have a choice...a choice that can set you free from your inner turmoil and struggles.

"Once gay, always gay?" That is what I used to think. Not anymore. Finding the true causes of my homosexual orientation gave me the spark, the hope, I needed to find the real me and relieve my inner turmoil.

You Don't Have To Be Gay contains the understanding, wisdom and direction I used to change my homosexual identity. And I'm not just talking about behavior or surface stuff. I'm talking about deep-down change. I no longer have the feelings, desires, temptations, orientation, or identity of the past. I am convinced you can experience this also.

You may find this change hard to believe. But once you have grasped the concept of gender identity development, I trust you too will conclude that you don't have to be gay, and that you also can overcome your homosexual feelings and desires. I sincerely hope *You Don't Have To Be Gay* will provide that spark, that hope, to all who read it.

Join me and discover the causes of homosexuality and the ways to overcome them.

Jeff Konrad

MIKE'S FOREWORD

November 26, 1985

Dear Mike,

I just got your letter. You better not kill yourself, buddy. You've got to give me the chance to help. I honestly believe one of the reasons you're sharing your feelings with me is because you want someone to help you. Well, I'm someone who wants to do just that, so give me the chance.

You keep saying I wouldn't understand how you feel, Mike, but I do. I was there. How many times do I have to tell you that I know what it feels like to want to die, to really want to die? I was suicidal for years. All I wanted was to get this life over with. I felt like I didn't belong here on the planet, that I didn't fit in anywhere. Believing I'd been born gay and given desires I didn't want, hadn't chosen and couldn't refuse, I felt helplessly and hopelessly trapped. No choices, no options.

Until now, you, too, have believed you don't have any choice…but you do, just as I did. Do you want to be homosexual or not? Choice is just another word for decision and you're the only one who can make the decision to change. I know it's not easy, Mike. You feel like you're all alone without any help, but you're not. I want to help you.…

Jeff

"You better not kill yourself, buddy." Jeff's warning leapt off the opening page of his letter to me with the force of a roundhouse right, jolting me more than any physical punch could have. I assumed Jeff couldn't comprehend the pain I was in—the confusion and agony—

that he had no idea of the depth of my self-loathing and desperation. Suicide seemed the only escape from being the only me I knew—a homosexual, or, as one of my relatives had crudely put it, a "faggot."

"You better not kill yourself, buddy." Those six words kept echoing in my brain until they penetrated through all the layers of garbage I had carefully wrapped around the idea of ending it all. Suicide as escape? No, suicide was just the ugly act of killing myself.

For months Jeff had been trying to make me see that an escape from the nightmare of homosexuality lay in terminating its hold on my life. I had to break old patterns of thought and behavior by coming to grips with their root causes. He freely admitted it wasn't an easy thing to do, but he stressed the fact that it could be done—providing I put in some honest effort. He was living proof that it was possible.

"You better not kill yourself, buddy." This time it finally hit me. In spite of my seeming desperation to die, the truth was that I so very much wanted to have what he possessed—a life worth living.

That letter marked the turning point for me. Until then, I had been resolutely paving my own way downhill by ignoring the help Jeff repeatedly offered while increasingly exploiting his faithful friendship. He shared facts with the power to change my life and even provided documentation. But they were revelations of such magnitude that I couldn't begin coping with them. It would have meant changing all my beliefs about myself and I wasn't about to do that—to start questioning my perception of who I was. After all, my identity was all I had.

He suggested certain courses of action, simple things like reading specific books and making new acquaintances outside the homosexual milieu. I dismissed these ideas because they required too much effort. Though he had given me an enormous amount of his time, energy, and compassion, I abused his dogged loyalty with arguments, whining lamentations, and excuses without end. Nonetheless, he hung in there, always keeping his hand extended in nonjudgmental love and concern. Ultimately, at the end of November 1985, his hand pulled me back from the brink.

How did he do it? Through the powers of compassionate love and prayer. More than that, what convinced me to try to change the course of my life was the sheer strength of Jeff's conviction that anyone who truly wanted to become emotionally free and whole to begin a new life could do so in the same manner he had.

"You don't have to be gay," he said, and at last I accepted the challenge. Today, I have validated his conviction. I don't have to be gay and you don't have to be, either. That's the simple truth.

However, when I wrote Jeff about my desire to end my life, I believed I was a 24-year-old born loser. I believed I had average looks, average intelligence, and came from an average social and economic background. I felt I had only one outstanding characteristic—I was homosexual. No one who passed me on the street would be aware of this flaw, of course. I wasn't limp-wristed; I didn't wear dresses. The worst impression I might have made with a stranger was that I looked slightly under-weight and completely unappealing in all other regards. My features were normal—brown eyes, brown hair, average height.

Socially, I appeared to be able to interact with other human beings in an acceptable way, even with women. My view toward women was certainly positive. I just didn't relate to them sexually. My straight friends would have described me as easy-going, perhaps a trifle shy, but possessing a good sense of humor and always dependable even when the chips were down. It would have never occurred to them that they really knew nothing about me. Still, none of that explained why I began looking in the mirror and screaming, "Why me, God? Why me?"

I couldn't remember a time when I hadn't felt "different." When I was very young I fantasized that I arrived on my parents' doorstep in a basket; it was the only way I could justify my complete lack of anything in common with them. I was emotional; my parents were stoic. My hair and eyes were brown; my mother's were raven and my father upheld the Aryan standard of blonde over blue—ice-blue, in his case. Later these childish doubts about my parentage were reinforced, somewhat ridiculously, I admit, when I couldn't break 5'9" in contrast to my father's solid 6'2".

Physical appearance aside, the most difficult challenge to growing up in my father's house was my role as his only son. All his hopes, and certainly all his fears, came to rest squarely upon my shoulders, and not one day passed that I wasn't somehow reminded of my obligation. My mother wanted me to be restrained and cautious. But my father wanted me to be like him—bold, quick-thinking, strong, confident, successful at all the so-called manly arts. Regrettably, confidence was the least quality I possessed, as might be expected, since I was always being called on to compete with him—and always lost the match.

I never really had any close friends. Unfortunately, I wouldn't let myself get close to my peers. I saw how cruel they could sometimes be to one another and I was terrified of ever becoming one of their victims. Throughout childhood I felt always on the edge. My only confidants were my older sisters. I appreciated their devotion, but they were not exactly the greatest role models for someone trying to follow in his father's footsteps.

The first clue I had that I might be more than just different surfaced when I went on an unfortunate hunting trip with my father the autumn I was thirteen. I hadn't really thought about the ramifications of hunting because I only viewed the outing as an opportunity to spend some time in my father's company, doing something he liked. The whole undertaking blew sky-high when he shot down a pheasant. My stomach turned as I watched the lifeless form plummet to earth. When it hit the ground with a soft, sickening thud, I vomited on the bile that had risen in my throat. My father was incredulous and ordered me to retrieve the bird while he reloaded his gun. I couldn't do it. His incredulity turned to fury and I believed he might actually turn his gun on me. Instead, he shot out the word "fairy."

Maybe I had denied my homosexual feelings before, but I doubt it, for I hadn't really gotten far enough into puberty to reach the stage of taking on any true sexual orientation. All I know is that from that day forward my father's accusation never left me.

After that incident there was truly no pleasing my father, and I no longer desired to do so except as a means of avoiding his full attention. In my confusion and guilt (I had let him down) I saw his angry epithet as a prophecy. I thought he knew something I hadn't known, that he recognized my imperfection for what it was even before I did.

When I entered high school the following year, he made sure I took all the shop courses and my mother made sure he didn't push me to go out for sports. She needn't have worried; it was clear he thought I was too much of a sissy to take up anything rough-and-tumble.

True loneliness set in during my high school years. Everyone else was either in a clique or a twosome; I was, as always, an odd man out. Everyone else had a good buddy or two; I didn't even have a dog anymore. When one of my sisters was found to be allergic to animals, my father got rid of my old cocker spaniel, Rex. I couldn't help thinking if I were only the young man my father wanted me to be, some other arrangement might have been made for Rex.

I don't remember much about my classes; to me academia was nothing more than a way of passing time. What made a vivid impression on me—scared me horribly, in fact—was the realization of my strong attraction to some of the guys, and as my hormone levels increased, the attraction became more physical. The other guys seemed to have everything I had always longed for. My need to be near them, to have some of their casual "macho-ness" rub off on me, was unbearable. I got through those four years without having a nervous breakdown, but I'll never know how.

After high school my parents expected me to go to college. Frankly, I would have gone anywhere, even into the Army, as long as it meant finally getting away on my own. I hadn't been at school two weeks before I had my first homosexual encounter. It was weird, exciting, a relief, and a painful affirmation of my "true" orientation. It was also a one-night stand. After all those years of acute loneliness, I felt driven to find someone with whom I could share an actual relationship. Fairly soon afterward, I took up with a guy who stayed in my life for the next two years. After him came Reed.

Reed had it all together: looks, clothes, car, career, everything. I'd never seen anyone so perfect in every way, except possibly my father. Unlike my dad, however, Reed possessed no affectation suggesting I had to compete on his level in order for him to like and respect me. I couldn't believe he was attracted to me; nothing in my life had prepared me for that sort of amazingly good fortune. Shortly after I met him, he accepted a job offer in San Francisco and asked me to move with him. I left southern California without a backward glance, overjoyed that of all the friends he had, I was the one he wanted with him most often.

A couple of years later I happened to run into Jeff at the Los Angeles International Airport. He was on his way to Hawaii for the summer and I was running away from another ugly scene with Reed, the latest in a long series. I knew the end had already begun for us; beyond that, I didn't know if there was going to be a tomorrow. Jeff seemed genuinely pleased to see me. I was intrigued by the indefinable way in which he'd somehow changed from the last time I had seen him, which was at one of Reed's parties. In the ten minutes we had together before he was called to his boarding gate, he completely overwhelmed me, first, with a short update on his life—he was no longer gay, even though I'd known him as half of a seemingly solid couple—and second, his instant recognition of the emotional state I was in.

"You look so happy," I said, "so fulfilled. How could you have gone through such radical changes without going right over the edge?"

"It's a long story," he replied, "and not as important as the fact that you look like you're the one who's about to go over the edge. What's wrong?"

"Another long story," I said. "I'm just about at the end of my rope, but that's nothing new, at least not for me."

"Mike, you're always going to be twisting at the end of that rope if you don't turn around and allow God to help you transform it into a lifeline. I know—I've been there and back."

"You haven't been where I've been," I argued. "You got out, man, but I'm stuck here until the day I die."

"You're wrong, and what's more, I can prove it," Jeff insisted. "I can tell you things..."

"Don't you understand, Jeff? It's too late for me! Way too late. I'm happy for you, but whatever worked for you just isn't going to work for me. I've been trapped since the day I was born."

Jeff smiled. "Listen, I'd like to write you from Hawaii and tell you a little about what happened with me. Will you read what I've got to say?"

"It's your stamp."

"Will you write back?"
"Yeah, sure. What are friends for?"

Michael G.

Dear Mike,

Hawaii is beautiful! Arrived in Lihue at 10:20 a.m. (1:20 p.m. California time) and was welcomed by a downpour that lasted just long enough to fully drench all of us trying to make our way from the plane to the terminal. Lihue really isn't very big—I think a sign said the population is 4000-something—yet it's the largest town on the island. That should give you some idea of how remote this place is. But guess what, they have a McDonald's here! Went looking for a cheap motel and found "cheap" meant only by appearance, not price. So I made a quick decision to live it up my first day here and checked in at the Kauai Surf Hotel.

Mike, you'd love it here on Kauai. It's about 80 degrees and I'm sitting next to a pool overlooking Nawiliwili Harbor, chief port of the island. Just ordered lunch from a cute little Polynesian girl, or was she Japanese...who knows? All I'm sure of is that a sandwich costs almost eight bucks! Such is life in Hawaii, at least for today. I have enough money to last me a little while, but I'll have to find a job pretty soon if I want to stay all summer.

I'm going down to Nawiliwili first thing in the morning to pick up my car. I know it sounds extravagant, but I was advised it would be cheaper to ship it out than to sell it at a loss in California and buy another here. Not to mention that when it's time to come home I can sell it for big bucks and recoup the shipping cost. So what the heck. It's supposed to have arrived here two weeks ago. I'll let you know tomorrow if it's still in one piece and already "gone native"—you know, wearing a lei on the steering column and all. After I pick it up I've got to get serious about finding a place to live, though. I bought a local paper so I can check the classifieds later this evening.

Still can't believe I actually ran into you at LAX this morning, especially after all this while. I mean, two and a half years is a long time for you to vanish without a trace when you haven't been busy robbing banks or something like that beforehand. Guess I have the typical Southern California attitude about San Francisco being a small town. During the flight over I kept thinking how strange it was that I spent a week up there last year and didn't see you anywhere.

Anyway, like I told you, Brian and I broke up in the winter of 1984, about a month after you disappeared. Strangely enough, another chance meeting similar to ours—this one involving an old high-school friend named Wayne—brought it about.

I passed right by without recognizing him (which indicates how much his appearance had changed, not early senility on my part), then he called out my name. If it hadn't been for his voice I don't think I would have known him. When I told him that, he laughed and said he had another surprise for me: he'd recently gotten married—to a woman! I was flabbergasted; all I could think was that it must be one of those "marriages of convenience."

Fortunately, however, I managed to refrain from saying so, but only by rather tactlessly demanding to know what in the world had come over him. His simple reply was that he was no longer gay. I didn't believe that for an instant, but you know me and my insatiable curiosity—I just had to get to the bottom of the whole thing. All in all we must have talked for six hours, throughout which I kept drilling him with question after question, trying to trip him up, find fault with his claims and the rationale behind them. To my utter amazement, though, I couldn't do it. In fact, the more Wayne told me the more I was convinced that he had truly stumbled onto something.

He credited all the positive changes in his life to a group of ex-gays down in Laguna Beach (of all places) and said if I wanted to go check it out he'd be glad to go along. Believe me, that first night I was such a nervous wreck I wouldn't have gone anywhere near Laguna Beach if it hadn't been for Wayne sort of propping me up and assuring me he'd stick to me like glue.

Well, to make a long story short, that first meeting just blew me away and for the next year I didn't miss a session. I mean, if it was Tuesday or Friday night, ol' Jeff was already spoken for. They talked all about going straight—how it was possible and how to do it. And these guys really supported me through all my initial doubts and questions.

Meanwhile, during that entire time, and despite countless invitations, Brian refused to go even once, although he always wanted to hear absolutely everything about what was addressed. After I had been attending the meetings for four or five months, we independently concluded that we really would much rather be straight and determined to try our level best to make a go of it.

To say breaking up was the hardest, the most painful and difficult thing I've ever done is an understatement. We both thought we could handle our separation, especially since we had talked about it for weeks beforehand. But when it finally happened it was almost unreal. I won't get into it right now, but suffice to say, we both went through some pretty dark days, and not always with flying colors. That's the downside, though, and the important thing is that it was worth every moment. I'm honestly the happiest I've ever been and that's far in excess of anything I ever imagined.

I'll write more tomorrow. Just wanted to let you know I made it here safely and say how good it was to see you again.

Until then, aloha,

Jeff

P.S.
Will send you an address as soon as I get one.

▸

23

Dear Mike,

Have you ever had one of those days you wish had never started? Today was sure one of them for me. Got up this morning and drove down to the Matson terminal to pick up my car, but—you guessed it—it wasn't there. The ship has been delayed for some reason or another in Honolulu and isn't expected until Thursday. Yeah, I was definitely a little peeved, especially since I'd been guaranteed in Long Beach that at the very latest it would be here by last Monday. I calmed down considerably, though, when I learned I'd be reimbursed for renting a set of wheels. Too bad I didn't take a so-called luxury car, huh?

Anyway, following that, I called some of the rentals listed in the paper, nine of which sounded good enough to investigate further. I then spent the entire day driving all over the island for nada. Most of the places were total dives.

Rounding things out, the weather has been the pits. Yesterday it rained no more than five minutes and then turned clear and sunny. Today it rained all day long. Everyone I've talked to says this is quite normal so I hope I get in step with it before long. On the way back to the hotel I stopped at that McDonald's I told you about. The rain and my disappointments really took the starch out of me, so I was glad to fall asleep around 7:30. Trouble is, I woke up at 11 and now the sandman is apparently off duty for a while. Oh, well. Hope it makes you feel special to know that I decided to write you instead of watching the boob tube. You rate over TV, buddy!

I know I've been complaining (please forgive an old friend), but actually, deep down inside I know things are going to work out for the best. They always do. I just have to be patient. That's been one of life's Big Lessons for me—and I still need to consciously summon it to mind on a daily basis.

I've been thinking a lot about our much-too-brief conversation yesterday and your reaction to hearing I'm no longer gay. Plainly,

25

you were curious, but beyond that I sensed a kind of hunger to know the how's and why's of my turnaround. Yes, I know what you said, but all the while we were standing there I seemed to see this person behind your eyes frantically trying to break through, looking for a reason to hope.

Now don't shut me off yet. Listen to me first, okay? If you had come up to me a few years ago and said what I just did, I probably wouldn't have believed a word you were saying, either. At face value, anyway. I mean, I thought I was doing okay, neither terribly happy nor terribly unhappy. I was in love at least, and I was loved in return. Brian and I had our disagreements, but life was going on, so what else did I need?

Wayne, however, made me take a look at my life from a broader view, whereas before I'd been seeing it with tunnel vision, the tunnel being my presumption that I'd been born gay, that I had no choice other than being gay. When Wayne caused me see beyond the little box I had cornered my life in, I realized for the first time the frustration, the hidden insecurities, the intense loneliness and despair I was truly feeling. It probably shouldn't have surprised me, but somehow it did, to discover also a great deal of anger. Anger at being something not "normal" or "right" by society's standards. Anger at society for making me feel different, making me an outcast. Anger at having to hide my feelings throughout most of my life.

Here's the kicker, though. The very same things that contributed to my homosexual identity were keeping me in bondage to all those negative feelings. Once I was freed from homosexuality, I found a huge transformation taking place in my whole personality. Where I used to be quite shy, I'm now nearly a certified extrovert. Where there was once massive insecurity about absolutely everything, there's now true confidence. I can't tell you in simple words exactly how good I feel, but *fantastic* isn't bad as a one-word description.

So how about doing me a favor? Like right now, this very instant. Take an honest look at yourself and your lifestyle. Get underneath your current depression and see yourself when you're not in Blues City. Do you see any real happiness there, any lasting sense of worth or security or love? Are you satisfied? It's possible that your depression is merely symptomatic of a greater pain. I guarantee you, though, that there is hope, that it is possible to change all these things. You don't have to be gay, Mike.

If you're interested in hearing more, I'd count it a privilege to share what I've learned with you. Remember, I've personally experienced all the things I will tell you. It's up to you, though, buddy. If you're not interested, I promise I'll shut up about it.

Since I haven't found a place yet, needless to say I still don't have an address. I'll keep you posted on how the house-hunting goes.

Your long-lost friend,

Jeff

Dear Mike,

Wow, what an incredibly busy week. Tuesday and Wednesday went pretty much the same as Monday. I was beginning to wonder what the heck I was doing here. But I hung in and sure enough the weather cleared up so at least I got to enjoy the scenery while driving around looking for a place to live. And now the good news: I found one!

Yesterday, while checking out a few more prospects, I stopped to get some gas. Now dig this, I'm standing there at the pump and this guy drives up in a car with California plates. I strike up a conversation with him and it turns out he needs a roommate! For some reason the thought of sharing a place with someone had never entered my mind. Anyway, he was on his way home, so he asked me if I wanted to follow him and look the place over. Then he added that it was out toward the end of the road, in some place called Haena. No sweat, I thought, not realizing that by "end of the road" he really meant, end of the road. You see, Kauai is basically round and has only one major road, which isn't continuous because of a mountain range (think of it as a donut with a piece bitten out of the top). I wound up following this guy to nowheresville, about a 45-minute drive from where we'd started in Kapaa.

Check this out—we get to his place and it's built on top of poles! Nonetheless, it's a beautifully decorated three-bedroom, two-bath house, fully furnished. The only drawback is its location way out in the boonies, since I need to find a job. I mention this small concern and he says it's been a major problem for him in the past because nobody wants to live that far out. But get this. Ray, that's the guy's name, works at a market only 15 minutes away and a girl there is leaving in three weeks to go back to Oregon. When I tell him I once worked as a supermarket cashier, he says that since he has to be at work at six o'clock, why don't I follow him down to the store and he'll introduce me to his boss. Would you believe it? I got the job starting in two weeks!

I'm stoked! Especially since I picked up my car this morning before moving my stuff out to Ray's. Can't tell you how good it feels to have my own wheels back. It was a little dirty but that's it, no scratches or dents. No leis either for that matter.

This will sound funny, but there isn't any mail service here, at least not this far out from town. The closest post office is in Hanalei (about 20 minutes from here), but when I went there to get a P.O. box, they didn't have one available, so I've had to put my name on the waiting list. In the interim, I'll be driving to Kapaa to get my mail, but I'm not complaining—it beats slogging all the way back to Lihue.

Write soon, okay? Use the return address on the envelope. Take care, buddy.

Your Hawaiian connection,

Jeff

Hi Mike,

For five straight days I hauled out to Kapaa just to check my mailbox. First, I'd look through the little window to see if anything was there and every day it was the same story: nada. But just to make sure I'd turn the combination to the right, then left, then back to the right, and open the door. Still nothing. Today, however, your letter was sitting in there, my very first. Thanks for beating out my first "junk mail" and/or stuff for the former boxholder!

Nope, I'm not working yet. June 1 is the big day and I'll be training for a week before Linda leaves. Shouldn't be any problems, it looks pretty basic.

Ray is proving to be such a terrific housemate; it's hard to think of him as my landlord, too. He's about my height, 5'10"-5'11", blonde hair and very tan. Ray's here mainly to surf. He works nights, but only four-hour shifts, so he can be free during the day, lucky dude. Since I'll be on mornings we won't be working together, which is probably just as well. Working and living with the same person could be a bit too much.

The house is set on phone poles because Haena is in the lowlands and tsunami tidal waves hit the island about every 11 years or so. Actually, the place belongs to Ray's parents who live in Newport Beach where his dad is some sort of big wheel in international trade. Normally they summer over here, but at the moment they're living in Hong Kong for a year. Nice little change of pace, wouldn't you say?

Ray's been showing me some of Kauai's hot spots. Yesterday after church, for instance, we went to Waimea Canyon, which just knocked me out. Imagine finding the Grand Canyon, with all its fantastic colors and hues, on an island in the Pacific. I'm amazed at how diversified this place is. One minute you can be someplace that looks like your typical Hawaiian postcard, then 15 minutes later you can be in a desert-like environment, and half an hour after that you can be in the midst of pine-covered mountains.

Saturday night Ray invited a bunch of his friends over to meet me and have a barbecue. Nice people. Most of them live out here on the north shore, but Ray's girlfriend, Pam—really cute—lives in Kilauea, about 25 minutes from here, and works as a waitress in Hanalei. Funny how there's this dichotomy here, just like in California, between people who won't drive any farther than they have to and those who really don't care. Want to hazard a guess as to which category I'm in?

It's really hard to believe how well things have worked out. I mean, my room is furnished to the max—I've even got a desk to work on my book (changing a homosexual orientation). Now that I'm settled I hope to get a lot accomplished on it, but you're right, my dedication to this project is probably going to be severely tested at times by the prevailing Polynesian ambiance.

I'm really glad you decided you wanted to hear more about my "big U-turn on the highway of life." Trouble is, there's so much to tell you that it's hard to know just where to begin. Guess the first thing I want to convey to you is hope and to do that I feel I've got to reiterate that you, too, have the ability within yourself to change your way of life, whether you feel like you do or not. If I could do it anybody can—and that even includes self-proclaimed hard cases like you, Mike.

Some things I've got to share with you are actually going to make your heart leap with excitement, which sounds hokey, I know, but I can't think of how else to express it. I absolutely guarantee you, though, that something inside will click when you begin to absorb these things and comprehend the truth of what I'm saying.

Generally speaking, I think most gays believe their homosexuality was caused by early environmental factors or that they simply had the misfortune of being born gay instead of straight. Either way, the end belief is that homosexuality is a fate over which the individual has no control, never having had a choice. I emphatically held that mistaken view. For as long as I could remember I had homosexual "tendencies," so my conclusion was that I'd been born homosexual. The fantastic thing, however, is that nobody's born that way, Mike, and that's why it's possible to change. It isn't a fate that's engraved in stone.

Here are a few quotes from some of the most widely recognized authorities on the subject of homosexuality. The first is by Dr. Reuben Fine, Director for the New York Center for Psychoanalytic Training. Dr. Fine stated in *Psychoanalytic Theory, Male and Female Homosexuality: Psychological Approaches*:

> I have recently had occasion to review the result of psychotherapy with homosexuals, and been surprised by the findings. It is paradoxical that even though politically active homosexual groups deny the possibility of change, all studies from Schrenck-Notzing on[ward] have found positive effects, virtually regardless of the kind of treatment used...a considerable percentage of overt homosexuals became heterosexual. ...The misinformation spread by certain circles that "homosexuality is untreatable by psychotherapy" does incalculable harm to thousands of men and women.

Dr. Edmund Bergler, in his book, *Homosexuality: Disease or Way of Life?*, said:

> The homosexual's real enemy is...his ignorance of the possibility that he can be helped.

And Dr. Irving Bieber and his colleagues concluded:

> The therapeutic results of our study provide reason for an optimistic outlook. Many homosexuals became exclusively heterosexual in psychoanalytic treatment. Although this change may be more easily accomplished by some than others, in our judgment, a heterosexual shift is a possibility for all homosexuals who are strongly motivated to change.

Seventeen years later, Bieber stated:

We have followed some patients for as long as ten years who have remained exclusively heterosexual.

Dr. Lawrence J. Hatterer writes in, *Changing Homosexuality in the Male*:

I've heard of hundreds of other men who went from a homosexual to a heterosexual adjustment on their own.

And Dr. Charles W. Socarides, of the Albert Einstein College of Medicine in New York, says in the *American Handbook of Psychiatry*, in his text, "Homosexuality:"

The major challenge in treating homosexuality from the point of view of the patient's resistance has, of course, been the misconception that the disorder is innate or inborn.

Here's fact number one, Mike: *homosexuality isn't an innate sexual problem, but one of gender identity.* You see, in order to change, to gain real, lasting freedom from your homosexual desires, you must first ascertain their origin, the actual "roots" of your homosexuality. It's imperative then that you understand your sexual orientation isn't caused by hormonal imbalances, or genetic or chromosomal abnormalities. Homosexuality is but a symptom—just a symptom!—of a confused, distorted, unaffirmed gender identity, of a disturbed personality which hasn't yet reached its maturity due to unresolved emotional turmoil and needs left unmet in the course of growing up.

Pretty heavy statement, isn't it? Almost insulting in fact. Nevertheless it's true. Every homosexual suffers in varying degrees from a gender identity crisis. So what do I mean by gender identity? Well, it's like this. Physiological sex identification is obvious—a person has either a penis or a vagina. But gender identity is our identification with our own sex, our sense of maleness (or lack thereof), and what we perceive to be masculine and feminine. Quite apart from anything physical, it's the perception we have of ourselves as being a male or a female, or something in between.

We know that biological differences between males and females are determined at conception. Gender identity, on the other hand, is a process that begins at birth. As children begin to explore and understand their own bodies, they combine this information with the way society treats them to create an image of themselves as boys and girls.

The crucial point here is *how we view ourselves*, for the breeding ground of homosexuality is a profound feeling of masculine inadequacy caused by the lack of being affirmed in our male gender identity.

Now, when I say you have feelings of masculine inadequacy, I don't mean you see yourself as a "fem," although obviously for some gays that's the case. There's a rather considerable difference between feeling inadequate as a male and feeling feminine. Stop and think for a minute. I'll bet you felt different from others while you were growing up, somehow less of a boy than the rest. Those feelings still exist in your life, whether you're aware of them or not, and this is part of what your homosexual drive is all about. There's a lot more to say on this particular aspect of the topic, but for now let's concentrate on gender identity and how it evolves.

Research clearly shows that who we are, how we think and behave, is a process of learning and living in the environment in which we're reared. You can pick up almost any book on human development, psychology, sociology, etc., and see for yourself how environment plays a major role in our development.

For example, in James Vander Zanden's *Human Development*, he says:

> Social-learning theorists take the view that children are essentially neutral at birth and that the biological differences between boys and girls are insufficient to account for later differences in gender identities. They stress the part that selective reinforcement and imitation play in the process of acquiring a gender identity. Viewed from this perspective, children reared in normal family settings are rewarded for modeling the behavior of the same-sex parent. And the larger society later reinforces this type of imitation through system-

atic rewards and punishments. Boys and girls are actively rewarded and praised, both by adults and by their peers, for what society perceives to be sex-appropriate behavior, and they are ridiculed and punished for behavior inappropriate to their sex.

He goes on to say:

Still another approach, which is identified with Lawrence Kohlberg, focuses upon the part that cognitive development plays in children's acquisition of gender identities. This theory claims that children first learn to label themselves as males or females and then attempt to acquire and master the behaviors that fit their gender category.

Vander Zanden also cites a striking example of how greatly the effects of environment can influence gender identity:

John Money has conducted research with hermaphrodites [individuals with a combination of male and female sexual organs] which reveals the crucial part that social definitions play in influencing a child's gender identity. One of his most dramatic case histories is that of the identical-twin boy whose penis was cauterized during circumcision. When the child was 17 months old, his parents decided in consultation with medical authorities that he should be raised as a girl. Surgical reconstruction was undertaken to make him a female. Since then, the child has successfully developed a female gender identification. Although the child was the dominant twin in infancy, by the time the twins were four years old there was little doubt about which twin was the girl and which the boy.

...On the basis of his research with hermaphrodites, Money concludes that the most powerful factors in the shaping of gender identity are environmental. "You were wired but not programmed for gender in the same sense that you were wired but not programmed for language."

Doesn't that all make incredible sense, Mike? Okay, so that brings us to this: what went wrong for the boy who grew up to be homosexual? What childhood experiences could have had such damaging effects on his gender identity? You're going to have to look into your past, as I did, to understand who you are and why you behave as you do.

All of us, gay and straight alike, are products of the environment in which we're reared. Our parents' attitudes, our home life, our relationships with others or, sometimes more importantly, lack of them, and even our perception of these events all contribute to the composition of who we become. More importantly, how we respond to any given situation today is frequently an unconscious, learned behavioral reaction from our past.

The purpose in digging for the roots of your homosexuality is to obtain insight into the formation of your thoughts. Specifically, it's not to relive painful memories but to discover how you think and feel about yourself and how this has affected the growth of your sexual identity. It is essential to discover how you acquired a homosexual identity because freedom from it and related compulsive behaviors will come only when you recognize and begin to deal with these early "root experiences."

It's time to get some sleep, so I'll wrap this up for now with the suggestion that you try concentrating on your *present* feelings and attitudes, looking for links to your past in them. I'm sure you'll find more than one or two key things that just might have affected your current identity. Let me know what you come up with, okay?

Until then,

Jeff

Dear Mike,

This place is really growing on me—despite the almost daily rainfall. Apparently, those of us on the north shore are favored with just a bit more precipitation than the rest of the island, but to make up for it everything out this way is terrifically lush and green. I'm convinced this is paradise.

Since we all had the day off Ray's girlfriend, Pam, came over this morning and the three of us drove to Ke'e Beach at the very end of the road. From there we hiked about two miles along the Na Pali coast to reach a really beautiful, secluded beach called Hanakapiai. "Secluded" in this case means that the only way to get there is by foot along the cliffs, the way we did, or by boat or helicopter.

No one else was there when we arrived and I got some inkling of what it must be like to be on a truly uninhabited island, particularly after Ray and Pam wandered off to see some waterfalls. I elected to stay behind on the beach, which turned out to be an excellent decision because they returned a couple of hours later covered with mosquito bites. (Maybe this isn't quite paradise after all.) In spite of their involuntary blood donations, we had a super day. The three of us get along really well together and always seem to be laughing, usually at Ray's instigation.

And so another peaceful evening arrives. Because of the mountain range we can't pick up any radio or TV signals, and there's no cable out here either. Nights are usually spent reading and listening to music, a pleasant routine custom-tailored for doing research on my book. Since Pam and Ray are in the living room playing a rather hotly disputed game of backgammon, I've decided it's okay for me to take the night off, too.

So, buddy, have you given any thought to my suggestion about trying to pinpoint a few of the factors contributing to your gay identity? I hope you have, but as I mentioned, it's imperative that you first recognize your condition is only a symptom of the real problem, not the problem itself. For far too long everyone has focused on homosexuality strictly as a sexual malfunction, an incurable disease. However, once you accept the viewpoint that homosexual behavior is just a *symptom* of impaired gender identity, you can see how it's possible to change that behavior. I mean, it's only logical that in order to solve a problem, it's necessary to know what that problem is. Once the problem is known it is much easier to find the solution.

Look at it this way, Mike. Think of homosexuality as you would the symptoms of a runny nose, sore throat, or congestion that accompany the common cold. There are plenty of symptomatic-relief remedies, but the cold itself lives on; no cure has yet been discovered for it. However, if you found the cure, you'd put an end not only to the aforementioned symptoms, but to the ailment itself. Don't get hung up in the analogy, just try to see my point because the same principle applies to homosexuality. If you get to the root problem (impaired gender identity) and deal with it, the symptom (homosexuality) will be eliminated.

This brings us back to the question of how someone acquires a gay identity—or better yet, how do you go about rectifying the situation and acquiring a strong, secure, valid gender identity? Have patience, because that's what we're going to tackle over my next few letters.

Before I continue, though, I need to set a couple of things straight. (No pun intended!) I can't possibly teach you all that I've learned, nor is that my intention. What I can do is give you an overview and steer you toward some of the proper sources where you can learn more on your own. If I'm not clear about something, just let me know and I'll try to clarify it. However, for complete documentation of what I'm saying or further detail, you're going to have to go to those sources yourself. I can't encourage you strongly enough to dig further. It's exciting, Mike, and more than that, investigating things for yourself and arriving at your own conclusions really makes a lot more sense than simply relying on someone else's say-so.

Go to the library, read some of the materials there on gender roles and identity, and I guarantee you'll acquire a sense of things falling into place. The reason I say to look for material on gender is because in my own quest for knowledge (or even clues), I used to pick up likely-looking books about, say, psychology, and immediately check the index to see if homosexuality rated its own heading. Frequently I was disappointed, but now I know better. When you start checking indexes for gender identity and/or roles (the part we're expected to take in society based on our gender), you'll be amazed at what a widely covered topic it is.

Speaking of reading, yesterday I found a fairly informative book called *Adolescent Psychology: A Developmental View* at the Kauai Community College library. Written by Norman A. Sprinthall and W. Andrew Collins, it elaborates on the effects of family in developing gender identification:

> Rightly or wrongly, the family has always been assumed to have major responsibility for gender-role development. Although other forces like the mass media, teachers, and the peer group also play a role, it is in the family where the most intensive opportunities for learning the rudiments of maleness and femaleness occur....
>
> As with other aspects of identification, the family characteristics that affect gender role learning most are the parents' nurture and warmth. In particular, boys who perceive their fathers as nurturing and supportive...are likely to match the cultural expectations about male...behavior relatively well. Although gender role learning shows sometimes quite different patterns for males and females, the father's role seems to be pivotal in gender role learning for both. For example...boys develop a masculine gender role most effectively when fathers are perceived as strong, decisive individuals who take an active role in the socialization of their sons. Masculine gender-role development is least effective when fathers are passive and mothers are dominant...the father's influence seems to help sharpen the distinctions among children who best fit the cultural stereotypes and those who match them less well.

I don't know about you, but I wasn't really surprised to discover that our fathers play a significant part in how we eventually turn out.

Clinical studies confirm what had already been my personal observation, that the greatest single common denominator among gays was a poor relationship with their fathers. But what I found astonishing was the extremely vast sweep of paternal influence, negative and positive, in affecting children of both sexes.

In her book *Crisis in Masculinity*, Leanne Payne states:

> It is the father (or father-substitute) who affirms sons and daughters in their sexual identity and therefore—because gender identity is a vital part of personhood itself—as persons.

Going back again to Vander Zanden's book, *Human Development*:

> Evidence suggests that in American society it is the father who plays the critical role in encouraging "femininity" in females and "masculinity" in males as culturally defined within the United States....
>
> The father also appears to be the main parent who prods his boys toward culturally defined sex-appropriate behaviors. A correlation exists between fathers' nurturance and their boys' masculinity as traditionally defined. When fathers combine warmth and understanding with dominance and high participation in child care, they increase the likelihood of "masculinity" in their sons. In contrast, it appears that boys from mother-dominant homes show less tendency to imitate their fathers and less overall "masculinity."

Accepting that fathers are crucial to appropriate gender development and that impaired gender identity can lead to homosexuality, it's important next to know how impairment takes place. Social science has adopted a word from the world of finance that perfectly expresses what's wrong with many relationships, no matter who's involved in them. That word is *deficit*. Homosexuals experience a critical deficit in their relationships with their fathers while growing up, meaning that normal psychological needs which should be met by the father/son bond are left unfulfilled.

Dr. Elizabeth Moberly tells us in, *Homosexuality: A New Christian Ethic*:

> A homosexual orientation depends...on difficulties in the parent-child relationship, especially in the earlier years of life.... Amidst a welter of details, one constant underlying principle suggests itself: that the homosexual...has suffered from some deficit in the relationship with the parent of the same sex.

She then goes on to clarify:

> In speaking of a deficit, it must be stressed that this does not always imply willful maltreatment by the parent in question, as distinct from unintentional or accidental hurt. But in every case, it is postulated, something of a traumatic nature, whether ill-treatment, neglect, or sheer absence, has in these particular instances led to a disruption in the normal attachment.

It seems inarguable that a boy needs a role model—someone to admire and pattern his life after, someone to imitate, someone to reinforce and affirm his own masculine behavior—in short, an attachment to and identification with his father if he's to become a "well-adjusted" heterosexual male.

Fathers who fail to be this role model generally fit into one or more of the following categories:

(1) Absent - physically or emotionally absent, workaholic, uninvolved in family life, fails to take an active interest in family affairs;

(2) Inefficient - withdrawn, avoids responsibility, rarely takes leadership in the home, a wimp, emotionally absent and immature; and/or

(3) <u>Hostile</u> - physically or emotionally abusive, angry, demanding, tends to be alcoholic, often resents his wife and children, someone to avoid.

Still, it's not necessarily what kind of father these men are but how *their children react to them* that can cause psychological damage, perhaps simply by blocking normal attachment to them.

A word of caution seems in order here, Mike. I'm not saying your father is the cause of your homosexuality; the situation is more complex than that. But the poor father/son relationship is the one common denominator to be found among homosexuals. This factor could hardly fail to be otherwise when fathers are such a major component of their sons' identities.

Look at your relationship with your dad. How was it? How did he treat you? How did you respond to him? Think about it for a moment, Mike. How did you feel around him?

Now what about this matter of detachment? To better enable you to grasp what we're after here, it's necessary for you to disassociate the feelings you have for your father now and remember how you felt about him as a child. Seek out your earliest recollections of him.

I remember the stories you used to tell me, so I know that your father caused numerous problems and significant psychological harm by his constant belittling and ugly drinking binges. Your father was anything but supportive and warm; instead, he was highly critical of everything you did or tried to do. Nothing seemed to please him.

For some guys, it may be only one unintentional act of their fathers that causes sufficient trauma to unwittingly break the needed bond of attachment. Even divorce can be traumatic enough in its effect on a child to cause a disruption in the normal emotional ties.

According to Dr. Moberly:

> Any incident that happens to place a particular strain on the relationship between the child and the parent of the same sex is potentially causative.

Obviously, a hostile father or father-substitute—such as a stepfather, guardian, or influential male teacher—may create detachment. Ill-treatment from this type of father will make a child withdraw, to erect walls between himself and his dad, which in turn can effectively block any love the father might try to give.

And then there's the absent father. Sprinthall and Collins write:

> In families in which the father is not present, either because of death or because of divorce or desertion, we might expect some problems in sex-typing.... One study...compared the play behaviors of father-absent 9 to 12-year-old boys with the behaviors of a similar group from father-present homes. The father-absent boys were less oriented to contact sports, were less competitive, and were more dependent on other adults than the father-present boys were. Furthermore, the effect was more pronounced the longer fathers had been absent from the home.
>
> But not all boys in mother-only families have problems in gender role learning. For example, when there are other sources of male influence or when the mother herself specifically encourages and rewards her son's masculine activities, there are few differences between father-present and father-absent boys. By adolescence the majority of father-absent boys have probably found alternative ways to learn the basic elements of the masculine gender role—from peers, other adults, and the mass media.

My dad could have been classified as an absent father. As you know, he was a workaholic who was never home, and I have very few memories of him prior to my twelfth birthday. He was always at the office and consequently not available to offer me the identification I needed. Then, of course, when I was twelve I acquired an extremely hostile stepfather. Now I don't believe this alone was enough to cause my homosexuality. There were a whole raft of other factors that came into play, which I'll be shedding some light on in future letters.

The most significant factor is that homosexuals *perceive* their father's behavior as signifying a lack of love for them. Naturally, we were hurt and created defensive detachments (we withdrew) to prevent further hurt and feelings of rejection. We thereby blocked ourselves from relating normally to our fathers. Consciously or unconsciously, we became unwilling or unable to relate. This failure to relate, according to Moberly, implies "that psychological needs that are normally met through the child's attachment to the parent are left unfulfilled and still require fulfillment." She isn't claiming that your homosexual drive is an urge for a father-substitute, nor is it an unconscious attempt to have sex with your dad. Rather—and it's essential to understand this—she's making the point that you're seeking *fulfillment of needs* that should have been met earlier through your father/son relationship.

I need to clarify something. I stated that homosexuals detach from their fathers to prevent further hurt and/or not to identify with them. For some this may have been an unconscious, subtle detachment. But for others, it was an overt vow not to be anything like their father. The severity of this detachment varies from person to person and is more obvious in some than in others.

When some men look at their father/child relationship, they see nothing wrong or out of the ordinary with this relationship. No traumatic experiences. No ill-treatment or neglect. They see nothing that could have placed a particular strain on their relationship to cause detachment. In fact, they don't even see detachment. So what about them?

I would venture to say that for some of these men under careful inspection, they too would identify areas of detachment or indifference. However, it's important to realize that detachment doesn't need to occur for unmet same-sex needs to exist.

The father doesn't necessarily have to do something extremely negative. Perhaps a father wasn't able or just didn't take the necessary time to affirm his son's gender. Possibly all this boy needed was a little more encouragement from his dad, a greater push into his masculine role, or more involvement and interaction from his father.

Detachment or not, same-sex issues are at the root of the problem. Again, it's imperative to understand I'm not looking to blame someone. I simply want to show you the role of the father for instilling and affirming an appropriate sense of "maleness" in his son's gender identity. Hang in there. It will all come together later as I share more with you.

I know I've given you quite a bit to digest, Mike, but it should really help you see the correlation between the relationship you had with your dad as a child and its effect on your gender identity. Write soon; I'm eager to hear your response.

As always,

Jeff

Dear Mike,

Today must be my lucky day. There were six letters waiting for me at the post office and one of them was yours! Thanks, buddy, it was good to hear from you.

To begin, I want to comment on one of the things you said. Of course I realize that some straight guys also had bad relationships with their fathers, but remember I stipulated that it's not necessarily how the father acted—more importantly, it's how the child *responded* to him. The emphasis I placed on the father/son relationship wasn't meant to blame fathers as the cause of homosexuality; that's an undeserved bum rap. However, the father's role in influencing his offspring's identity has long been established; he is a pivotal factor in shaping his son's gender identity and gender role. While a messed-up gender identity is the major cause of homosexuality, many things contribute to that condition.

Eventually, Mike, you'll see that homosexuality is multi-faceted, deeply rooted and quite complex. Many things lead to a homosexual identity, but we'll deal with them one at a time, so don't get bogged down over any one concept. Some of these things you'll relate to instantly and others you won't. Wait for the overall picture to develop. I assure you that in time it will become clear how you acquired your current identity.

Next, please don't apologize for not accepting my every word right off the bat; playing devil's advocate will help prove my case. Come at me from all directions and ask as many questions as you like or can think of. I know the things I have told you are both answers and the path to the answers because they've worked for me and many, many others. And it's not just because this works that I believe in it; it's because it's true. It clicks. Something inside says, "Yes, this is it. This makes sense."

Your questions and comments are nearly a verbatim rerun of what I said to Wayne when he first began helping me. I had plenty of doubts, too. You don't need to agree with me on every point, but just stay open. Listen to what I'm saying and test things to see whether they're true. As time goes on, as you learn more, you'll see for yourself what's true and what isn't. I'm certain you'll ultimately discover, as I did, that your doubts come more from not seeing the whole picture than from any fundamental disagreement.

Let me tell you exactly my perspective, Mike. Homosexuality is so complex that if you jump at every little thing I say, that is, thinking it's either the answer or the cause, you're going to miss the whole point. What I'm trying to do now is give you a foundation, a basic understanding of how you became homosexually oriented. A cornerstone of this foundation is the knowledge that you weren't born gay—fact, not theory or opinion. Research, some of which I've cited in previous letters, has established that fact. If you're really skeptical, check it out.

I'm mainly reading research material, and I have discovered excellent books and articles showing that homosexuality results from emotional issues, not alleged biological causes such as hormonal or genetic. I'll refer you to them as I find them.

One such fact is from Tim LaHaye's book, *What Everyone Should Know About Homosexuality*:

> Scientists who have run extensive tests on male and female homosexuals have found their hormonal level to be the same as heterosexuals. After studying androsterone and the effects of estrogen therapy, two doctors writing in the *John Hopkins Medical Journal* reported that "when extremely effeminate males (homosexual or heterosexual) have been tested by these means, they have shown entirely normal hormone levels." Other tests have verified these findings, and some have uncovered an even higher ratio of male hormones in homosexuals than in heterosexuals. To date there is no scientific evidence to support the notion that homosexuality is inherited.

I don't think you want to go to the bother of digging up a copy of *Science*, specifically Volume 211, 20 March 1981, page 1316, so

I'll just give you this one little pertinent bit from "The Effect of Prenatal Sex Hormones on Gender-Related Behavior":

> The available data...suggest that sexual orientation mainly follows the sex rearing and identity, and therefore is based on social learning rather than hormones.

This is just an example of some of the studies that have been conducted to prove that homosexuality is not caused by biological factors. Other authorities reinforce this conclusion. Again, from LaHaye's book:

> Dr. Evelyn Hooker, famous for research on homosexuality, states, "There is no evidence that homosexuals have faulty hormone levels, or that their sexual orientation can be changed with hormone injections." Dr. Charles Wahl, a researcher in this field, adds, "The vast preponderance of evidence clearly indicates that homosexuality is a learned disorder and is not genetically inherited." On the basis of all known scientific data, it is safe to say that one's genetic and biological make-up does indeed determine his sex but not his sexual preference.

Dr. Charles W. Socarides, a psychiatrist who has written and spoken widely on homosexuality, writes in his article, "Homosexuality: Basic Concepts and Psychodynamics":

> Homosexuality, the choice of a partner of the same sex for orgastic satisfaction, is not innate. There is no connection between sexual instinct and the choice of sexual object. Such an object choice is learned, acquired behavior; there is no inevitable genetically inborn propensity toward the choice of a partner of either the same or opposite sex.

And Masters and Johnson, the most widely-known authorities in the field of human sexual behavior, state in one of their books, *Human Sexuality*:

The genetic theory of homosexuality has been generally discarded today.

It seems clear that the biological causation theory has been refuted. Unfortunately, there are people who want you to believe otherwise. I have heard different gay activists make statements such as, "Presently, there are studies being conducted in laboratory animals to prove homosexuality is innate."

They make it sound as if the mere fact that someone is conducting tests means that the conclusion they want—biological causes for the homosexual condition—are assured and it's only a matter of time before that fact is established. Of course, people who make such statements have their own personal or political agenda. They can't make their case for attaining "minority status" unless they have an inborn condition that can't be changed.

Sure, such studies are being conducted and have been for decades, but they won't change the truth. *There is absolutely no conclusive scientific evidence to prove that people are born gay. Homosexuals are no different, biologically or physically, from heterosexuals. You weren't born homosexual. That's a fact, not a theory.*

If homosexuality had been scientifically proven to be innate, don't you think this amazing discovery would have been on the covers of all the national news magazines? Furthermore, how would they explain all the people who have changed their homosexual orientation if indeed homosexuality was caused by biological factors? My genetic make-up hasn't changed, but my orientation has!

You weren't born homosexual, but as long as you think you were, you have no hope of changing. (If you're born gay, then that's it, that's the way you are, right?) Once you make the connection that you acquired those feelings, desires, attractions—that they were, in fact, learned—then you have reason to hope. *Learned behavior can be unlearned.*

So for now, Mike, accept that the root of your homosexuality is a gender identity problem and that fathers play a big role in developing their sons' sense of gender. Acknowledge also that there was a deficit in your relationship with your father when you were growing up: specific needs that should have been satisfied through a good, healthy father/son relationship have instead been left unfulfilled and unmet. This is the essence of your homosexual drive—to fill that "love vacuum" that's been eating away at you for years.

It's important to recognize that we're not born fully developed, mature human beings. Maturity is a process through which we grow from one stage of development into the next while forming and securing a sense of who we are. In fact, studies show that real maturity demands this progression of stages in growth. Progression, however, from one stage to another, demands that certain prerequisites and needs be met. You can see then that the homosexual, with needs left unsatisfied from the father/son relationship of his childhood, has been left behind in a particular phase of growth.

Dr. Moberly addresses that point directly when she states:

> The central factor in all cases is that needs that should have been met through the parent-child attachment remain yet to be met. What the homosexual seeks is the fulfillment of these normal attachment needs, which have abnormally been left unmet in the process of growth.

Two needs that should have been met through attachment with your father are first, a strong sense of your male gender identity, and second, his love and approval. These are essential needs for healthy progression in growth and maturity, and in your life, Mike, they are needs that still have not been met, and thus define two major elements of your homosexual drive.

Remember that group Wayne took me to in Laguna Beach? There's another one in Santa Monica called Desert Stream whose leader, Andy Comiskey, conducts a seminar on personal transformation.

In one of these seminars Andy said:

> Our sexuality not only distinguishes us as male and female, but compels us to interact with others—to know and be known. That process of interaction begins as we are

interacted with as children. Our early relationships are utterly significant, as they mirror back to us our first glimmer of who we are. We are not born with a secure sense of identity, confident in gender and the self-worth required to love and be loved. We develop our identity, and the sexual undertones of it, as we begin to interact with those around us.

The majority of our early identification takes place with our peers—neighbor kids about our own age and classmates at school. When a boy receives affirmation of his masculinity from his father, he gains confidence in his own identity and is then able to successfully interact with his peers, further enhancing and developing his identity. In our case, the lack of being affirmed by our fathers inhibited us from establishing healthy interaction among our male peers, which further prevented proper identification and affirmation.

Contrary to popular belief, Mike, the homosexual dilemma isn't difficulty relating to women but *difficulty relating to men*!

Again, from Dr. Moberly:

> The homosexual condition is itself a deficit in the child's ability to relate to the parent of the same sex which is carried over to members of the same sex in general.

Detachment from your father and the corresponding deficit in same-sex love-need created a weak foundation for your gender role learning. Instead of feeling secure in your gender, you felt inadequate. Deprived early in life of a secure identity, you were then deprived of developing the heterosexual identity you were meant to have.

Now don't be too quick to dismiss this, Mike. Explore your feelings first and be willing to dig beneath the surface. How do you feel around other guys, especially on a one-to-one basis? What goes on in your head, what emotions start churning? Do you experience feelings of low self-esteem? Of inadequacy? Do you feel you don't fit in? What?

I'm not talking about when you're with your gay friends. What's important is how you feel when you're with a straight guy. How comfortable are you? From now on, start questioning yourself so you can get in touch with what you're feeling. Notice how you respond mentally and emotionally to "heterosexual" men. (I don't like to use words like "heterosexual" and "homosexual." We are *all* heterosexual by nature—it's our identity as men that became distorted. Your heterosexuality is in a dormant state and needs to blossom and come forth. But for the sake of our correspondence, I will use these terms for clarity.)

There's so much more to say, Mike, but I'm going to stop here because I want you to go back and reread this letter. Once again, please don't write off anything at first glance. Search, really search, within yourself for possible connections and work at getting in touch with your feelings. Analyze your thoughts and break them down so you can see their true source. Dig for the roots of your being.

I care for you so much, Mike. Write when you can and take care.

Your buddy,

Jeff

Dear Mike,

I know you're going to get this letter the day after, if not the same day as yesterday's letter. I really wasn't planning on writing again until I heard from you, but there's just so much I want to pass on that I can't wait. I mean, I could wait, but I don't want to. It's such a drag not being able to talk with you face to face, not only because I'd rather discuss these things in person but because letter-writing takes forever. Guess I'm frustrated because I want to go on to other things which contributed to your homosexual identity, but I'm not sure if you fully comprehend the ground we've already covered—specifically, the impact parents have on their children, especially the father. Please, for your own sake as well as mine, go to the library and read material about gender identity. Do some research on your own; it'll be beneficial for you and me both to check out what I've been telling you.

Something I said toward the end of yesterday's letter keeps bugging me because I don't think I stressed it enough. It is vital—it is crucial—it is essential—that you start getting in touch with your true feelings. It's an extremely important element of your journey toward growth and transformation that you learn to dissect and analyze your thoughts and desires to discover what's at the source of how you feel. Unfortunately, you can't rely on feelings alone, for they'll often deceive you, Mike.

A good way of getting in touch with the source of your feelings is to keep a journal. Many times you may feel a certain way, but you don't know why, and the uncertainty bothers you. Most of us at that point concentrate solely on the feelings, but our minds are so jumbled up nothing seems to make sense and our thought processes are so fast it becomes difficult to pinpoint the source. You'll discover that as you write down your problems, many times you'll find the answers right in front of you. Writing things down forces your thoughts to slow down and be collected. As you gather your thoughts you can sort through them, come to grips with them, and see them for what they really are.

Not only does keeping a journal help you come to terms with your thoughts and feelings, but it's also a good measuring rod. It's a fact of life that most of the time progress and growth happen very subtly. When I first began keeping a journal it frequently appeared that nothing had changed for me, that I'd made no progress whatsoever. I mean, I still felt gay and I was still thinking homosexual thoughts and desiring homosexual activity. Looking back at my earliest entries, I see that what I felt at the beginning was utter hopelessness—all I wanted to do was die. A month later, though, the entries were more positive and showed I'd learned many new things. So another definite advantage of keeping a journal is being able to see growth through hindsight.

Of course, I must say I didn't see progress in all entries. Whole sections of my journal are taken up by periods when I was not doing well and not caring. Still, by writing these thoughts down I was able to learn more effectively from the experiences. I could trace the steps that led to certain outcomes, and that helped me from making the same mistakes over again.

Also, the business of being able to look back and see how far you've come gives a tremendous inspiration when you're feeling down in the dumps about your present situation. Let me give you an example of what I mean. I had a conversation with my dad a year after he had a stroke that had left him partially paralyzed. Despite the fact that he was going to physical therapy three times a week, his speech remained affected, he couldn't use his right arm and hand, and he needed to walk with a cane, for quite frequently his right leg would give out on him completely. All in all, it seemed he really wasn't getting any better than when he'd first been stricken. I stopped by one day to see him at work when I was really bummed and told him how depressed I was because I didn't seem to be making any progress toward ridding myself of my sexual attraction toward men. "Tell me about it!" he grunted, referring to his somewhat negative feelings about the progress he was making in recovering from his stroke.

He then went on to tell me one of the most profound and everlasting things I've ever heard:

I've been going to physical therapy for almost a year now and some days I don't want to go at all. I think, *What's the use, I'm no better off now than I was a year ago!* But every now and then I can do something I wasn't able to do the month before.

Just this morning I was able to put my foot up on my desk without lifting it up there with my hands. Improvement had taken place even though I hadn't realized it. It wasn't until I saw the result of all that hard work that I believed progress had taken place.

Now if I'd quit whenever I felt like it, I never would have been able to get any better. And this same lesson applies to you, Jeff. You have to hang in there and give it all you've got. Your day will come when you'll see yourself feeling different. It may not be a total picture yet, but a little here and a little there adds up. Soon enough you'll notice growth and see yourself feeling differently than you did before.

I can't begin to tell you how many times I went to my journal and reread sections of it for encouragement. There were depressing days when I wasn't doing well and I was thinking, *What's the use, I've failed again.* But after reading parts of my journal, I could see just how far I'd come. A lot had changed; I had grown in many ways. I just needed to recognize I had more growing to do. I could not fall into the trap of thinking I hadn't left the starting gate.

So start writing in the enclosed journal; that's why I'm sending it to you. And here's a tip about journal-writing: Don't think you have to write in it every single day because that only creates an extra burden, an added resentment. Write when you feel like it. If a few days go by without an entry, so what? The important thing is to start. Over time your journal will become a real friend. You'll feel better after writing in it and getting things off your chest.

Question yourself as you write. Get beneath the surface. This isn't to be a diary of all the things you did during the day, but a personal journal of your deepest thoughts, feelings, desires, questions, answers, defeats, victories, etc. (Okay, I'll concede there are times when you'll need to incorporate what you did and who you saw to clarify a point, but I trust you understand what I'm driving at.)

For your journal to work most effectively you must be as honest with yourself as possible. You'll be amazed at what you can learn from this alone. I realize it's scary, but believe me it's worth it. I'm also way ahead of you on your next objection, Mike: to help promote this honesty, find a good safe place to keep your journal, a place where nobody will find it. I keep mine inside a combination-locked briefcase because I agree that honesty is encouraged once you've alleviated the fear of someone discovering your deep, dark secrets.

I wanted to write something here to motivate you further, to encourage you to use the journal I'm sending. Instead, I just keep coming back to this one thought: *It's a must that you keep a journal.* Bleak, depressing days are sure to come your way in the future and when they do, it's imperative you have something to fall back on to gain a better perspective of things. Discouragement will blind you to whatever progress you've made if you don't have a reminder of your accomplishments entrusted to your journal.

So go to it, Mike. Be honest; tell the bad as well as the good. Spill your guts. You'll gain profound insights into yourself.

Your friend always,

Jeff

Hi Mike,

Thanks so much for your letter, buddy. I can't tell you how glad it made me. I actually had tears in my eyes after reading it. I was that happy for you! When I didn't hear from you for a couple of weeks, I was really concerned and didn't know if you'd given up on everything, or what.

How wonderful that you did some digging into gender identity on your own. It's really exciting to see what you've learned. Hearing that these matters are now confirmed for you just blows me away, especially in light of your first few letters when you were so defensive that you were ready to attack everything I said. I told you that you could gain hope and strength through understanding your basic situation! The more you learn, Mike, the more motivated you'll become, mainly because of your growing recognition that you're not destined to be a victim of circumstances beyond your control, that you can, in fact, do things to achieve proper gender identity development and maturity.

Anyway, to answer your question, I started my job about three weeks ago and I really like it a lot. The people I work with are great, though strangely there's only one Hawaiian in the bunch. The rest are all "haoles" (pronounced "how-lees") like me, mainlanders and/or Caucasians. Funny, every time I think of home, I think of it as back in the U.S., completely forgetting that Hawaii is a state, too. When people here refer to California as being part of the mainland it's like they're talking about a foreign country, so I guess I'm not the only one who has trouble keeping their geography and history straight.

Since most of the guys I work with speak pidgin (part-Hawaiian, part-English), I'm starting to pick it up also. If something tastes really good, it's now "ono," and whenever Ray or I see a good-looking girl, one of us is bound to say, "Hey, brah, check out the wahine." (Pronounced "wah-hee-knee.") It's never going to qualify me to be an instructor at Berlitz, but it's fun.

You know, I really lucked out when I met Ray. He's such a great guy, real easygoing, and just bound and determined not to ever let a single moment happen that might cause me to feel left out. This weekend we drove just about halfway around the island to a place called Poipu on the south shore. Actually, Poipu is as far south as you can get on Kauai without driving into the ocean.

Anyhow, we stayed with a friend of Ray's there, another Jeff, and let me tell you having two Jeffs in one house was a bit much. All day Saturday, anytime someone asked for Jeff, we both answered. Fortunately, that night an old episode of "Father Knows Best" came on the tube and everybody decided I looked like Bud, so that's what they started calling me, ergo end of confusion. I kind of hope it sticks; it's sort of fun having a nickname. (I never had a good nickname before, only bad labels.) We really crammed a lot into two days and I would have loved to stay longer but I had to be back at work this morning.

Okay, I guess that's enough of today's installment of "How Jeff's Summer In Hawaii Is Progressing." Let's get back to you, starting with a mini-review of what we've got so far. Basically, homosexuality is a symptom or by-product of an unhealthy gender identity. The homosexual feels inadequate in his gender role—not necessarily feminine—and as you've confirmed in your own studies, the father is a major factor in the acquisition of his son's gender. In order for a person to mature and evolve into heterosexuality, certain needs must be met.

For instance, Dr. Elizabeth Moberly states:

> From the present evidence it would seem clear that the homosexual condition does not involve abnormal needs, but normal needs that have, abnormally, been left unmet in the ordinary process of growth. The needs as such are normal; their lack of fulfillment, and the barrier to their fulfillment, is abnormal.

So now we know that same-sex love-needs and identification for boys are normal, legitimate requirements usually met by their fathers during early childhood. They are then later reinforced by factors outside the home such as peers, teachers, media, and society as a whole.

The picture is definitely beginning to take shape, isn't it, Mike? As little boys our perfectly natural needs for same-sex love, acceptance, identification and affirmation weren't met. Because we were insecure about our masculine adequacy, we never ventured out to legitimately fulfill these needs in the larger world. Moberly, by the way, calls these needs "homo (same)-emotional" which is very apt. You have the same homo-emotional needs as other men. In fact, your homosexual drive is actually a reparative homo-emotional drive, a continual attempt to repair or remedy earlier deficits and fulfill those still-existent needs.

It should be clear by now that homosexual behavior will never satisfy your emotional needs. Instead, it only increases and intensifies them. Equally obvious, and one of the greatest tragedies, is that most homosexuals are unaware that these needs exist in them. They only know what they feel—a sexual attraction to other guys.

As a result of all the things just mentioned, our self-image becomes distorted. I was keenly aware of having feelings that society said weren't normal, which caused me to doubt myself and wonder who I was. Since these feelings, thoughts and desires were said to be homosexual in nature, I started questioning my sexuality: *Am I gay?*

The feelings were real enough—strong desires which only grew stronger with time. I always hoped they'd go away, hoped I was just going through a phase and that as I got older they'd just vanish, like acne or something. The irony here is that I was nearly right; all I needed was to complete my same-sex identification process through the fulfillment of my same-sex needs. (Once I did go through the same-sex identification process those feelings did disappear.)

Of course, I didn't know my problem was the lack of fulfilling my homo-emotional needs. All I knew was that I felt different and alone, possessed by feelings other boys surely didn't have. The older I became the more deeply my doubts about my sexuality became entrenched, and thus created a gay self-image.

In *Psycho-Cybernetics*, Maxwell Maltz says:

Whether we realize it or not, each of us carries about with us a mental blueprint or picture of ourselves. It may be vague and ill-defined to our conscious gaze. In fact, it may not be consciously recognizable at all. But it is there, complete down to the last detail. This self-image is our own conception of the "sort of person I am." It has been built up from our own beliefs about ourselves. But most of these beliefs about ourselves have unconsciously been formed from our past experiences, our successes and failures, our humiliations, our triumphs, and the way other people have reacted to us, especially in early childhood. From all these we mentally construct a "self" (or a picture of a self). Once an idea or belief about ourselves goes into this picture it becomes "true" as far as we personally are concerned. We do not question its validity, but proceed to act upon it just as if it were true.

Thus the problem with the person who has labeled himself a homosexual—he thinks he's gay and interprets his normal (but unmet) homo-emotional feelings the wrong way. And based upon his feelings he continues through life reinforcing his gay identity, further hindering the identification process and preventing unmet needs from being met. It's a terribly vicious cycle that can be stopped only by understanding same-sex needs and satisfying them through proper channels.

"Homosexual" is a label you put on yourself because of certain feelings and desires, defined by society as being gay in nature and misinterpreted by you through lack of understanding as to their real origin. A well-adjusted heterosexual man is one who has had these needs met and fulfilled satisfactorily. Dr. Moberly says:

> To "stop being a homosexual" means to stop being a person with same-sex psychological deficits.

When you were growing up, your primary psychological need was for same-sex identification. It still is. The lack of being affirmed in your masculinity inhibited you from establishing interaction with your male peers which further prevented identification from taking place. What's missing in your life now is identification with other males in a non-sexual way, identifying with them and being one of them. Your new goal, Mike, is to meet these same-sex deficits without sexual activity, maturing psychologically from a homosexual self-image into a heterosexual identity through fulfillment of these unmet needs.

Explore the possibility that as a youngster or adolescent you misinterpreted your feelings, misreading your attraction to other males as erotic in origin, not realizing the attraction was rooted in the need to identify with and be accepted by members of your own sex. Begin to see yourself differently, not as you think you are but as you really are—a 23-year-old man. You aren't a homosexual, Mike, because there's no such thing as a homosexual, only homosexual behavior. When you label yourself a homosexual, you're accepting an identity which is not only invalid and unnecessary, but unfulfilling and ultimately very damaging.

Since relationships with other males remains your primary psychological need, you must set about attending to this deficiency, interacting and establishing healthy, non-sexual, same-sex connections. Make new friends with some straight guys. Get to know them, hang around them, allow yourself the opportunity to experience the feeling of "being just one of the guys."

Sure, I know it's all easier said than done and that it takes a certain amount of courage to sail into these uncharted waters, but it's necessary for your well-being, Mike. If you didn't already have "a certain amount of courage," our correspondence wouldn't have gotten to this point. Besides, your ol' pal Jeff is here to give you pointers, so stop worrying, will you?

Wow, it's gotten really late, so I'd better say bye for now. How about writing back as soon as possible, okay?

Your pal,

Jeff

Tuesday
July 2, 1985

Dear Mike,

I feel terrible! Please forgive me if I gave the impression that going out and establishing new friendships is no big deal. Believe me, I know how difficult and scary it is—even the thought of it was frightening for me at first—but let's not worry about it for the moment, okay? What I'm trying to do is appeal to your intellect. All I wanted you to recognize was that same-sex needs must be met by members of our own sex, so don't concern yourself with new relationships yet. First, let me delve a little deeper into the acquisition of a homosexual orientation.

In my last letter I asked you to try to see yourself for who you really are and not as the homosexual you think you are. Once you truly realize that the so-called homosexual is basically driven by unsatisfied *normal* needs, you'll find it easier to view yourself differently. Dr. Elizabeth Moberly covers this topic in detail in her book, *Homosexuality: A New Christian Ethic*, which I've concluded is a must-read. You've got to get a copy; it's excellent.

If you can't find it in any of the local bookstores, or would prefer sending away for it, write Regeneration Books, P.O. Box 9830-K, Baltimore, MD 21284. Ask them to send you a free catalog of their books on overcoming homosexuality. (Are you getting the feeling I really want you to read this book??? I do want you to read it because she really covers the homosexual dilemma from A to Z, start to finish.)

For all that I've been saying to sink in, for you to fully comprehend all the points I've tried to make, you absolutely have to do some introspection, dissection, and analysis of your feelings and desires. Don't accept them for what they appear to be, but follow them to their true source because these feelings and desires are the things you must deal with. Do you recall me saying that we're all a product of the environment in which we were reared? That our home life, our parents' attitudes, and the people we interacted with all contributed to the persons we are today? Although these things mainly registered on an unconscious level, for better or worse they molded our personalities and identities. That's why it's essential you look into your past. It's the only way to discern how your current self evolved.

Some of your childhood experiences caused you to emotionally withdraw which stopped that growing process in your life. Now you're stuck in this stage of growth until you examine these particular roots and begin to see ways in which you can grow and mature as you were intended—to become the man you were meant to be and have the potential to be—according to all the laws of God and nature.

Working through this maturing deficit will come about as you discover those areas which you still allow to direct and control your present behavior. Look back, Mike. I'm sure you recall how certain experiences affected you; now recall how you reacted to them and how this made you feel about yourself. I'm talking about those experiences that had an unfortunate, overwhelming influence on how you viewed life, distorting your perspective of yourself and others.

Let me throw in a caution at this point. Too often people use their past to justify their current behavior, so remember that you're not probing your past life to find excuses. As long as you're searching for excuses, such as blaming your hormones, genes, or environment for your actions, you'll never experience transformation. You'll only be deceiving—and hurting—yourself. Don't rationalize your situation, and don't try to justify your attitudes or behavior.

The key component to recovery is to stop blaming others in order to avoid taking responsibility for your own current actions. What you want to do is recognize how your environment influenced your self-concept. Once you see the connection to your past you can start dealing with it.

I'm sure you've heard plenty of people claiming, "Well, I'm this way because my parents spoiled me as a child," or "I turned out badly because my parents treated me poorly," or "This or that happened and that's why I act the way I do," and so on. Perhaps for the most part it's true, but these people will never change. They accept their present condition as an irreversible by-product of their past, not realizing they do have control over their current behavior and future destiny.

Many of your reactions to your childhood experiences were childish responses because, of course, you were only a child. Today, however, you're no longer a child, Mike. These feelings no longer need to dominate your thoughts and actions. The first step toward actualizing transformation is accepting full responsibility for your present behavior. Don't allow your past or the concept of self it created to control your feelings and attitudes. Locate areas in your life where you need to change and no longer permit yourself to be a victim of the self-destructive image created by the child in your past.

Yes, I know, another matter of easier said than done, right? Okay, there are two terrific books you should read that specifically address this subject. One was written by W. Hugh Missildine and is called, *Your Inner Child of the Past*. The other is *Putting Away Childish Things*, by David Seamands. Of general interest to anyone who's begun to catch on that his past contains some aspects that need to be dug up and dealt with, these books provide a better understanding of what I'm talking about and show how to get in touch with true feelings.

Make no mistake, these feelings are deeply imbedded and require time and patience to overcome, but remember, Mike, you're worth it. In time, the evolution of your homosexual identity will become evident. You'll be able to cope with your desires because you'll understand why you have these feelings and you'll know their true source. Half the battle is realizing you weren't born a homosexual, that nothing is wrong with your hormones or genes. Behavior can be modified, whether we're talking about alcoholism, overeating, drug abuse, pyromania, or homosexual practices. (Ultimately, though, your self-image needs to change because healing from homosexuality is much more than just "behavior modification.")

I grew up a very shy, introverted kid—a loner for the most part, except for hanging around the neighbor kids who were usually younger than me. I felt terribly insecure and inadequate around guys my own age or older; so uncomfortable in fact, that I tried to avoid them as much as possible. The sad thing is I never questioned why I felt this way; I just knew I did and tolerated it. Dutch psychologist,

Gerard van den Aardweg, in his book *Homosexuality and Hope* discusses this "gender inferiority complex."

> The child or adolescent who is stirred by homo-erotic fantasies and interests has inferiority feelings regarding his sexual identity or "gender identity;" in other words, about his being manly.... A boy then feels inferior *compared with other boys* as to his boyishness, toughness, sturdiness, sporting capacities, daring, strength, or manly appearance.... Variation on this rule can occur, but the general line is unmistakable. Basic in this kind of inferiority feeling is the awareness of not really belonging to the men's...world, of not being *one of the boys.*

What set me up for a gender inferiority complex? As with most men who struggle with homosexuality at some point in their lives, my relationship with my father was the primary root.

As I've said, my dad wasn't home much in those days, so my needs for a role model and some same-sex affirmation weren't taken care of. Now, if absence alone was all I'd experienced in my relationship with him, I doubt it would have been sufficiently influential to attribute to my homosexuality, though it contributed to it in a major way. But again, as I've also said before, many other things were involved.

For instance, my parents never displayed any verbal or physical affection, and I interpreted their inability to express love as meaning that I must not be lovable, that something must be dreadfully wrong with me. Even though my parents actually and truly loved me, for the most part I never received it. I was always doing everything I could think of in an attempt to earn their love, but never slowing down enough to just accept it the only way they knew how to show it. Believing I was unlovable produced a low self-worth and a poor self-image, which only fed my feelings of being unlovable in a non-ending, nightmarish cycle.

Take my word for it, this wasn't any small thing for I truly felt unlovable. I thought they loved my brother but not me. Maybe a lot of that was just second-child syndrome—you know, the firstborn gets a lot of stuff, while the second kid seems to only get hand-me-downs. But whatever the reasons, I felt unlovable and unloved. Through that old 20/20 vision of hindsight I've learned an incredibly valuable lesson from this one aspect of my childhood. Though environment is a leading factor in the formation of our identity and in conditioning us in many ways to behave as we do, it's not always past events and circumstances that cause our pattern of behavior. Frequently, it is simply *how we interpret and respond to these experiences* that shape our future actions.

Although I usually wasn't aware of it or didn't feel it, the reality was and is that my parents loved me. And it wasn't necessarily how my parents actually treated me; it was more how I thought they were treating me. The point I want to make here, Mike, is that what *actually* transpired in our childhood wasn't as important as what we *thought* was happening. The development of our identity is dependent upon how we *interpret* reality, how we *perceive* the manner in which others treat us, and not necessarily on reality itself.

My parents loved me; they just didn't express it the way I wanted them to. I wanted to be touched and held and told that I was loved. They didn't do that, however, and I reacted as a child who felt unlovable.

Not only did I feel unloved, but I was hurt by my dad. For example, whenever I cried while growing up, he would always tell me to stop acting like a woman because crying to him was effeminate behavior. I also wanted a stuffed animal but my dad refused because once again he believed no boy should have one. He scorned a lot of things that I thought were normal wants and activities, not just for me but for any child, because he thought they were feminine.

His disapproval didn't make me feel feminine but it did add considerably to my feelings of inadequacy as a boy. After all, according to him, boys don't cry and don't want to play with stuffed animals—I did both.

Now I don't want to give you the wrong idea here. My dad wasn't a mean person or anything of the kind. As a matter of fact, he was a very nice, giving person. The point is, it's not so much how my dad was, but how he wasn't. I needed someone to encourage me and, yes, at times push me to do the things I should have been doing as a boy.

The key word is *encouragement*, instilling confidence and prompting me to do non-solitary things—activities involving other guys; there shouldn't have been only discouragement from doing things that didn't matter. What I needed was for my father to help build me up, affirm me in my progress toward manhood.

When this wasn't forthcoming, I reacted by pulling back from his machoism and male chauvinism. This detachment from him, and the corresponding deficit in same-sex love-need it created, eroded whatever foundation I had for gender role learning. It left me feeling insecure, inadequate and confused in my gender identity.

As a result, I chose to stay where it was safe and familiar rather than venturing out and discovering on my own that I was really okay. Convinced I didn't need anybody, I withdrew and became a loner. The problem with this behavior was that it further prevented me from identifying myself as a male. By remaining alone and aloof, I wasn't able to exchange ideas, thoughts, fears, questions, etc., with other boys. I denied myself the opportunity to discover the feelings of my male peers and how they responded to different things in life. Of course, this self-enforced separation nourished my belief that I was the only person who felt the way I did.

You must remember I wasn't aware of the concept of same-sex needs; all I knew was how I felt. As a young boy I was aware of my physical attraction to other boys and although it certainly wasn't sexual in nature at first, I didn't know the difference. By reviewing my feelings much later in life, I was able to pick up a few clues about what had really been going on inside me. The adult Jeff realized that all the younger Jeff had really wanted was to belong and have some male friends. I wanted to play baseball and not feel like a sissy. I wanted to joke around and have fun with a bunch of buddies. I wanted what I thought every other guy had—I wanted to feel like a normal guy.

You can imagine the long-term effects on a kid who watches everything from the outside and never gets involved. By not hanging around other boys while I was growing up, I couldn't identify with them in a healthy way. Watching from the sidelines, I admired them, envied them, and wished I was them. I wanted to belong, to be approved and accepted by them.

Not only was I lacking in a secure gender identity and gender role, I also lacked any sense of identity with my male peers, which created an even bigger deficit in my life. As I missed out on that whole aspect of living and the attendant process of learning, an intense amount of envy, jealousy, rejection, and longing sprang up in its place. I guess it's almost redundant to say that it greatly influenced me. I was always looking at other guys, but I never realized that all I was trying to do was to identify with them in some way, or wishing I could. Not being aware that I had common, normal, homo-emotional needs, I concluded that something must be wrong with me.

What I want you to pick up on from all this discussion is that there are more contributing factors to your homosexual identity than might appear at first glance. In addition to my father not being there for me physically and emotionally, and not instilling confidence in my masculinity instead of in some ways robbing me of it, a major root cause in my life was the belief that I was unlovable. The ramifications of not feeling lovable were very significant. All these negative feelings, coupled with my insecurity as a male, prevented me from going out and establishing normal peer interaction which would have allowed me to be a part of the normal same-sex identification process and could have given me the affirmation and feedback I so desperately needed.

Interaction is essential to growth. I just can't put enough emphasis on this. Personal development depends upon connecting and socializing with others, especially with other males. How we see ourselves and others is the basis that forms our identity, and your identity and self-image are dependent on identification with your own sex. It's through interaction with your same-sex peers that you secure a sense of who you are as a male.

For the time being, Mike, why don't you just think about—take time to digest—these things and see if there's any correlation between what I've described and what you see when you probe your own life. Unearth these things so you can begin to break them down and analyze them. I'd like to hear about the roots you find that may have influenced the way you think about yourself. Write back soon, and in the meantime have yourself a great Fourth of July.

Oh, I almost forgot. Everybody is still calling me Bud. Even Ray. And to answer your question, you can call me Bud. I'm glad you like the nickname. So do I!

Your pal,

Bud

P.S.

It's a little strange signing my name as Bud, but I like it all the same.

Dear Mike,

    After dropping off your letter yesterday at the post office, I went to get my car serviced at the VW dealer's in Lihue. I was waiting in the customers' lounge reading a newspaper and who should walk in but Robert. Remember him, one of the guys we met down in Cabo San Lucas? I'd forgotten all about him living over here. In fact, I hadn't seen him or talked to him since that Christmas party some years ago in Malibu, the one you didn't show up for. Anyway, he'd come in to get a new fuel pump for his Bug, and I have to admit it was another case of me being recognized first. Only after he'd walked up and asked if I'd been in Mexico about four years ago did the lightbulb go on in the attic.

    Man, you wouldn't believe how much he's changed—and all for the better. I mean, even if I hadn't known him, I would have wanted to because he just radiates a confident zest for life and personal contentment. Since we both had some time to kill, we went down the street to get a bite to eat and shoot the breeze. (By the way, macadamia nut pancakes are out of this world!)

    Naturally, I asked him what he'd been up to and he said he had become a Christian. We talked about that for a while, but that's not why I'm mentioning this. Turns out he was living in West L.A. the past couple of years while going to that group I told you about in Santa Monica, Desert Stream! I was blown away by the news that he'd turned himself around, too. Isn't that fantastic? I'm incredibly happy for him. We're going to start meeting every Monday for breakfast. He's really interested in my book project and is chock-full of helpful ideas for it.

    I told him that you and I had reconnected, and he was awfully glad to hear you're trying to get your life back on the track. He said the two of you had a long, in-depth talk while we were all down in Cabo about how unhappy you both were. He told me that Mexico was the turning point for him, because here were six gay couples, for the most part all unhappy and stressed out about their situations, yet doing nothing to improve things.

Did you know he tried to kill himself a week after getting home from that trip? He said the "wallow"—his word—of drugs, booze and sex had left him feeling emptier than it seemed possible to feel and still be alive. He couldn't escape the realization that life was pretty sad if you had to be high to go on with it and not think about it. Of course, he was right, you know. Even though I didn't put away anything stronger than a Dos Equis, I spent a lot of time in Mexico wondering why I wasn't any happier than I was and if I'd ever be happy being gay. But since I didn't think I really had a choice, I just kept quiet and hoped things would get better.

All the rest of the guys have broken up and are back into the bar scene, but maybe you already knew that. I really feel for them. The only one I've heard from is Daniel, who's still working in Hollywood. He calls me every now and then, usually when he's depressed and has had a few drinks. He's so terribly unhappy all the time, but whenever I try to talk to him about it, he just tosses off a couple of glib statements about how he knows it's his own doing, but blah, blah, blah, and so he continues to do all the wrong things for all the wrong reasons. Thinking about him makes me especially glad that you decided to do something about your situation.

So how are things going for you? Is more of this material I've been talking about starting to make sense? Quite a number of things I've mentioned will become much clearer to you once you start reading those books I recommended. I know you haven't had an opportunity to lay your hands on them yet, but please be sure to do so as soon as you can. It's really a small investment of time and money compared to the return you'll get in speeding up your recovery process.

And while we're on the subject of books, I've got another one for you called *Homosexuality: Laying the Axe to the Roots*, by Ed Hurst. In it, Hurst shows how even things such as envy, rejection and fear can contribute to a homosexual orientation, and he accords them full root status. Just as your relationship with your dad was the root of your gender identity problem, these are roots to your overall personality and identity as a whole.

I've already told you about several of the major roots of my homosexual identity and how each one branched out into the next, making me a pretty messed-up kid. Well, almost as if to put the icing on the cake, when I was 11 or 12 years old, a rumor surfaced about a neighbor kid and me. At first it appeared to be no big deal, but the ultimate outcome was such that I know my life would have been different if it had never happened.

It was the summer between sixth and seventh grade, a time when I was looking forward finally to being in junior high. A guy named Dennis and I were fooling around in our "fort" one day, playing soldier and pretending to get shot. This activity soon metamorphosed to playing a combination of soldier and doctor, so you can imagine where we kept getting shot. Now that I'm older, of course, I know this type of "sex play," comparison and curiosity, is common to a lot of guys; it's just a way of seeing how you measure up to your friends. Anyway, a few of the other kids in the neighborhood found out and though it was a drag for a while, the whole thing eventually died down and I forgot all about it by the time school started.

Even if I hadn't forgotten by then, I soon would have, because in junior high I got my first girlfriend. I was a shy boy and although I was very attracted to Kathy, I didn't make any moves toward her. Her friends had to set us up together. But after that, what fun we had eating lunch together, walking home from school, and spending endless hours on the phone with each other. I was considered really cool by my peers for having a girlfriend and naturally I was feeling a lot better about myself, even almost normal. I mean, someone really cared about me and listened to me.

This feeling of normalcy quickly came to an end, however, when that rumor from the past summer resurfaced. It not only resurfaced— it resurfaced bigger than life. The kids were saying that Dennis and I participated in oral sex! It seemed like that was all anyone at school talked about. The odd thing was they weren't really talking about me but about Dennis. Everybody knew who he was. He was really popular at school and was involved in sports. I, on the other hand, was just a nobody.

I vividly remember when sitting in my history class watching a film on the Civil War, a scene flashed onto the screen showing a guy blowing a bugle and the narrator saying, "Gabriel, come *blow* your horn." At that point someone yelled out Dennis's name and the whole class roared. I could have died of embarrassment.

From that time on, I pretty much reverted to being a loner. I didn't want to get involved in anything at school for fear of being singled out as Dennis had been. Even in eighth grade I was still hearing about it from time to time. It was, bar none, absolutely the most humiliating experience of my life, so devastating that when a group of high-school coaches came by to give a pep talk aimed at recruiting our involvement in high-school sports, I wouldn't even consider it. Not that I didn't want to, I did, but I was afraid that if I was ever in public view for a sports event, someone might yell something embarrassing. I couldn't handle it.

I allowed that one lousy rumor to mess up my whole life. Until then I'd merely been just a kid on the block with a few hang-ups. I didn't think I was a homosexual, although I was aware of my obsession about other guys. Sure, my identity was already on shaky ground and I did feel inadequate in my masculinity. Yet I might have received enough affirmation from my peers to correct that if the rumor had not escalated.

After all, things were already going in the right direction. Having Kathy as my girlfriend made me feel like the other guys, which might have helped me interact and identify with them. But the fear of further humiliation just nipped everything right in the bud. I broke up with Kathy and withdrew from the very things that could've helped me. I didn't pursue the interaction I needed to heal my gender identity problem. Instead, I became consumed with my attraction toward guys in general, and in particular, those who were living the sort of life I wanted.

Without my knowing it, this obsession was a reparative drive to meet same-sex needs. Something inside me was drawing me toward the very thing that would have met those needs and stopped the attraction. However, I didn't know about such needs—all I knew was how I felt. And as time went on I was "taught" that these feelings meant I was a homosexual, or that at the very least, I had homosexual tendencies. Unfortunately, I accepted this fallacy as the unchangeable truth.

You see, this is what guys who are attracted to other guys think. Society doesn't really provide them any other way to go and that really infuriates me. If only I'd been told that I simply had same-sex needs—normal, legitimate needs—I wouldn't have had to go through all the pain I experienced as a result of my ignorance. That's the whole reason I want to write a book. I want guys to know that they're not gay just because they have certain feelings while growing up.

Those are some of the roots that affected my identity. You've got your own, I know, but I hope that by sharing mine I've shown you how certain childhood experiences can influence you and steer you off-course. To eliminate your homosexual condition, Mike, it's vital that you work all the way through to the deepest roots of your homosexuality. You need to discover the cause of your attraction toward men because at the very core of this attraction lie several needs yet to be met. By now you should be able to see at least the vague outline of your needs for acceptance from men, identification with other men, same-sex love-need (non-erotic), and a sense of belonging.

Part of my attraction and pull toward guys was a natural, inner, reparative drive to meet same-sex needs, but probably an equally compelling urge was my unconscious, all-consuming envy of a lifestyle I desired. Yet the situation was even more complex than that. I began to be consciously attracted to guys physically and then sexually.

How did it happen? When I found myself attracted to another guy, what was I feeling? Whenever I tried to figure it out, I never got any further than physical, sexual magnetism. Then one night at a meeting of New Life in Laguna Beach, (the group I've told you about), someone asked me what kind of male I found attractive. What physical traits or characteristics appealed to me? While I was mulling over a response, he asked me what kind of person I wished I was. The insight I gained from these questions was astounding: *I was attracted to guys who looked the way I wished I looked! Envy was the root of all homosexual relationships I aspired to.*

Why did I possess so much envy? It's such a cancerous monster of an emotion—one I actively despised. The person who raised these questions talked with me a bit longer, but wouldn't hazard a guess in answer to my return question. He left it up to me to discover the source of this malignancy within myself. Ultimately, I found that my attraction to men related directly to my feelings of inadequacy in my masculinity. I was attracted to guys who had characteristics I deemed masculine.

I've since found this to be the case with all my gay friends, including Daniel. It's not just coincidence that he, lacking body hair, finds men attractive who have heavy beards, hairy arms and chest, etc. This feature really turns him on. He once told me that kissing an unshaven guy makes him crazy. From his description of how much he's aroused by everything from five o'clock shadow to full-grown beards, I could easily picture him trying to suck somebody's beard right off his chin as if he were trying to acquire it for his own. In his mind, however, all he knows is that a day-old growth of facial hair turns him on.

A passage in Ed Hurst's book repeats this line of thought:

> Somewhere in the course of my first interview with a male counselee, I ask two important questions. The first is: What kind of guy do you find attractive? The second is: If you could change anything about yourself, what kind of person would you like to be? In 98% of the cases, the answers to both questions are nearly identical.

In *Crisis In Masculinity*, Leanne Payne develops this critical equation a step further:

> After such a sufferer states what it is he admires in the other man, I ask him this question: "Do you know why cannibals eat people?" As he shakes his head in the negative, with varying degrees of astonishment, I proceed to tell him what a missionary once told me: "Cannibals eat only those they admire, and they eat them to get their traits." Those who succeed in feigning insanity or some other equally undesirable trait do not end up in the pot.

Hurst goes on to say:

A guy who admits to preferring men of a certain physical stature usually wishes that he could look like that. Someone who is searching for a man who "has his head together" will often admit that he is lacking in stability. A man who falls far short of society standards for masculinity will often search for a "real man" as a sexual partner.

Many who admit to a strong genital fixation will also admit that they feel cheated in their own genital endowment... it doesn't take a genius or even a doctor of psychology to make the connection here. Behind these homosexual temptations...behind these homosexual "orientations"...is a root problem of envy.

This is what Hurst says about his own past identity:

My image of myself as a man was a big zero. Was it just coincidence that I wanted a "real Man" to come into my life? My emotional stability wasn't the best. I was nervous and very high-strung. Was it only coincidence that my "dream man" was quiet and gentle, yet strong and resolved? I was short and stocky and soft in appearance. The man of my dreams was 5'11" and masculine. (He didn't have to be a he-man.) I had a distinct feeling that I didn't "measure up" in my genital size. Could this have been a factor in my becoming a "size queen?..."

Was I just one extremely mixed-up case or were my traumas the traumas of most of the gay society? Our counseling experience has shown that I was not an isolated case; nearly all of the people we have counseled have experienced one or more of these types of misguided envy.

When we pause to consider this, we realize that man has often tried to acquire or reclaim through sexual expression that which he did not have. The picture of the older man trying to reclaim his long-departed youth by marrying a girl young enough to be his daughter demonstrates this tendency vividly. Within the gay society the most sought after partners are those who seem to embody youthfulness and innocence. Is it coincidence that these correspond with two of the greatest traumas known to gays—that of growing old and the burden of guilt? (Friends, I ask you not to read into my statements. I have not said that most homosexual persons are child-molesters. From my experience most prefer "youth and innocence" coupled with at least a high school education.)

And Mike, we don't just envy those qualities of others that we lack, but also those qualities we already possess but haven't recognized. Payne writes:

> What they admire in the other man will be their own unaffirmed characteristics, those from which they are separated, can in no way see, and therefore cannot accept as part of their own being.

I know in my own life I didn't see any masculine characteristics. I dwelt so much on the negative that it blinded me from seeing the positive. People would honestly and sincerely tell me nice things about myself, but I never received it. Here I was, 5'11", good-looking, nice build with a decent amount of hair on my arms, legs, and chest (the very kind of male I was attracted to), but I didn't recognize it.

Why? Well, men who are unaffirmed in their masculinity often don't see their own masculine traits. They see only their undesirable traits, or they're so consumed with what they want that they don't recognize what they have. As a result of not being affirmed, they suffer from a poor self-image and are unable to accept their own characteristics. They end up unable to accept themselves.

On a superficial level, I believed I was okay. If anyone had asked if I liked who I was, my answer was an emphatic yes. I really thought I was secure in who I was. However, not until I started examining my roots and observing their connections to my behavior did I see things as they really were.

Although I thought I was emotionally stable, my actions told a far different story. I had insecurities and inhibitions buried so deep that I didn't even know they existed. That's why I keep harping at you to get to the roots of your homosexuality. You need to discover that things frequently aren't what they appear to be.

So much more to say, Mike, but so little time. I'll write more later when I get the chance.

Take care,

Bud

Hi, Mike!

Sounds like all of you had a great time over the Fourth. We celebrated here too, naturally, but without fireworks. Instead we staged a big luau at the house. A few of the guys helped Ray and me construct a sort of thatched roof over our picnic tables, using bamboo poles tied with twine for the framework and palm branches laid across the top to block the sun. Looked pretty good, if I do say so myself, or as Ray put it in pidgin, "Shaka, brah," meaning, "Terrific—well done, bro."

I swear, there must have been at least 100 people here, and each brought their own culinary specialty. What a feast—all sorts of salads, breads, vegetables, fruits, and desserts. While we were busy making our bamboo masterpiece, others were digging a fire pit and some of the girls raided the plumeria bush in the front yard to make fresh leis for everyone.

A friend of Jeff's provided the pig that we roasted. He killed it earlier that morning by tying it up, hanging it by its hind legs and slitting its throat. I'm glad he did it at his house, because it's not the sort of thing I would've cared to watch. As it was, I sampled everything that was served except for the poor pig. Everyone said it was super, but a few vegetarians and I managed to resist without feeling in the least deprived.

Let's see…what else is new? Oh, yeah, I got a letter from Daniel this week. He said he finally found "Mr. Right" in the form of someone named Roger. He and Roger were "made for each other," he said, and "nothing will get in the way this time." Sure. It's really too bad. I mean, I know how he feels and what he wants, but I also know it won't last. You should see his letter; it's all Roger this and Roger that. He has the guy so high up on a pedestal that he's just got to fall and let Daniel down. If only Daniel weren't so overly emotional—I'm really afraid of what he might do when this relationship fails.

Now, to your letter. To answer your question about how your unmet needs and/or envy could have been translated into homosexual activity, I'd say it has to do with your misinterpretation. As you entered adolescence you carried all of this emotional baggage from childhood with you. In addition, you were bombarded with other intense, deep, emotional sensations. Because you didn't know how to legitimately fulfill these needs you eroticized them.

Dr. Elizabeth Moberly puts it this way:

> The fact that homo-emotional needs are often, though by no means always, eroticized, has tended to distract attention from the significance of the homosexual condition in itself. It is not surprising that someone who has attained physiological maturity should interpret his or her deepest emotional needs as sexual, but this is to mistake the essential character of these needs.

Remember, Mike, the homosexual condition is a non-sexual condition. Yet the vast majority of the time it's eventually eroticized. Unfortunately, by eroticizing legitimate needs, the condition then becomes a sexual one. Because the homosexual does not comprehend his true, non-sexual emotional needs, he feels irresistibly compulsive to migrate toward other males, and ultimately, he's led to conclude that his attraction is sexual in nature.

Sexual response is a learned behavior. For example, you taught yourself to respond sexually to your homo-emotional needs by eroticizing your desires. This eroticizing took place over an extended period of time, of course, and once you taught yourself this method of responding to your impulses and desires, your mind continued to interpret emotional input in the way you'd unconsciously programmed it.

Your inappropriate response to unresolved emotional needs solidified the confusion to your sexual identity rather than resolved it. Consequently, you interpreted your eroticized emotional responses to infer a sexual preference for men.

I hope I've answered your question, Mike, and not merely muddied the water. To tell you the truth, I'm really beat tonight—too tired to write anymore.

Affectionately,

Bud

Dear Mike,

Just received a letter from a friend of mine in Orange County who has assumed a gay identity. He has been seeing a counselor once a week in an effort to get free from his homosexuality. The reason I'm telling you about him is because I don't want you to fall into the same trap.

For over two years Mark has been shelling out $50 a session, four or five times a month, with very little to show for it. His counselor has linked part of Mark's problem to his dad, and while that's okay, what isn't okay is that he's got Mark concentrating on trying to repair the father/son relationship in order to change his orientation. This isn't going to change the homosexual identity Mark's taken upon himself. Meanwhile, Mark is getting more and more frustrated by his father's unwillingness to participate in this remedial exercise.

It's not that I don't think restoring Mark's relationship with his dad is a great idea—it's just that it won't bring about Mark's recovery. It's the deficits that resulted from this poor relationship that caused Mark's homosexuality, not the relationship itself.

Don't get me wrong here, Mike. I'm not opposed to people seeking help from psychologists. I know, in fact, they can be quite helpful, but I just don't see that Mark's counselor is really helping him. I really don't think the man is challenging him enough. All Mark seems to be getting for his money is a sounding board. He should be getting help in setting goals and receiving advice on ways to achieve them. Furthermore, if you seek counseling, make sure the psychologist has experience in dealing with guys *overcoming* homosexuality. It's a drag having to teach your counselor at $50 an hour.

About setting goals, you ought to draw up a list of your own, Mike. Be realistic, though. For instance, you shouldn't set down that you want to be healed next week, or anything like that. Obviously, you'd be thrilled if that's what happened next week, but we both know that it's not a realistic goal. Your ultimate goal, of course, is to move out of homosexuality into heterosexuality, but you can't put a time limit on it. Now I can almost hear you saying, "Hey, Bud, this is a swell idea, but what's the point of it?" That's simple, the point is to have a game plan.

This is the way I went at it. I first listed on one sheet of paper all the things I felt contributed to my homosexuality: feelings of inadequacy in my masculinity, feelings of being unloved and unlovable, fear of rejection, fear of failure, fear of being humiliated, envy (and more envy), low self-esteem, poor self-image, feelings of being a "pansy," inability to play sports, lack of coordination, fear of trying new things, etc., etc. On another piece of paper I then listed goals I set in order to overcome these contributing factors. I needed to identify with other males, meet same-sex love-needs, start taking chances, learn new ways to communicate, develop new interests, and so forth. But this wasn't specific enough. Your goals need to be things you can realistically zero in on, something you can obtain and measure.

I had to set goals—in writing—and then set tasks to achieve these goals. The tasks had to be simple at first or I knew I'd quit out of despair. For example, I wanted to identify with other guys and start enjoying some healthy interaction with them. That was a goal. Now I needed to set some tasks for myself that would lead to achieving this goal. Since I'd always wanted to play sports and thus be like other guys, I established a secondary goal. However, it would have been ridiculous for me to immediately join a community baseball team because I wasn't prepared and I didn't have the skills. I made joining a community baseball team one of my goals and set different tasks to get me there.

The first thing I had to do was learn how to play baseball. I registered at a local junior college for beginners co-ed slow-pitch softball. Co-ed was an important factor because I knew the other guys in the class wouldn't be real serious jock-types. When I found myself talking more with the girls in my class than the guys, I set myself the task of making a conscious effort to converse with another guy. The more I did this, the more I could see that the other guys in the class liked me well enough and thought I was okay. Receiving this acceptance enabled me to talk with them more and that laid the groundwork to establish some healthy interaction and identification. The following semester I took a softball class for guys only. It was scary, all right, but I wanted to achieve my goal, and I did.

Note that this was just one goal and it required several tasks to accomplish it. All in all, I must have had 100 such goals and an even greater number of tasks to conquer in order to obtain them.

I'm not saying that you should start off with that many tasks, Mike. I realize it's way too much to contemplate at this point. But how about setting yourself the task of being bold enough to introduce yourself to some guy you've never spoken to at work? Or, if the people where you work know you're gay, maybe you should set yourself the task of finding a new job or requesting a transfer to another store. It's important to give yourself the best possible conditions for your new identity to grow, and that might just mean a new environment.

I also recommend that you avoid making long lists. It might be too overwhelming. Keep them short, maybe five tasks per list. Let the fifth task be to *make a new list*. Like this:

1.
2.
3.
4.
5. Make a new list!

It's not a one-time thing, Mike. When you finish one list, begin another. Keep gaining ground. Look for new ways to bring about the desired transformation.

Here are three important steps for you to follow regarding the tasks you set: (1) Write down what you felt about the task before you attempted it; (2) Write down how you felt while doing it; and (3) Write down how you felt after finishing the task.

Use your journal to record all this information and be as concise as you can; try to get to the center of what you're feeling. I know it sounds like much busywork, but believe me, it's not. The insight you gain by doing this is incredible. I think you'll really enjoy it and I know it'll encourage you to do the other tasks you've set for yourself.

Whatever you do, whether you record them in your journal or not, save these lists. Begin checking off the tasks as you complete them. As you do, you will create a sense of accomplishment that will help motivate you to tackle other goals and tasks.

So start devising some short-term goals, buddy, and let me know what tasks you come up with to accomplish them. I promise you, the rewards are well worth the effort. Take care and write soon, huh?

Your brah always,

Bud

Hi, Mike!

Well, it's about time. I'd nearly forgotten what your handwriting looks like. Called you several times this past week, but nobody was home, I guess. How are things going for you? There weren't any hints in your letter and that makes me wonder—and worry a little, too.

What about those goals, buddy? Have you established any yet? Set some tasks? I want to hear about them because I'd like to give you some feedback.

Don't know about you, but I think it's time for you to start doing something with all the stuff I've been telling you over the past few months. In other words, it's time for you to be challenged.

Here's a quote that belongs in everyone's permanent collection:

> *Knowledge is the beginning of action;*
> *action is the completion of knowledge.*

Pretty heavy, isn't it? Comes from an old Chinese philosopher named Wang Yang-Ming (c. 1490 AD), who pretty much summed it all up in that one sentence.

Having the head knowledge isn't enough to bring about transformation. You have to put that knowledge into practice and prove to yourself that it does in fact work. Knowing what you need to do isn't the same as getting it done, and intellectual insight doesn't bring about healing. Head knowledge needs to be turned into heart knowledge and that only happens through experience.

So get on the stick, Mike. You've got more than enough knowledge to start converting some of it into action. What do you honestly have to lose, buddy? I know it's foreign and scary, but once you begin reaping the benefits of fulfilling same-sex needs, you'll never want to return to the gay lifestyle and you're going to wish you'd started earlier.

This letter is intended as a swift kick in the butt, guy, to get you moving in the right direction. Hope I've at least motivated you to sit down and write out some of those goals and tasks. How about doing it tonight, okay???

Write soon,

Bud

Monday
August 12, 1985

Dear Mike,

I'm sorry. Really I am. I didn't mean to sound insensitive or come down on you like a ton of bricks. Believe me, Mike, I care for you a great deal and wish you could know how much you mean to me. It's often difficult for me to convey this in my letters, but I love you even though it doesn't always sound like it. There are just times when I get so frustrated at my inability to get across what I'm trying to say that I wind up slamming everything together in one harshly worded statement…and for that, I sincerely apologize.

Please, in the future always remember that underneath anything and everything I say exists my strong brotherly love for you. So read between the lines and see the concern and affection that's there. I want you to make it through this, Mike. I know you can do it, but you have to stay motivated. And that's all I was trying to do in my last letter—just keep you motivated.

You keep saying that I don't understand how you feel, but I do. When I first decided to "go straight," I felt the same as you. I think these feelings are common to most ex-gays during their transition out of the gay lifestyle. Learning new things is seldom easy. It produces a lot of anxiety and tension, which just piles up on top of all the stress that led to the attempt to learn new stuff in the first place. Dealing with all these feelings can be a real bear, but you've got to keep at it to fulfill your goals.

You're absolutely right—the unknown is frightening. That's why one of the biggest roadblocks to recovery is fear. People usually are afraid to try new things, but you can't let fear stop you from living, keeping you stuck in your homosexual identity and prevent you from developing emotional wholeness. You've got too much going for you, Mike, to let fear hold you back from actualizing your dreams.

Think about this very seriously for a moment—what's the worst that could happen to you as a result of facing the unknown? The absolute very worst, I mean? Aren't we really talking about people-to-people issues here? What I'm trying to say is that when you break it down, we're talking about elements you're already familiar with, but just put together in new ways. You've got to take some risks to facilitate the healing process. The more risks of this nature that you take the less hold your fears will have on you.

I've got two mottoes in life that I'm determined will see me through to the end of my days:

OVERCOME YOUR FEARS;
DON'T LET YOUR FEARS OVERCOME YOU.

RUN TOWARD THE THINGS THAT FRIGHTEN YOU.

Stay with it, Mike. Allow yourself the exhilaration of conquering your fears. Let yourself experience the tremendous satisfaction of relating to other men as you were meant to.

Sorry to end this letter so soon but Ray and I are going surfing! Will write more tomorrow.

Bud

P.S.

Oops, I forgot something. To answer your question of how I can help you meet your same-sex needs, I have to see a list of some of your immediate goals. Like I said, I went back to school in order to begin attaining mine. I also switched jobs. In the past my working relationships have been primarily with women. So, I got a job which gave me possibilities for more interaction with men. It gave me the opportunity to receive affirmation from them, and to identify with them.

Now please don't misunderstand me as did another friend of mine when I suggested he go back to school. After about a year's coaxing, he finally took the plunge. I didn't hear about it until six months later. He informed me he'd taken my advice but that nothing had changed, that he hadn't met a single person. When I asked him what effort he'd made toward meeting people, he replied very succinctly, "None."

Going back to school isn't the goal. It's a means of meeting your goal. Once you're there you will need to set yourself a task for, say, the week, and perhaps it will only be introducing yourself to just one guy. Or maybe it would be no more than taking a seat next to a guy you'd like to know. Whatever the task is you've got to take the initiative, you've got to take the risk. Someone else might speak to you first, but there's healing in it for you if you make the first move.

Over and out, buddy. Write soon.

Hi Mike,

As I was surfing yesterday, I thought some more about your last letter. You know, when you talk about homosexuality as feeling so natural and right, I'm familiar with those feelings, too. Homosexuality is familiar to you, Mike. You're "comfortable" in your gay identity because it's all you have known, not because it's right for you.

Sure, you might then ask how I account for the fact that on those occasions in the past when you've had sex with women, you found yourself preferring men. A couple of reasons come to mind. I don't know whether you had sex with a male first or a female, but the odds are that you probably fooled around with other guys as a kid. If that's the case, then as I've mentioned before, you taught yourself to be attracted to men sexually through eroticizing your same-sex needs.

Since sexual behavior is a learned response, you must realize that your particular sexual behavior is the result of misinterpreting your homo-emotional needs as sexual desires. (Forget about the common experience of mutual masturbation that many adolescent males engage in at least once. If their same-sex needs are being met they soon outgrow this activity. I've got a reference about this somewhere in my notes. I hope I can find it. If I do, I'll attach it at the end of this letter.)

Now if the case is that you had relations with a female first, you need to look at how you were feeling at the time. Recall what's at the core of homosexuality: masculine inadequacy, gender confusion, deficiency in same-sex needs, etc. Even though you were pursuing relationships with girls to the extent of having sex with some of them, your primary need at that time in your life was still homo-emotional.

Homosexuality feels natural because your desires and impulses are so strong and real. What you thought was your "homo-*sexual* drive" is actually an innate, proper drive to correct homo-*emotional* deficiencies. This homo-*emotional* drive is a God-given drive, so to speak, a reparative function built within the human mechanism so that it can right itself. It pulls you toward other guys to satisfy your homo-emotional needs, but not on a sexual level. Instead of meeting these needs in legitimate, non-erotic ways, the confused male acts upon these impulses through sexual expression.

Your desires and emotions won't become heterosexual in nature until you take care of your same-sex needs. Remember, healing involves growth—advancing from one stage of development into the next only when the old stage has been in all ways outgrown or fulfilled. Your unmet needs will, as long as they're unmet, block you from proceeding into the heterosexual stage.

Even though you say homosexuality feels natural and right, you've been very unhappy in the gay lifestyle. Doesn't that indicate it's time to move on? Take a few steps to the edge of the nest. Trust your built-in mechanism that says you can fly. Flap your wings. Venture out of the familiar and soar onward and upward to new heights, new goals, new experiences. These things offer freedom, Mike. They offer healing.

You'll never know what's out there just waiting for you unless you give yourself the chance to find out. So go ahead and try; take a few risks. And don't forget, I'm with you all the way.

Your friend who loves you very much,

Bud

P.S.

Yep, I found that reference I was looking for. It comes from the Institute for Sex Research, founded over three decades ago at the University of Indiana by biologist Alfred C. Kinsey:

> The Kinseyans define a homosexual as anyone who has had more than six sexual experiences with a member of the same sex. The first Kinsey report on male homosexuality revealed that 37 percent of all American men had had at least one homosexual experience between the onset of puberty and old age.

It should be remembered, however, that the findings of 37 percent incidence among males were weighted by the inclusion of adolescents. Among boys who are coming of age, mutual masturbation or "circle jerks," or even fellatio is common, but such activity is usually a passing phase in the development toward mature adult sexuality and rarely presages their sexual behavior as grown men.

That's from Dr. Robert Kronemeyer's book, *Overcoming Homosexuality*. I also agree with what Sprinthall and Collins have to say on the subject in *Adolescent Psychology*:

Surveys indicate that fewer than 5% of college students consider themselves to be exclusively interested in members of the same sex. However, perhaps 20% or more of young people have one or more homosexual experience sometime during their late childhood or early adolescent years. Thus homosexual contacts seem to be somewhat more common than true homosexual preferences, in which only persons of the same sex are seen as possible affectional partners. Indeed, it has been suggested that homosexual contacts among both adolescent boys and girls are quite common but have no lasting implications for normal sexual development. In fact, we might think of typical same-sex contacts in the early adolescence as mutual masturbation rather than as the acting out of a true homosexual preference. In other words, boys, or girls, as couples are involved in exploring sexual feelings rather than expressing their attraction to one another. A difficulty often arises, however: *Adolescents themselves assume that because they found such experiences pleasurable, they may be homosexuals.* As in many other instances, *how we label or explain our experiences is often more important than the experiences themselves.* [Emphasis added]

Did you notice Kinsey stated his definition of a homosexual was someone with seven or more same-sex sexual experiences? I think that number was chosen because of his knowledge that it's common for guys to experiment with same-sex contacts. And as Sprinthall and Collins said, those experiences "involved exploring sexual feelings rather than expressing their attraction to one another."

But for many children, their early experimentation with sex "defines" their sexual identity. Brad Sargent, Director of Research at Exodus International, elaborated on this point at one of his lectures. "Sexual experimentation can combine with other predisposing factors to almost seal the child's fate by giving them the powerful sense of excitement during sexual arousal with members of the same sex." He illustrated this principle by sharing the story of Ken:

> One rainy Saturday afternoon, sometime about 4th grade, Clint and I were playing in the basement at his house and something very odd happened. We were playing a pretend game of "dress-up." Not women's stuff, but character things, like Halloween costumes. Clint suddenly started grabbing me and holding me close. I was being seduced! He was 11 or 12 and I was 10 or so. I felt revulsion and nausea, but also a strange feeling of secret excitement.
>
> I remember thinking that I should run away from this scene at the time, and tell Clint's folks and mine what had happened. But guilt, shame, and an odd delight overwhelmed me together in a deceptive recipe. I also didn't want to lose one of the few friends I had! I told no one about this incident for many years. Peer pressure had its payoffs, unfortunately.
>
> Clint initiated things, but it wasn't long into junior high days before I took the controlling initiative…having Clint come over to my folk's house before and after school. We got into some pretty heavy fantasies and sexual practices for 7th graders—including oral sex.
>
> Many, many times I see the course of my whole life almost unalterably set by that one afternoon; wishing, hoping I could go back somehow and re-do it differently, like a time traveler from the '60s TV show, *Time Tunnel*.

It's sad to think of all the kids who are mixed-up and really confused simply because of their ignorance of their inner needs, or because of sexual experimentation. It could all be so easily avoided by educating them about same-sex needs and the development of gender identity, not just in college or high school, but in junior high.

A friend recently wrote me that as she was driving to work she noticed a marquee in front of an intermediate school that said, "It's easier to build a boy than to mend a man." How true.

Kids need to hear this stuff early in their adolescence, and society shouldn't be afraid to talk about such things because the consequence of perpetuating ignorance about the matter too often leads to homosexuality. A kid needs to know that having same-sex contacts doesn't make him a homosexual. So many boys are bewildered about their identities after that sort of experience and they should be told not that it's okay, but that it's common. They need to learn what's behind their feelings, so they don't have to wonder and worry about themselves when they find pleasure in such experiences.

I'm currently reading an excellent book called _The Rejection Syndrome_, by Charles Solomon, that pertains to how some kids assume they're homosexual when they find same-sex contacts pleasurable. Solomon states the following in his book:

> What we know to be true, or what we think to be true, can have a direct impact on the way we feel—both emotionally and physiologically.

If you thought you were gay—interpreted your desires as such and acted upon these feelings in a sexual way—then found pleasure in the experience, you can see how you'd feel about yourself. You would be reinforcing what you thought to be true—believing you were gay when you weren't.

Many boys have these experiences during adolescence but don't wind up thinking they're gay because of them. Why? I think we can safely assume it's because they're secure in their gender identity— they've had their homo-emotional needs met sufficiently. Their same-sex contacts are merely an exploration of adolescent sexual

103

feelings. The crucial difference is that this exploration isn't carried any further in that direction.

However, the guy who hasn't had the same secure emotional background might assume such experiences are a confirmation of his "homosexual tendencies." Thus his homosexual identity solidifies, based on a misinterpretation of his feelings.

Solomon offers a grand example of perception-and-response:

Imagine a person who might be driving down a super-highway at 85 miles per hour. Classical music is playing on the radio, and the driver seems not to have a care in the world. Suddenly a car appears out of no-where, with lights flashing and siren blaring. The knowledge that he may be facing a trip to court, a big fine, and points on his driver's license may all flash through the driver's mind in an instant of time. There may be a queasy feeling in the stomach, as well. Then, as the patrol car pulls closer and the person is ready to pull over and face the consequences, suddenly the patrol car pulls around and goes on to answer a more urgent call. Now a new set of emotions begins to appear, based on new knowledge received in the mind. What was thought to be true, that he was going to be ticketed for speeding, resulted in fear and the emotions were upset and caused a corresponding physiological impact, the queasy stomach. As the situation was reversed, the new knowledge resulted in a change in the feelings, psychologically and physically, but a certain amount of time must pass before the process takes place and the person fully recovers.

What we believe is true about our condition can very definitely affect the way we feel. As the information comes that changes our beliefs, so will our feelings change...but a lifetime of emotional patterns may not reverse themselves without some time lapse and without constantly reminding oneself that the old information...is no longer true.

It definitely takes time to recover, Mike—to shed the old ways of thinking, feeling, reacting—but what joy you can experience during this time! As you permit the old, misconceived ideas of yourself to fall away, you'll begin to see the real you emerge—better, stronger, capable of finally loving and respecting yourself. So don't be discouraged that the process takes time. Instead, take heart from this new vision of yourself.

Okay, I'm really signing off for good now. Talk to you soon.

Dear Mike,

Isn't there some way you could take your trip to Mexico sooner than next month? That way you'd be back in time to still get in on the start of school. I really think going to Orange Coast or Saddleback would be good for you. I realize school's always there, but this term would be such a good time for you to sort of dip your toes in the water by starting up some healthy relationships with guys your own age.

I don't want to nag, so I won't say any more about it, but please, Mike, see if the guys you're going to Mexico with would be willing to leave a couple of weeks early, okay?

Nothing new here and I'd better get going before I'm late for work. Oh, yeah, I forgot, I did get a letter from Daniel. Things aren't going very well between him and Roger—that was awfully quick, wasn't it? Maybe you could give him a call just to see how he's doing. It would give him quite a lift and remind him he's got friends who care.

Let me know what you decide to do regarding school and Mexico.

Aloha,

Bud

Dear Mike,

Thanks for the letter. Yep, I got your postcard and it sounds like you had a good time (???).

Before I go any further, I want to tell you in black and white that I'm really in a good mood, and that my heart is full of love and compassion for you, so please don't read anything into this letter that isn't there, okay?

Let me also stress that I'm not mad at you. Disappointed in your behavior, yes, but I'll get over it. I thought something like this would happen when you told me who you were going with to Mexico. Sorta sounds like a reprise of the trip four years ago and for that I'm sad. You've learned so much, Mike. Are you going to throw it all away now?

Please let me know what you're feeling because I'm not sure how I should write you anymore. Do you still want to change? Was Mexico just a fluke, or are you planning on hanging around those guys? I know they're your friends, but they're not good for you.

You sounded almost boastful in talking about the things you did down there…where are you coming from, Mike? I just can't tell from your letter. Remember, I'm NOT mad at you, I'm just somewhat confused. Write soon.

Your friend,

Bud

Dear Mike,

I just want to comment on a few of the things we talked about last night. It really sounds to me as if you're trying to find every possible excuse for not starting to initiate steps to help you climb out of the pit you're in. For everything we talked about on the phone, you managed to come up with a flimsy excuse as to why you couldn't do it. You've got to be careful, Mike, to avoid the trap that I fell into at first. I thought if I knew this information—POOF!—I would be changed. I believed that somehow, through osmosis or something, this knowledge would automatically transform me. It doesn't work that way, though. *You've got to put this knowledge to work and make things happen.*

Another thing is that you should look at the positive. Don't dwell on the negative. Start noticing the things you *can* do and not just the things you can't. Do you see how the way you're looking at the healing process has to affect the outcome? If everything's viewed in negative terms, recovery is going to be a negative experience. If all you see is, "I can't do this and I can't do that," you're eventually going to quit out of despair and frustration. Let yourself see things as they really are, the things that produce life and healing. Then you'll stay motivated to carry through.

I'm afraid you've been looking at this whole process in the wrong way. Your focus can't be on not behaving homosexually, for that's only going to suppress your feelings, which will cause more damage and lead to a relapse of destructive behavior. Where your focus ought to be is on healing past hurts, meeting same-sex needs, and obtaining the male identity you truly desire.

I know I've already said this a zillion times, but I'm going to keep on repeating it until it sinks in. If you don't start dealing with the roots of your problem, then the problem will not only continue to exist but will actually grow. This will keep you stuck in your homosexual state.

Think of these roots as weeds. If you merely lop off the part that's exposed, the weed grows back. You've got to get to the roots—the very source—and pull them out to stop the weed's regrowth.

Did you ever draw up a list of things you thought contributed to your homosexuality? How about those books I recommended that deal with negating harmful feelings and attitudes developed in childhood? Remember, *Your Inner Child of the Past* and *Putting Away Childish Things*? Read them, Mike, please. Do it as a personal favor, or for any other reason you can come up with that's sufficiently compelling to get you to do it.

I guess the bottom line is this: you've got to start converting knowledge into action. Don't just sit on it because time will go by quickly and you won't see much change. Then you'll say these things don't work. *The only way they can work is if you apply them.* Enough said.

One last thing, though. Remember our agreement? I'll continue to help you in any way I can and be your friend, but you've got to be honest with me. Let me know how things are really going for you. I want the truth—not what you think I want to hear—even if it's "bad." Otherwise, how can I give you decent advice and effective feedback? This isn't to insinuate you haven't been honest in the past, but I just want to encourage you to remain so.

Aloha,

Bud

Hi, Mike!

Boy, I can't stand the way the media gives out "positive" portrayals of the gay lifestyle. Seems like there's something pro-gay every day on the tube. In fact, one particular barrier to changing my orientation was the way the media treated homosexuality. When I didn't think I had any choice about my identity, this type of attention made me feel better. I was thrilled about the coverage given to the plight of gays. Homosexuals were depicted as just your average, normal, male on the street, except for one small matter—they were attracted to other men.

Later on, when I was leaving that lifestyle, I'd be doing just fine until I saw something on TV portraying homosexuality as an "alternative" lifestyle. And that would throw me into a tailspin. I'd instantly feel defeated and old feelings would haunt me. Seeing other guys promoting the gay life touched a vulnerable spot in me. My gut reaction wanted to stand up and scream out in agreement: "Yes, yes, that's the real me. I'm gay!"

Now I know why I felt that way. It took most of my life for me to accept my homosexual feelings, and once I did I felt so relieved. The struggle to deny those feelings was over. I was no longer alone. By identifying myself as gay, I felt connected with those gay advocates showcased on TV. Since homosexual thoughts and desires had filled the majority of my past, it's no wonder I was pulled toward anything on the boob tube that displayed gay life as normal; I wanted to feel normal. What a great relief and comfort it was to discover there were other guys with similar feelings...I wasn't the only one.

Even when I'd begun the process of changing my orientation, I still had an overwhelming residual sense of a gay identity—I "felt" I was gay. Over the years my perception of who I was had been solely based on the foundation of my homosexual identity. And though I had recently been taught I wasn't gay, I couldn't turn off my feelings like a light switch. It was necessary for me to re-educate my response to those feelings, which ultimately changed them.

News coverage and movies really romanticize the gay lifestyle; they don't show the more common day-to-day struggles and soul-searching. I saw one movie that portrayed the hero as being discontented only while coming to grips with his homosexuality. Once he found his "true" identity, he lived happily ever after with "Mr. Right." It was a blatant attempt to sell homosexuality as gratifying and fulfilling, but that's so far from the truth, it stinks.

I really hurt for all the people who are misled by this type of presentation because I understand precisely how they feel when they encounter it. It made me feel that perhaps it would be possible to live a normal life as half of a homosexual couple once society accepted such arrangements as being within the sphere of normalcy. Even if such a thing were to happen, the majority of homosexuals would never find or keep a mate. They're engaged in an endless search to have their needs met by another man and no one man can meet those needs.

It's appallingly common in the gay community to have literally hundreds of sexual partners over a lifetime. This isn't just my own opinion—it's an established fact. The Kinsey Institute conducted perhaps the most thorough study on this issue. It reported that 43% of the white male homosexual surveyed estimated they'd had sex with 500 or more different partners—28% had sex with over 1,000 partners. (*Homosexualities: A Study in Diversity Among Men and Women,* by Alan P. Bell and Martin S. Weinberg, 1978, p. 308.)

These guys go to bars and baths, city parks and public rest rooms in desperate attempts to satisfy their desires. Yet all they achieve, at best, is temporary gratification of their sexual drive, and afterward, they're left with profound feelings of loneliness, rejection and frustration.

They all believe their troubles will end once society stops discriminating against them. They're sadly mistaken, but what other hope do they have? They have to pin the blame on someone for their unhappiness, and society makes a convenient scapegoat.

Meanwhile, the media focus their attention on a few gay spokesmen who try to convince the world that they're happy and content as homosexuals. I'm sure some of them actually think that they are happy. If you feel you had no choice in your sexual orientation…well, the strong will survive and eventually have to believe they're happy with what they're doing.

On the other hand, any homosexual who truly looked within himself and made an honest appraisal of what he saw, would have to admit to the turmoil in his life. Just look at how many alcoholics and drug-users there are in the gay community. They're trying to live their lives by entertaining themselves with drugs to keep their minds off their problems. Avoidance and denial are a whole lot easier than confrontation and reality.

Don't let the media rip you off, Mike. Stick to what you know is true. Follow the facts instead of feelings and emotions. Follow the things you've learned. Hope to hear from you soon.

Your pal,

Bud

Thursday
October 3, 1985

Dear Mike,

Please don't think I'm ever going to give up on you, buddy. I'm not mad that you went to a gay bar. Just disappointed. Yet my disappointment isn't so much in you as for you. You can't see it at the moment, but you're suffering additional harm each time you go to bars and/or engage in homosexual behavior because you're reaffirming a gay identity rather than moving away from it.

I am ticked off at Rich, though. He knows what you're trying to do, yet he continues attempting to dissuade you. Why can't he leave you alone? Have you been totally up-front with him about your intentions for the future? Does he know you're really committed? Or do you give him mixed signals, indicating this is something you're just giving a try? You need to be firm with him, Mike. Tell him to back off and let you live your life the way you want. Don't let him cause you to lose sight of your goals.

I don't care what he says; he's not as happy as he'd have you think. If you believe you don't have any choice, then you make the best of what you've got, right? So when Rich says he never had any choice, that he was born the way he is, what's he left with? He has to either deny or accept his feelings. The gay movement would have you accept "homosexual" desires. Rich accuses you of denying and suppressing your feelings. I say that you've got a third choice: see your desires for what they actually are, not what you think they are or what others tell you they are.

Granted, there are homosexuals who appear quite happy in their lifestyle, but I doubt that appearance would hold up under close inspection. When Brian and I were out with the boys, we looked like the perfect couple. It appeared that everything was going just fine for us. I thought I was happy for the most part because I only saw what I wanted to see. I only wanted to remember the good times. I didn't want to see the fights, the insane jealousies, the insecurities, and all the other garbage.

117

You're only seeing Rich when he's up, after he's had a few drinks, etc. If you really think his life is so wonderful, I challenge you to spend some time with him apart from the bar scene and apart from any homosexual activities. See how he is on a day-to-day basis, when there's nothing to entertain him and nothing to keep his mind occupied and off his problems. See how he handles life then. Listen to him. Observe the real Rich, not the guy you think he is or the person he wants you to believe he is.

Do you really and truly think he can be happy the way he lives? I'll bet you any amount of money he isn't. I don't care what he says, he isn't, Mike. More than likely, he's really experiencing a tremendous amount of anger, emptiness, and depression.

Let me relate to you some observations from Dr. Robert Kronemeyer's documented book, *Overcoming Homosexuality*, and then you tell me if you still think Rich is a genuinely happy guy:

> Saying "I am happy" neither describes nor confers a state of happiness. There can be a psychic interest in putting a gloss on appearances. Some of the most hopeless people have enough neurotic pride to try to conceal their inner turbulence with a cheery countenance—the best defense against letting others or, more importantly, oneself perceive the depths of one's unhappiness. There often is a messianic mission to "sell" homosexuality as a viable road to fulfillment.

Does that sound like Rich? Read on:

> Most homosexuals strenuously defend their way of life and—quite correctly—their right to "be Myself." Many of them honestly believe they are happy, "normal," and operating at full potential. Given the opportunity to change, they would choose to remain as they are. They assert that if it weren't for the bias and uptightness of "straight" society, they would have nothing, absolutely nothing, to complain about....

One of the benchmarks of homosexuality is promiscuity; it connotes the intensity of underlying fear and panic. The need for "proof" of desirability is insatiable. Driven from partner to partner, the gay skips from one "conquest" to the next along the interminable yellow brick road to "love everlasting." His sexual compulsion is like the drug addict's need for a fix or the alcoholic's unquenchable thirst. "To be gay is to go to the bar," lamented one male in a series of profiles of homosexuals, "to make the scene, to look and look, to have a one-night stand, never really to love or be loved, to know this and yet to do this night after night, and year after year...."

Three out of ten homosexual men have never had a relationship that survived the one-night stand, and most gay men have never had an exclusive relationship with another gay that lasted as long as six months....

Symptomatic of their distress is the difficulty that gays have in falling asleep at night; in one survey, three-quarters of the gays reported sleep problems. More than half of them confessed they sometimes or often drank too much. (It has been estimated that the rate of alcoholism among homosexuals is between 20 and 30 percent, or three to four times the rate of all American adults.) Two-thirds said their hands trembled enough to bother them. Forty percent were apprehensive about having a nervous breakdown....

The homosexual, whatever his accomplishments may be, is by and large an extremely tense, anxious, depressed, and bitter person just below the glossy exterior. Anyone who has desperate inner tension, constant jealousy, antagonism, envy, cynicism, and is often self-pitying can hardly be described as "happy" or "gay."

And that's all without mentioning the high incidence of hepatitis and other sexually transmitted diseases, let alone AIDS. It's amazing how the AIDS epidemic has spread the way it has. And it is no longer a threat just to the homosexual community. AIDS is afflicting intravenous drug users, people who receive blood transfusions, and even now individuals through heterosexual and bisexual contact. To me that's unbelievably tragic. I'm sure you've seen the headlines by now that Rock Hudson died of AIDS yesterday.

Can you honestly say the homosexual lifestyle is a happy one? Do you still think Rich is as happy as he claims? I'm not saying he fits into each of Kronemeyer's descriptions, but just look at the statistics. Look at your other gay friends and listen to how they talk about their present and future expectations. The reality of homosexuality is that it's a depressing life, Mike. For your own good, please don't listen to Rich. For reasons even he may not be aware of, he's trying to sabotage your efforts.

Try to make some new friends, maybe at work where you feel the most comfortable. Start by initiating casual conversation with a guy you'd like to get to know. In time, when you feel more at ease with him, take another bold step and ask if he'd like to get a bite to eat during your lunch hour. Or maybe go to a sports event or movie together. The important thing is to start somewhere. Set out to cultivate new friendships, ones that'll add to your growth, not diminish it.

That's what I did when I first came out of the lifestyle. I started developing new friendships with guys during softball games, and at school, church, and work. It helped me a lot.

Hang in there, Mike. I'm pulling for you.

Your friend,

Bud

Dear Mike,

So Malibu's on fire, again. I called Jimmy when I first heard about it and he said the flames jumped right over his house. Then they landed down again on that old shack of his out back, destroying it in about two seconds flat. No big loss there, right?

Apparently, my dad's place escaped harm altogether. He said the fire never got closer than 100 yards. That's sure a far cry from the big blaze of 1978. I remember being up on the roof, trying to keep it sprayed down, and watching our neighbor's house burn to the ground. What a nightmare. Hopefully, this time won't be as bad.

Thanks for your honest letter. I'm sure it was difficult for you to write it and I appreciate you all the more for it.

Believe me, there were definitely those times when I just wanted to shove all this material aside and give in to my desires. Many times I did. I didn't care about the cost involved. It didn't matter that I was only adding to my problem by reinforcing my homosexual identity. I needed a fix—and for a few fleeting minutes, it seemed to work. There was always a price to be paid, however, a setback of some sort or another.

It's amazing how something that takes just a few minutes can control your whole life, I used to think. But I was only seeing homosexuality in sexual terms. When you believe such statements as that, you're basically saying your entire life is determined by your sexual drive. Sure, there were times when that's exactly how I felt. However, when you look at the problem from the perspective of all your newly acquired knowledge, you know you're not searching for sex, but for your masculine identity and fulfillment of your homo-emotional needs.

Since I was there once, I've got a reasonably good idea of how difficult your struggles are. I know it's easier to gratify your sexual desires. It is easier to feel victimized and give up. It's easier to kick back and relax, and let whatever happens happen. Easier, yes, but not

121

better. Easier, but not fulfilling and lasting. It's easier *at the moment*, but not in the long run. Mike, if you take the path of least resistance, you won't find your true heterosexual identity—you'll just stay stuck where you are.

We all have sexual longings. When these desires are gratified, it *does* bring us pleasure. However, it *doesn't* do a thing to satisfy the same-sex needs driving them. Sure, it feels good to have the attention of another guy, to be sought after, to have sex, and so on, but what are the long-term effects? The fact that you enjoy the attention of another guy—what's behind that, Mike? Identification, belonging, acceptance from a male—even if it's in a perverted way—that's what's motivating you to be sought after by another guy and you need to recognize this.

I think every gay man knows to an extent what led to his homosexual orientation. He might not be able to put his finger on it precisely at first, but once some light is shed on possible causes, things become much clearer. If you took the time to look, you'd see quite clearly the events and circumstances that created your condition. I always had a vague idea of why I was gay. Now it's even clearer to me because I can see how my unaffirmed gender identity gave me a weak foundation.

Insight and knowledge alone should motivate you to do things to promote healing. However, I found what really keeps you going is *experiencing the fulfillment of these hidden needs.* It's satisfying and stimulating beyond belief, Mike, and that will inspire you to continue to grow.

Don't stop now! Don't give up before you even try! I know it's hard, but that's just for now, at the beginning.

What else is going on? Why do you continue to avoid things that will prompt healing in your life? Do you really want to change? Remember, just knowing this information isn't enough; you have to apply it.

I don't know what else to say at this point, except please write soon.

Your bro,

Bud

Wednesday
October 30, 1985

Dear Mike,

Hey, buddy, next time you're feeling as down and out as you were Friday night, please give me a call—collect or any other way. I want to be there for you. I'm really sorry I hadn't thought to tell you before now that I'm not any farther away than the phone. I mean it, anytime at all. I don't care whether it's three or four in the morning, or whatever. If you're down, running it all by someone who cares can really make a difference. So don't forget, okay?

I understand your concern about establishing satisfactory hetero- sexual relationships, and I know how impossible it seems to you at this point that there could be any physical fulfillment in being straight. I wasn't at all sexually attracted to women, either, but that'll change for you just as surely as it did for me, so give it some time.

What you can and must deal with at the moment is your overriding ambivalence towards males. Put an end to your uncer- tainty and start taking some positive steps toward achieving your goal of healthy, affirmative relationships. Make a calculated deci- sion to change, Mike. Merely wanting to change in an on-again, off- again way isn't enough.

You have to do whatever it takes to stop the progression of your gay identity and that means, among other things, you've got to stop going to gay bars. When you go to those places you're just nurturing negative behavior patterns and thought processes, and reinforcing your homosexual condition.

You need to do some self-analysis, Mike. Engage in a little introspection. Search for what's behind your compulsive behavior. How were you feeling Friday night before you went out? In your letter you said you were lonely and that you were seeking compan- ionship. Is it possible that your real need or desire was simply a friend? You also said you were bored and horny, which made you decide to hit the bars. Was it actually sexual desire motivating you, or was it something else that triggered your trip to the bars?

123

From what you told me, this is my analysis of what happened. You were depressed, bored, and lonely. Watching the guys next door playing basketball made you envious. You compared yourself to them and consequently felt inadequate. You wanted to be with someone you could relate to, someone who would accept and appreciate you, so you decided to go out.

First, you stopped by the gym to get all pumped up. Then after showering and putting on just the right attire to get maximum attention, you headed for the bar. You got a drink, began to relax, and then were ready to bask in the attention you were to receive. Feeling better, you told yourself that this was exactly what you'd needed. The ritual seemed to work once more—temporarily, anyway—until the following day and the process begins again.

My question for you is this—when will it stop?

You need to understand what's going on. Your normal needs are being misinterpreted as erotic desires, and because you see them as such, you try to fulfill them in sexual ways. Homosexual behavior, though, is the very antithesis of what you need and consequently you'll never be satisfied. You're constantly in search of the one guy who'll do it all for you, Mike, and he doesn't exist. The answer, the solution, lies within you.

The next time you get the desire to go bar-hopping, try to ascertain what your true needs are at that moment. Analyze how you're feeling. Dissect your desires. See if there isn't a link between what's superficially sexual and the very real feelings of loneliness, boredom, frustration, hopelessness, anger, etc.

Here's something to memorize and carry with you the rest of your life. Whenever you're depressed or just down in the dumps, stop or halt everything—whatever it is you're doing—and think for a minute: Am I *H*ungry? Am I *A*ngry? Am I *L*onely? Am I *T*ired? *H-A-L-T*. Nine times out of ten, your depression is caused by one of these things. Once you've figured out which it is, you can deal with it and put a halt to the blues.

Going through my journal this morning, I was trying to find accounts of experiences I'd had that you might relate to, and I came across a real gem—a day that encompassed every one of the feelings just mentioned. I was tired from working several weeks in a row without a day off. I was hungry because I'd resolved not to eat before dinner-time in an attempt to counteract my rather gross consumption of junk food the night before. Angry over pigging out like that, I was down on myself, and capping the whole thing off, I felt terribly lonely.

Instead of taking a nap, getting something to eat or calling a friend, I stayed indoors, feeling sorrier and sorrier for myself. Then I got angry at God for not taking pity on me and doing something about my situation. I knew better, but this was just one of those times when I didn't want to pull myself up—I wanted someone else to do it for me. Right, I know that's about as negative as you can get, but that was me at that particular moment, and I'm trying to be as honest with you as I can, Mike.

So how did I ultimately respond to all this? I called Brian and naturally we wound up seeing each other. Sure, I knew what I should have done, but I chose a moment's pleasure and satisfaction instead of seeking long-term results. I took the easy way out, without any concern for my future and the goals I'd set, and I had to pay a pretty stiff price as a result. For literally weeks after that hour I spent with Brian, I had to fight down even stronger desires to see him and be with him again. I'd seen some real changes in my feelings toward him up to that point, but a lot of it was lost in just that one hour. What a mistake.

I needed to acknowledge my behavior was irresponsible, that this behavior, coupled with my attitudes and thoughts, was keeping me in a holding pattern slanted toward more homosexual conduct.

As you can see, it's how you respond to your desires that will determine your future identity. The more you interpret and respond to your feelings as homosexual urges, the more deeply etched they become. Without consciously considering your feelings, you habitually reinforce the label you've placed upon yourself. You need to recognize that these feelings have as their beginning legitimate needs and/or normal desires.

"*H-A-L-T*ing" will help you see these feelings for what they really are!

I had to learn the hard way, through trial and error, but you don't have to go through all that. You can learn from my mistakes. Try to tune into what you're really feeling, what you really need. I assure you, once I started putting the acronym into consistent practice, *H-A-L-T* saved me a lot of grief.

I'll write you later, but right now I've got to get ready for work. Hang in there, Mike. You'll be okay.

Your buddy,

Bud

Dear Mike,

Sorry I haven't been home. Ray and I are thinking of buying ourselves 12-speeds, so we flew over to Oahu for a couple of days to check out some bike shops. We just got back this morning and the first thing I did was listen to my phone messages.

Mike, you sound really awful. I couldn't make out much of your first telephone message at all because you were crying so much. All I managed to decipher from the rest was that you had gone to see Reed and after walking in on him, found him with another guy.

What's happening??? I've been calling you all day, but nobody answers. I was hoping that at least Dave would pick up the phone, but no go.

Why didn't you tell me you were seeing Reed? Do you still love him? What's the story, Mike? What about all these sexual encounters you've had in the past few months?

I'll try to call you again tonight.

Next day 8:00 p.m.

Mike, I tried calling you from work today during my breaks and I've continued calling ever since getting home. I'm really worried now, buddy. Please, PLEASE, call me as soon as you get this letter. I don't know if you're there and just not answering the phone, or what's going on.

I hope you didn't think I was trying to avoid you or something when you only got the answering machine. I want to be there for you, buddy, but I can't always be at home. If I'm not in, leave a message telling me where I can reach you. If you're home, but not answering the phone in case it's Reed calling, just let me know what sort of signal I should use to get through—you know, one ring, hang up and then call back, or whatever. Call soon—please.

Bud

Friday
November 15, 1985

Dear Mike,

Wish you would've called, but I'm grateful for the letter. What a relief to know you're okay. I've been half-crazy worrying about you. No, I don't hate you, and no, I'm not mad at you. How many times do I have to tell you that you shouldn't feel that way?

So what are you going to do now? You can't just sit in your room for the rest of your life. How many days of work have you missed?

Although I've long accepted that life is full of surprises, I've got to admit that your relationship with Reed was one of the bigger bombshells I've encountered recently. I'm sorry you had to go through it alone. It must have been very painful, and I know that it's still agonizing. Breaking up is a horrendously difficult thing to do.

At least now I know why you've been so reluctant to put any real effort into re-orienting yourself. I expected some resistance, but not nearly as much as you've given. You may not want to hear this, but I'm going to say it anyway. I don't believe in coincidence. All of this is happening for a reason—to force you to start on your new life by breaking you loose from compelling counter-influences out of your old life. Even though it doesn't feel that way to you now, I honestly believe it's for the best, Mike.

I don't know if this will make you feel any better or not, but when I deliberately chose to break up with Brian so I could change my lifestyle, I felt like I was suffering all the more for having consciously decided to bring that misery down upon myself.

I was in emotional, mental, even physical anguish that words cannot describe. Breaking up was a necessary step for me to take and somewhere deep inside I knew that, though it didn't seem to relieve any of the pain. Now you couldn't pay me to go back with him. There's no sum of money in the world that would make going back worthwhile. My life today is 900 million times better than it ever was when we were together. I'm thankful we broke up—Brian is, too.

Gotta go now. Ray's car broke down yesterday so I have to pick him up at work. I'm really glad you're okay. Just hang in there. I know what you're going through, Mike, and I'm praying for you. You'll make it. If I could, then you can—and that's a guarantee from a friend who loves and supports you.

Always,

Bud

P.S.

Don't worry about ruining it for me at this end. I've got my own phone so Ray never heard the messages.

Dear Mike,

I'm really worried about you. When you talk about suicide, are you just telling me how bad you feel or are you seriously thinking suicidal thoughts?

No matter how hard or bad things get, suicide isn't the answer. I was suicidal for years. At least once a day for three entire years I contemplated killing myself. It was always on my mind. I even tried it once by taking an overdose of pills, but thank God, I failed.

And again a few years ago, I'd lost all hope and motivation. Utterly depressed, I felt I just had to die. I thought death was the only way to escape my despair. Sitting with my dad for a few hours one Christmas morning, I told him I just couldn't go on, that I didn't want to try anymore. He knew I was serious and I could see the concern on his face. For the longest time nothing he said about it mattered to me. I felt sorry for him, sorry I was hurting him, but that was it. Then the more he talked to me, and the more I talked and he listened—really listened—I felt a little better. Not much, but at least a little.

Yeah, he knows about my past. I was drunk one night with a friend of the family, running off at the mouth, and one thing led to another until I totally spilled my guts to her, including my intention of killing myself. She told my dad within hours. Normally, I would have been furious that she'd told him, but at that point I just didn't care anymore. Since I thought I was going to end it all very shortly anyway, it didn't really matter to me what my dad thought.

I wanted to die—I really did—and I would have killed myself if it weren't for that talk with my dad and another conversation I had with someone else. Remind me to tell you about Vern Hunt some-time, Mike. If not for him, I know beyond any doubt that I'd be dead today.

My point is, death isn't the answer. I made it through those rough times and I'm very thankful I'm still alive. I've found that life is a wonderful gift, and it can be for you, too, but you have to make it happen.

Call me, Mike. Call me everyday if you need to. I want you to make it, and I know you can. Don't worry about the cost. We can split it, or if you can't afford it, then just call collect. That's not important. What is important is that I'm here for you, no matter what. Swallow your pride and talk to me, buddy. Get things off your chest and don't keep them to yourself, because when you're feeling this low, they're getting more than a little distorted.

Write if you can. Call me whenever. I care very much, Mike. Remember that.

Lots of love from your friend in the islands,

Bud

P.S.

It's just occurred to me that you may think I was "gently suggesting" you tell your folks about your homosexuality. I wasn't, Mike. I don't think it would be wise at all, unless you think they'd receive it in a good way. From all I know of your father, though, I don't think he'd respond as you'd like him to and I know you don't need any extra grief right now. I'm sorry if I gave you the wrong impression about it at first.

Over and out.

Dear Mike,

Wow, terrific timing on my part, huh? Sorry I wasn't here for your call but don't worry, the answering machine didn't cut you off last night—I got the whole message. (If you happen to catch it again, just remember it's voice-activated and will record a message up to five minutes long.)

I hope you didn't see Reed, but if you did, I understand. I ran to Brian a lot of times when I was feeling down, even when I knew that while it would make me feel better at first, I'd only feel worse later. Not so much because of guilt, but because it just wasn't satisfying. The feeling never lasted. It was just a fix to get me by.

There were many nights when all I wanted to do was quit, to just stop trying, and to accept the fact that I was gay and always would be. I wanted to run back to Brian and live happily ever after. The only thing that stopped me was the input I'd been getting from the group, the knowledge that it wouldn't work—not with Brian, not with any guy. Yet there were easily 1,200,682 times—give or take a few—that I tried to talk myself into believing that things would be different with somebody else, even if I couldn't make it work with Brian. It wouldn't have been any different, though, and it won't be for you, either. It's the nature of that life—or more precisely, the troubled nature of those living it—that guarantees the same old problems will surface in every relationship.

You still sound pretty down, Mike. How about taking a week off and coming over here for a visit? I've already checked with Ray and he says you'd be more than welcome. If it sounds like a plan, you'd better book a flight pronto. Ray tells me there isn't much leeway for last-minute travel arrangements between now and Christmas. I think it would really be good for you, and I'd love to see you, so try, okay?

Gotta run. Let me know what's up as soon as you can.

Your friend,

Bud

Dear Mike,

I just got your letter. You better not kill yourself, buddy. You've got to give me the chance to help. I honestly believe one of the reasons you're sharing your feelings with me is because you want someone to help you. Well, I'm someone who wants to do just that, so give me the chance.

You keep saying I wouldn't understand how you feel, Mike, but I do. I was there. How many times do I have to tell you that I know what it feels like to want to die, to really want to die? I was suicidal for years. Absolutely all I wanted was to get this life over with. I felt like I didn't belong here on the planet, that I didn't fit in anywhere. Believing I'd been born gay and given desires I didn't want, hadn't chosen and couldn't refuse, I felt helplessly and hopelessly trapped. No choices, no options.

Until now you, too, have believed you don't have any choice…but you do, just as I did. Do you want to be homosexual or not? Choice is just another word for decision and you're the only one who can make the decision to change. I know it's not easy, Mike. You feel like you're all alone without any help, but you're not—I want to help you.

To show you that I do understand what you're going through, I'm sending you part of my journal to read. It's you I trust, Mike, so please, please, keep it confidential and don't let anyone else—not even Reed—go through it. Okay?

You're about to enter the Twilight Zone:

* * * *

Friday 11/5/82
Malibu, California

I don't know why, but I'm at Dad's house for the weekend. Seems so odd to recognize that it's really a very pretty day—the sun's out and there's just a hint of a breeze to push all those billowing

135

clouds across the sky—yet looking outside just magnifies my pain. Looking inward, I see only emptiness, shattered dreams, lost hopes, loneliness without end. Isn't there any way out of this?

Seconds turn into minutes, into hours, days, weeks. What am I doing living minute-to-minute or day-to-day, when I'm always thinking I'm not going to make it to the next, only to find myself still existing with months gone by? I feel like I'm living in an invisible prison, but "living" is hardly the right word for merely enduring, for barely maintaining, for just scraping by.

I honestly can't bear much more. There aren't even any words available to convey this agony, so why go on trying to cope with it? I feel like there's so much inside I want to say, but I just don't know how anymore. I want to scream out my anger, but what would it accomplish? Just another noise in the universe. So pain remains and that thing called future is surely in jeopardy. Death equals solution, my only way out.

Saturday 11/6/82

Malibu, California

How can this existence be called living when society dictates every move? I don't want to go on like this. I'm so tired of the lying—of the continual, non-ending lies necessary to being accepted. After all it's not "me" who's being accepted—it's who they want me to be, but not me. How long will I have to go on making excuses? Why can't I just be me, the real me?

Still, I can't really blame them. Even saying it to myself it sounds strange, "homosexual." It's unacceptable as a word—a "dirty" one, in fact—and so much worse as a fact than as a word. However, I can't help what I am and how I feel. I'm attracted to men and not women, and I'm in love with another guy.

Why must things be so complicated? Why must deceit be as common and as necessary as breathing? Why???

I waited all my life for the day I fell in love—the Great Moment of All Moments. And here I am today, 27 years old, in love with a guy who's 24. In love...and yet such ambivalence toward the relationship. How is it possible to love something so much while hating it even more? I love being loved, feeling loved. I find enormous

136

pleasure in the intimacy we share, in loving and caring for Brian— but these things aren't satisfying. Something's missing. So the search goes on and I don't know what I'm looking for, except something that will last, something that will satisfy me and stop this aching need. Why is it that things with Brian were satisfying at first, but aren't any longer? The only satisfaction I find in our relationship now occurs while having sex, and even then it doesn't satisfy my inner longing for something else.

I just feel so continuously empty—perhaps because everything we do is so secret. We're always hiding, trying to protect ourselves, afraid of being found out, unable to live like other couples, normal couples. What would people say, what would they think? Maybe the strain is just too much for our relationship to overcome. I don't know. Maybe all I'm really seeking is acceptance. Accept us and leave us alone and I'll be happy.

We do have happy times. They're just between us though. And even those are being eroded and destroyed by how others think we should live. Or maybe I should be blaming myself for letting "them" control my life and actions to the extent that I don't feel free to do anything without considering all possible consequences?

I feel so weighted down—like I'm being crushed alive by my circumstances—without enough strength to fight back. I don't even want to fight back anymore. Life's done such a good job of dictating everything for me so far, ruthlessly telling me to do this and not to do that, to dress, talk, and act like everybody else, making me wish I was like everybody else, so that I could feel normal and know what it's like to really be accepted. Can't they understand I'm not like everybody else! I'm a faggot!

I didn't choose to be gay—I hate being different—yet I've never had any say in the matter. So it seems perfectly fitting now that I've had more than my fill of all the pressures and fears—to take the one action I can call my own. I just want to be free from this hell I'm living in.

Monday 11/15/82

Seal Beach, California

Insomnia is going to drive me crazy—is already making me

crazy. Another restless night…I don't know how much longer I can stand just lying there wide-awake, especially when I'm so exhausted. What's causing this latest curse? Last night I was beat from not sleeping the night before and intentionally kept myself awake until late so I could sleep the night through. It didn't work. I was awake from 1:30 a.m. till sometime after 5:00 a.m. The more I tried to just drift off again, the more impossible it became. I tried everything from clearing my mind of all conscious thought, to changing position, to getting up and making a sandwich; but nothing worked. I merely got infuriated and more tense by the moment. Why can't I sleep—why, why, WHY???

Then a new day begins. Just getting out of bed seems impossibly exhausting. I want things to be different—normal people don't go through this. It seems I'm always hoping for tomorrow and my tomorrows never come. The hope is vain, or else it's just plain false. Tomorrow is always like the day before—or worse.

I'm so tired. Every single movement takes extraordinary effort.

Things between Brian and me are the pits. All we seem to do nowadays is argue, and over the stupidest little things. I can't believe we allow ourselves to do this day in and day out. When will it stop? What will it take to make us quit letting our lives be governed by insecurity and jealousy? I just don't feel like I have any control over the person I am.

Monday 11/22/82
Seal Beach, California

I've been too depressed to write this past week. I really think life has come to an end for me. Nothing's going to shake me out of this and I don't much care. The only thing I want is to talk to Brian about how I feel, but he doesn't understand how someone could want to die, and he doesn't want to listen.

Thursday 11/25/82
Seal Beach, California

What began as a short walk on the beach this Thanksgiving Day lengthened into a seven-hour period of intensive self-examination. I was all alone except for an occasional seagull wheeling overhead.

How I envied their freedom, their simplicity of life when mine is so full of confusion and doubt.

Now that I'm out of school I need to start making some decisions, some plans for my future. Instead, every thought I had today was consumed with the concept of death as a means of escaping this wretched existence. I found it impossible to concentrate on developing plans for a future.

Being alone on a traditionally "family" holiday didn't help any. I want so much to be with loved ones at times like these and it really hurt to know Brian was at his family's annual gathering, enjoying a plentiful feast, while I was roaming the shores of the Pacific, alone and lonely, again. Wouldn't it have been wonderful if they'd known the truth about us and had invited us as a couple to share in the festivities of the family? That could never be, though, not with his family. As for mine, I neither know nor care. With everyone living so far apart and each doing his or her own thing, it's not much of a family anyway. I don't even want to think about it, not anymore.

From this time alone on the beach today, a poem:

Choice: To be alive, to live with a lie,
to be honest and live.

Being alive isn't worth living. Death?

To live with the lie brings a bit of happiness,
but is a hard and difficult path to follow.
It's frustrating, lonely, and empty not being true
to oneself and others. It's joy not heard,
love not shared, honesty not seen
or missed.

Honesty? Life doesn't want to see the truth—
it's "sinful, repulsive, abnormal, and wrong."
Life's cruel, non-understanding. It says there's
a choice, but there is none. The decision was made
as readily as with my brown hair and hazel eyes. And

I've since cried until I could no longer cry. I've
prayed, begged, and bargained for naught.

Death appears—again—to be a choice, my own.
It taps me on the shoulder daily, offering me rest
and peace of mind. It's been three whole years now,
and Death's lure has become ever so strong. A
selfish way out, indeed, but Life's left no room
to look elsewhere. Feeling sorry for myself, some
would say, but not any longer, I answer. Just tired.
No sympathy wanted, just rest from the struggle.

Friday 11/26/82
Seal Beach, California

Funny, I've been writing in this journal for over a year now and
all during that time I've dreaded the idea of anyone else ever seeing
what I've written. I thought I'd die if that ever happened; I worried
about dying accidentally and leaving this behind. That's why it
seems so funny that I'm now about to entrust the whole thing to
whomever might be interested in it. For a year I've been writing to
myself, yet what follows is meant to be read by others. By reading it
you'll understand me better and oddly I take some comfort in that.
I'm just sorry it's come too late.

This will be my last entry. I don't know how to begin writing such
a difficult thing as this. For some of you, what I'm about to do will
come as a complete surprise, and yet others of you have seen at least
a glimpse of what I've been going through. I want you to know that
I've postponed suicide for the longest time because of an infinitesi-
mally small amount of hope that I might somehow change. Now I've
discovered that when hope vanishes, so does all motivation to live on.

For those of you to whom I talked some about my suicidal
thoughts, I can easily put myself in your shoes: *if only you'd known,
if only you'd said this or that, if only you'd done more to help, if
only*...unfortunately, this isn't one of those situations. There aren't
any if's and there isn't anything anyone could have done to change
things.

140

For literally years now, I've been thinking of this as the only sure way out of my pain.

Every detail has been planned and replanned to minimize the trauma this is going to cause. I didn't want any of you to have to be the one who finds me dead and have to suffer the rest of your life every time you had to go out in the garage or something. I thought of going away to do it and leaving a note behind, going someplace like Mexico where I'd never be found or at least never identified, but then the uncertainty would've been even more painful for you. This way really seems best for everyone except the paramedics. Hopefully they'll be veterans conditioned to this sort of thing, though I realize it's scarcely likely they prefer dealing with the remains of someone who's blown his brains out. I regret the necessity of such a messy way to die, but I want to make certain this time. You never knew that I tried to kill myself before, about eight years ago, with pills, but as with everything else in my life, I didn't do that right either.

With an end to the pain in sight, I can't rationalize staying around any longer. I'd only prove to be even more of a burden than I've already been, and I want to leave while I still have friends. I understand what a drag it is for someone to always be depressed—talking about ending it all—whenever you see them. By telling you I felt suicidal, I wanted you to truly know how desperate I was for help, but in reaching out to you that way I guess I was mostly just living off your strength and energy, trying to exist long enough for things to get better. They didn't.

Know that I'm happy now and rejoice with me in that. No more struggling to try to be someone I couldn't be—the fight is over. I'm really very sorry for the pain I've caused. I love you all very much.

Jeff

Saturday 11/27/82
Lake Arrowhead, California

How things change! Today was the day I was going to kill myself, and instead here I am at Lake Arrowhead, booked into a comfortable room overlooking the water, surrounded by the eternal serenity of mountains and pines. Dark storm clouds are closing

141

swiftly on the ridge across the lake, something I'd ordinarily find a perfect accompaniment to whatever gloomy mood I was in, yet today it's a scene that enhances the cozy contentment I'm feeling.

When I returned from my walk yesterday, I found a message on my answering machine from Carolyn, who was driving up from La Jolla. She wanted to know if I had time to get together for an hour or so this morning. As soon as I heard her, I wanted to say, "Well, sure, but I'll have to reschedule this other little thing I've got planned...."

I really did want to see her, though, and bless her, she took one look at me and asked what was going on in a way that meant she really wanted to know, regardless of whether it was good or bad. Nobody could've been more surprised than me, though, when I heard myself saying I wondered what she thought of me.

Sitting there across the table from her I realized I had to follow up on what I'd just said and tell her the truth. After all, she'd be finding out soon enough when the news of my suicide reached her. In any case, at that moment the thing I most desired was for Carolyn to understand me. Unable to put it off any longer, I fumbled for some way to break it gently, and then just said flat-out that I was gay.

I hadn't been aware I was trembling, but it hit me at the same instant I registered Carolyn's reaction—her eyes filled with tears. She reached across the table, gripped my hand, and then said, "I love you."

Just like that. I was utterly dumbfounded, practically in shock. Of all possible responses, that was the very last one I'd anticipated. I don't know how long I just babbled all sorts of stuff at her before finally calming down enough so we could have a real conversation. We then talked until we were both emotionally exhausted.

At the end she gave me some money and told me to get away by myself for the weekend and get my priorities in order. Since Brian is leaving for a ski trip right after work with a friend of his, Carolyn's idea and generosity couldn't have come at a better time. One last remarkable thing about our encounter was that she absolutely insisted I start putting my thoughts down on paper. It enabled me to reveal at least one area of my life where I've been doing the right thing by my standards as well as someone else's. Carolyn has just got to be the best stepmother and friend in the world.

So here I am, not dead at all but very much alive. The rock I'm sitting on feels like a block of ice, but everything around me is so beautiful I don't want to budge an inch. I can't begin to express how good I feel, like some captive part of me has finally been freed.

I just reread what I wrote yesterday and the contrast between how I felt then and how I feel right now is so incredible I can scarcely relate to yesterday's entry. I've decided to rewrite the poem:

Choice: To be alive, to live with a lie,
to be honest and live.

Being alive isn't worth living. Death?

To live with the lie brings a bit of happiness
but is a hard and difficult path to follow.
It's frustrating, lonely, and empty not being true
to oneself and others. It's joy not heard,
love not shared, honesty not seen
or missed.

Honesty? Life doesn't want to see the truth—
it's "sinful, repulsive, abnormal, and wrong."
Life's cruel, non-understanding. It says there's
a choice, but there is none. The decision was made
as readily as with my brown hair and hazel eyes. And
I've since cried until I could no longer cry. I've
prayed, begged, and bargained for naught.

Death appears—again—to be a choice, my own.
It taps me on the shoulder daily, offering me rest
and peace of mind. It's been three whole years now,
and Death's lure has become ever so strong. A
selfish way out, indeed, but Life's left no room
to look elsewhere. Feeling sorry for myself, some
would say, but not any longer, I answer. Just tired.
No sympathy wanted, just rest from the struggle.

Now I have finally chosen, just one, from only three.
Choosing the third, I envision what the outcome may be:
an insensitive ear, lack of compassion, jeering laughter,
outright rejection...A strenuous task lies
directly ahead, I think.

I told my family today. To my surprise and delight
it was a beautiful and treasured moment shared.
Would you believe they love me still!
Perhaps even more.
Such a relief, an unbelievable alleviation of fear;
Encouragement and acceptance of myself for who I am.
I am Gay!

Tried to call Brian, but he's either not home yet or has already gone. Can't remember what I said in the note I left for him, but whatever it was, it can't even begin to say what's happened in the world today. This is just too wonderful to be true. I feel so incredibly free. I'm going to live a normal life, tell the world I'm gay and not worry about it, live openly with Brian in the way I've always wished to do. No more lies, no more hiding. We're not roommates, we're lovers.

This is going to help our relationship so very much.

Sunday 11/28/82
Lake Arrowhead, California

I can't believe it. My outlook is even brighter this a.m.! I have this massive sense of strength and confidence that doesn't feel like it'll ever quit and I hardly know what to do with myself because I want to do everything. Carrying this secret around for so many years, always being an outsider, you really begin feeling that you're crazy. I never realized just how desperately I needed someone to confide in, someone who would simply listen and accept me. (Was it really family acceptance that I needed, or did I really just need to accept myself? Perhaps both. Probably both. It's almost as if I hadn't accepted it myself until I told Carolyn.) After fighting these feelings for so long, and then lying to everyone, pretending to be straight so

I could preserve a steady place in their regard, it's absolutely fantastic to finally be true to myself from my heart on out.

Later...

Sure wish Brian was up here with me. Everybody seems to be paired off with someone and I can't stop thinking about him being with Heather, having fun with her instead of being here with me. I've got so much I want to say to him and share with him; guess I just miss him and I'm feeling lonely.

Later...

Met a couple of guys downstairs in the gym who've invited me to a party in their room tonight. They're both really good-looking, very nice, and indisputably "straight" (both made a point of telling me that a lot of women would attend). Wish I didn't always feel so inhibited and awkward whenever I'm around guys like them. My mind just seems to go blank, like we have absolutely zero in common to talk about, and whatever I manage to say comes out sounding so stiff, I might as well be a ventriloquist's dummy. I'm sure my terror shows all over my face.

Later still...

Instead of eating in the hotel, I decided to go down to the village. Wouldn't you know it, getting out of the elevator I ran into the same two guys again. I was instantly uptight and felt I was going to start stuttering uncontrollably. It's so stupid because I wanted so badly to appear normal, cool, at ease—like them. To my surprise, however, apparently none of my ridiculous stress visibly manifested itself. They acted like we were all old acquaintances and asked me to have dinner with them. I declined—naturally—and said I was on my way down to The Mac as an economy gesture, then nearly had a seizure when they chorused "Great!" and invited themselves along!

It was terribly awkward being with them, and yet at the same time it was somehow really fulfilling. I thought I wanted the whole world to know I was gay, but it suddenly hit me how good it felt to be with those two without them knowing. On the other hand, the whole time we were together I couldn't stop wishing they were gay, too (they really are both very good-looking). I don't know...it's hard to describe my feelings right now.

Anyhow, on the way back we ran into some people they knew

who were heading for the local pub until the party starts, and I wound up being invited to join their merry little group. I tried to get out of it by saying I was meeting a friend at eight, which of course led to the invitation being extended to "her, too," so I had to stretch the story a bit further and explain that "we" were going to be "busy catching up" for the rest of the night. This elicited all the usual remarks and didn't make me feel a whole lot better about trudging back here to watch TV by myself.

Why do I let my inhibitions keep me from experiencing so much of life, of what everybody else does? It sounded as if they were going to have a lot of fun, but I was positively terrified of joining them. I don't even know precisely what I was afraid of, except maybe I was scared of looking like a jerk, or even worse, a fag who'd somehow strayed into the midst of these good-looking straight people. Oh, well.

Monday 11/29/82
Seal Beach, California

All day long I was really jazzed over finally getting to tell Brian about my talk with Carolyn and how good I feel about being gay and being with him. This new freedom is nearly impossible to contain and I want so much to share it with him. Now he's called to say he'll be staying in Mammoth one more night. I was so disappointed I cried after he hung up. I mean, I've waited all day just to see him walk through the door, to tell him how much I love him and need him and have missed him. I'm so bummed now.

Tuesday 11/30/82
Seal Beach, California

I feel utterly miserable and so let down. Brian just left for work after not getting home until noon. He wasn't in the best of moods anyhow, from having to get out on the road at dawn, and I should've known better than to try talking with him, but I just couldn't wait to share the excitement of the past few days. The instant I started telling him about my conversation with Carolyn, though, he began tensing up. I wanted him to know how fantastic it made me feel, but he just

146

got ultra-defensive and paranoid, and started carrying on about what his family would do if they ever found out about us.

"Who cares?" I said. "Are we supposed to live out the rest of our lives just for others? What could be better than simply being true to ourselves and starting to genuinely *live* for a change?" He just couldn't seem to see that there has to come a time when we recognize that what matters the most is how we feel about ourselves, not what people think about us. I told him that if his family really loved him, they'd only want whatever makes him happy, but his response was that I don't know his family, that they'd disown him in a moment if they knew.

We argued for the rest of the afternoon. All my hopes and dreams wound up being shot down just as quickly as they originally surfaced. Now what? I can't endure the same old secret lifestyle we've had for the past three years. I'm tired of it, really bitterly tired of the confusion and lying and guilt that goes with it. Maybe he'll feel differently in the morning.

Thursday 12/2/82
Seal Beach, California

Time hasn't worked to our benefit at all. Today Brian and I had our worst argument ever—and that's really saying something.

I'm sure that trying to please everybody but yourself eventually drains most people—it certainly has me—but Brian is apparently immune. He seems perfectly content hiding behind the facade that we're just roommates, while I'm sick to death of being "in the closet." Although I've always hoped that someday we'd be able to just be ourselves regardless of whether we were with family, friends, or strangers, I now realize—after three years—that this isn't possible for us. Brian's unwilling.

What a "Catch-22" situation. I love him so much I'd rather die than be without him, yet if I stay imprisoned in our same old totally restricted, hush-hush relationship, it will kill me. It's such a lonely existence being forced to keep your fondest memories to yourself, and it really hurts to see others who are able to express their feelings

147

of love openly and freely. I want our friends and family to know we're in love, and to be recognized as a couple.

So now what do I do? I feel indescribably sad and I wish I wasn't so weak because I always turn to the same answer for relief. Whenever I think of it, I feel at rest. No more conflict and strife.

Sunday 12/5/82
Seal Beach, California

I'm too depressed to write, mainly because things between Brian and me are at an all-time low...and then there's Christmas. I hate the holiday season. I don't think I can make it through another...it only magnifies the loneliness.

Friday 12/17/82
Malibu, California

I had to get away from Brian, from the ever-growing tension between us. Since Dad is in New York, I've come here. Seemed as good a place as any.

Watching the sun settle down into the ocean from this wind-sheltered corner of the patio, I've realized that there is one thing about December I enjoy—sunsets are much more dramatic at this time of the year. (Maybe it just seems that way because of the gin & tonic I brought out here with me. I'm really beginning to feel the effect from reversing the usual ratio of one to the other.)

Sure wish I knew what I'm going to do with my life. Looking back at how long it took me to work up the courage to terminate myself last month—and then again, how easily I abandoned the plan at the 11th hour—I just don't know. Right now my only desire is to be dead, to get it over with and find out what life was supposed to be all about. I don't have the guts for it, though. Maybe after a few more drinks. I'm such a sickening wimp.

Saturday 12/18/82
Malibu, California

Sometimes I really feel like I'm living out some French guy's idea of black comedy. I was sitting in the dark last night, diligently working away at my fourth "shot of courage," when I heard the

148

doorbell ring. I couldn't imagine who it was and I really didn't care, since I had no intention of answering it. But the next thing I knew, here was this big figure coming around the side of the house—Vern. He said he was driving through Malibu and decided to stop and see if anyone was home.

He looked so cold. I felt compelled to invite him inside, even though I wanted to be left alone in the worst possible way. He proceeded to make himself right at home, getting something to drink out of the fridge, and then parking himself in the living room where I'd deliberately left the lights off, hoping he'd take the hint. But no. So we sat there, neither of us saying anything about anything, and he was doing most of that. I was close to screaming when he suddenly said, "Why don't you tell me about it?" My automatic response was to start making up just a simple little rundown of complaints common to everyone, but with nothing to lose I began spilling my guts.

The more I revealed about myself and my life, such as it is, the more certain I became that there wasn't any way out except the one I always came back to. Also, the more I talked, the more I wanted to say, explain, confess, get across—not just from my head, but from my heart and soul. At some point, probably a couple of hours into all this, Vern had to tell me to slow down and take a break, that we had all night to cover things because he wasn't about to leave, considering the state I was in.

When he said he thought that drinking had probably made everything seem lousier than it really was and that I'd see things differently in the morning, I told him about last month and read some parts of my journal to him. Reaching over to turn off the light again, I was stunned to see tears streaming down his face. Seeing that kind of response on a burly 25-year-old ex-football player, I don't know, I was more deeply touched than I ever would've thought I could be. I mean, why should he care at all, really?

For the rest of the night he tried to show me the more positive side of things, but he didn't say anything I couldn't counter with some validation of my view that it's useless to go on. Nonetheless, when he left this morning, he told me there has to be a better answer than mine and swore he wouldn't stop searching until he found it.

So far, he's called three times today to make sure I'm okay.

Sunday 12/19/82
Malibu, California

Again today Vern has called three times to check up on me. I can't believe it. He also asked me if I'd consider going to see a minister about my "problem," to which I could only respond that I didn't think a dose of hypocrisy was what I really needed.

My disappointment in the religious establishment is a longstanding grievance. I mean, sin is sin, and yet many so-called Christians treat homosexuality as the worst thing on the face of the earth. To clarify what I meant, I told Vern about my experience the time I went to see the pastor of the church I used to attend. The pastor said if I "really wanted" to change, I would. All I had to do was to stop all homosexual thoughts and behavior. Even when he was allegedly praying for me, all he was doing was preaching at me and not lifting up my needs to God whatsoever. I'll never willingly go through that humiliation again.

Monday 12/20/82
Malibu, California

Brian called again today. He's concerned about me and misses me. I miss him, too. What am I going to do?

Vern called twice to see how I was, and mentioned that a pastor told him he'd heard of a ministry for homosexuals in West L.A. He says he's going to do some "major sleuthing" tomorrow and will let me know what he finds out. He's just too sincere and earnest in his efforts for me to say, "thanks, but no thanks."

Tuesday 12/21/82
Malibu, California

The holiday season is only adding to my confusion.

There are people absolutely everywhere with smiles pasted to their faces. Where did they all come from? The streets are jammed with Christmas shoppers rushing frantically from one place to the next. Why? Why do people wait for Christmas to share a little love with one another? Why do they have to have an excuse, a birthday or holiday, to express these sentiments? Why can't we all just let our facades fall, cut loose our stupid inhibitions, and love one another?

Tuesday 1/4/83
Seal Beach, California

What a surprise to have made it through Christmas. Vern's called everyday, including Christmas morning. I can't, for the life of me, understand why he cares so much. What can I possibly have to offer in return?

He's found an organization in Santa Monica called Desert Stream that's supposed to help gays go straight and has talked several times to a guy there named Tim. Now Vern wants me to call him myself, but I said no. All this Tim could offer is false hope and I've had my fill of having my hopes raised for nothing.

Why do I go on? Do I really still have some shred of belief in the future, some expectation that things will change? Or is it merely Vern's strength that's sustaining me? He cares so incredibly much and I don't want to hurt or disappoint him if I can avoid it…but what should I do? I can't go on living in limbo, and I know I can't change. So why am I hanging around? I need to do something decisive soon. As it is, I'm only prolonging the inevitable—again.

Wednesday 1/5/83
Seal Beach, California

Brian, complementing the sensitivity he's been showing the past few days, brought home some flowers for me this afternoon. I love him so terribly much! Why can't things work out right?

Now even my daily chat with Vern has gone up in smoke. He called this morning to see if I'd changed my mind about contacting Tim at Desert Stream, but when he kept pushing the issue, I got mad. I told him quite bluntly that he doesn't have the vaguest idea of what it's like to go to some church organization seeking help, only to have people there act like you're the scum of the earth and beneath their contempt. I won't be subjected to that again. Besides, I tried doing what I was told the last time I saw a minister and my homosexual feelings only got stronger, not weaker.

Thursday 1/6/83
Seal Beach, California

Poor Vern. He called to apologize for getting on my case

yesterday, and we had a good, long talk. Clearly, he only wants to help and is trying the best way he knows how. I'm almost at the point of meeting with Tim solely for his sake, in the hope that it'll make him feel a little better.

Monday 1/10/83
Seal Beach, California

I've just made an appointment with Tim for 2:30 tomorrow. Let the record show that I expect precious little to come of it.

Tuesday 1/11/83
Santa Monica, California

I feel like screaming. However, since I'm on the pier and there are several hundred other people around, I'd better not.

I've just left Desert Stream—surprisingly, quite an impressive outfit, well-organized and very professional—after spending a little less than an hour with Tim. Presumably, most people who come through their door are apprehensive to some degree, so before getting down to cases, he gave me some background on himself and the organization. It helped break the ice considerably to learn that despite his straight-looking appearance, he used to be into the gay lifestyle and had a lover for a year or so.

I didn't have any trouble telling him all about Brian and me, but once he said I needed to break off the relationship, everything else just started going in one ear and out the other. The only thing I could think about was that I couldn't live without him. Actually, Tim had quite a lot of good things to say, things that made sense and all, but it's just no good to me. Brian's my everything. Life has no meaning without him.

I feel worse than ever. Before I had no hope of changing, and now I see that it's possible, but only at high cost and with great difficulty. I really do feel like screaming from all this frustration.

Wednesday 1/19/83
Seal Beach, California

I can't get the stuff Tim told me out of my head. Do I want to live

152

this pit of an existence, kill myself, or find out how life as a male is meant to be experienced?

Saturday 2/5/83

Santa Barbara, California

What started out as just a short drive along the coast turned into a three-hour journey, bringing me here. It's such a quaint and sleepy sort of place, I almost feel at peace. I was actually calm enough to stand in line at Häagen-Dazs for an ice cream cone.

Now that I've just fed the last of it to a half-dozen pigeons who seem to view this bench as a lunch counter, I'm forced to take up the big "if" again. My conclusion is that I'm either just a gutless coward about killing myself or I have some hidden hope of changing. I really feel like I'm stuck somewhere between the two, with something pushing me toward the latter and something else pulling me the other way. Maybe Tim and his people do hold the key, but I can't leave Brian. I could never do that. It hurts too much just thinking about it. Dying would be easier.

Later...

It just goes around and around. I should know what I want—everybody else does.

Again,
I am here again.
Surrounded by darkness,
blinded by its density,
I look around me to see nothing
but the pain this darkness brings.
The strain of trying has taken its toll,
the will to persist has disappeared.
I can see a speck of light ahead
if I concentrate hard enough.
But it's exhausting and
I'm extremely tired.
Too tired to try
anymore.

They say suicide is a permanent solution to a temporary problem, and I suspect that under most circumstances, that's true. The thing is, this isn't temporary; it's not going to go away in time. I didn't just lose my job, get broken up in a car wreck, or run into some financial setback. This is my life we're talking about. My sexual desires are a part of me, a part that makes up my whole nature. Time heals a lot of things, but it can't alter homosexuality.

So what am I waiting for?

Wednesday 2/9/83

Seal Beach, California

Maureen called tonight and asked me to go to a church down in Orange County with her to listen to a group of guys talk about how they got out of the gay life. Since Brian was at work and I was feeling lonely, I said yes.

I was fine until we pulled up at the "church," a converted movie theater, with quite a crowd milling around out front. One look and it was full-fledged panic time for me. I made Maureen go around the block and park way down the street because I had to have time to think, to conquer my fear that everyone would take one look at me and know why I was there.

As it turned out, most of the church members were in attendance because this is normally their Bible study night. And, of all things, the guest speakers were ex-gays from New Life Fellowship, the same group that Wayne went to in Laguna Beach! I nearly fell off my chair when they were introduced.

There were six of them altogether, and each one gave personal testimony as to how he was once actively homosexual but is now free. Their sincerity was so convincing that we stuck around after the meeting was over because I wanted to talk with one of them. A lot of other people there had the same idea. It took a good 45 minutes before I got my chance. Despite the interrogation he'd already undergone, Eddie said he'd be glad to answer my questions. So I started firing away at him and the responses he gave were just as forceful as his earlier remarks. At the end he asked me to come to his group's Friday night meeting, and I said I'd try to make it.

Friday 2/11/83
Seal Beach, California

I've just come back from New Life Fellowship—what ambivalence I feel about all this stuff. In principle, I agree with everything they're teaching, but it ultimately means leaving Brian.

The founder of New Life, David Steege, told me not to worry about that for now, but to first concentrate on learning how I acquired my homosexual identity and deal with the roots that caused it. He said I need to get back on my feet, gain some strength and insight, and that I can worry about Brian later. Everything, he said, will come in time.

* * * *

Now do you see where I'm coming from, Mike? I really *can* say I know what you're going through. And, true to what David, the New Life director, said, everything does come in time if we work at it and allow it, buddy. So will you give some more thought to contacting Desert Stream? Its format is quite similar to New Life and it's close to where you're living. I know it's frightening to think of going to a place like that by yourself, but Robert is coming to California for a couple of weeks and if it's okay with you, I'll give him your phone number. He's going to one of the meetings and that might be a perfect time for you to go.

Think about it, please. Going even once would help you immeasurably.

I'll try to call you Saturday night around 9, for sure, and probably before then. If we don't manage to connect before, try to be home then, okay?

Hang in there, buddy. Remember, I really love you—and I really want you to be around a few more years. Sixty sounds like a good round number.

Talk to you soon,

Bud

Dear Mike,

It's raining cats and dogs today. Have you ever wondered how that saying got started? Anyway, not much to do on rainy days here except read or write, so you're the "beneficiary" of today's weather.

I really wish I could give you an easy formula to follow, an instant cure-all or something, but life doesn't seem to work that way. I'm sure you've noticed that already, but reality doesn't lessen my desire to provide you with the "extraordinary." Since I can't, though, I can only ask you to keep in mind that your problem stems from improper growth. You must grow out of where you are by the fulfillment of your homo-emotional needs, and that's going to take time.

I remember the first night I went to a New Life meeting. I called Wayne, told him I'd seen some guys from there at a Bible study, and had been invited to attend a regular session. I was hoping he'd repeat his previous offer to go with me, and he did.

We arrived a few minutes late and when the group's leader saw us walk in, he acknowledged Wayne by name and then asked me to introduce myself. I could've died on the spot, although there were only about 20 people present and I was only being asked for my first name. After I managed to do as asked, the meeting continued for a while, then open conversation was initiated. At first, I determined not to say anything, but rather to just sit back and observe. However, I had at least 100 questions I wanted answered, and I finally decided I might not have another chance to ask them.

Right up front, I told the group where I was coming from. I told them I had a gun to my head and that if they didn't offer a viable alternative, I didn't feel there was any other alternative except pulling the trigger. (I'd even prayed to God before the meeting and asked Him to use this group to heal me instantly. Otherwise, I had no alternative but to give up and kill myself; I didn't believe I had the strength to go on unless *something happened*.)

Well, Mike, of course nothing happened that night—except that glimmer of hope I'd seen at Desert Stream somehow now grew measurably brighter. Didn't seem like much at first, but it was enough to keep me going until the group's next meeting.

The first few weeks were a real struggle, but one day I realized that the more I learned, the less I wanted to die. I grew stronger and stronger, soaking up as much information as I could get my hands on. With each passing day, greater expectations and dreams for the future filled me. The impossible was impossible no longer. Doors I'd thought were closed stood wide open. Hope and knowledge took the place of my fears and doubts. I saw all of life through new eyes. Where only darkness had existed before, I now saw bright, shining light. I was so inspired and encouraged by what I was learning that I decided to break up with Brian—within three and a half months of my first meeting with New Life!

This isn't to say that I did it on my own. Without the loving support of Maureen Dunn and Vern Hunt (and his roommate Bob Smith), I wouldn't have made it—no way, no how. Period.

Initially, I thought it would be a breeze living apart from Brian. We'd discussed it and everything seemed fine. A friend helped me get all my things out of the apartment while Brian was at work, and still I felt perfectly fine. It wasn't until that night that it hit me—we weren't together anymore. After three years, it was suddenly over. I cried, buddy. I cried, and cried, and cried.

The head of New Life, David Steege, came over to try to comfort me. He even took Maureen and me out to dinner, and tried to assure me everything would be all right. Deep inside I guess I knew that it would be, but I sure wasn't prepared for such pain—I physically ached from the emotional turmoil.

If I hadn't learned as much as I had by that point, I would have crawled back to Brian that night. The only reason I was able to stay away was because we'd both agreed the gay life wasn't fulfilling. We both wanted more out of life than what we experienced, and we decided to give our all to shedding our gay identities.

Though I knew all this in my head, my heart and emotions were telling me a different story. I woke up the following morning feeling worse than the night before. Whenever I managed to stop crying for a moment, I'd just burst into tears seconds later. It was terrible. I absolutely and sincerely doubted my ability to make it through the time necessary for my pain to diminish, let alone for it to disappear.

That's where people came in.

Vern called me every day. Since Vern, Bob and I were good friends in college together at Pepperdine University, Vern convinced me to take Bob into my confidence as well. Once Bob found out, he started calling me several times a day as well. They made themselves available to me around the clock. I confess I called them more than once long after I was past the worst just to feel their encouragement and support wrap itself around me. I'm alive today because these guys loved me.

Then there was Maureen—the best of the best. I stayed with her a while. She was my rock and my strength. She was there for me every minute of the day, comforting me, going through most of my hell with me, holding my hand all along the way. Take my word for it, Mike, you can't do this on your own. Lean on somebody when you're feeling down; don't try to carry it by yourself. I'm here anytime you need me—day or night; just call.

The pain you feel *will* go away, although I know full well it doesn't seem possible now. Believe me, though, it does fade away. I'm living proof!

Let me be there for you in the interim. Let Robert into your life, too. He honestly desires to be your friend and help you however he can. Why don't you drop him a note and arrange to spend some time together while he's in Santa Monica? I wouldn't suggest it if I didn't believe you'd benefit from it, buddy; I love you too much to play games with you.

Until I talk to you next, please remember I love you.

Your friend always,

Bud

P.S.

Have you ever thought about getting an answering machine? A lot of times when I felt so down I thought I'd die, listening to my messages made all the difference in the world to me because people called—knowing I wasn't home—just to let me know I was being thought of, that I wasn't alone. It helped me through some of the darkest days mankind's ever known. Won't you think about it?

Dear Mike,

Sure wish I was there to give you a big hug—sounds like you need one.

You know, you really gave Dave and me a gigantic scare last weekend, buddy, taking off the way you did. (Of the two of us, I feel worse for Dave, since he somehow feels that because he lives with you he is more responsible for your well-being.) You've gotta admit, you haven't exactly been acting like we shouldn't worry about you.

I know you're feeling about as down as anyone can be, Mike, but if you don't stop dwelling on the past and holding onto the feeling that you're beaten, you're going to turn this thing into a self-fulfilling prophecy. That's just how I got to the point of wanting to die.

Looking over my entire life, it didn't seem worth living. The more I dwelled on it, the more depressed I got. I wasn't rationally thinking of ways to improve my situation. Rather, I was just immersing myself deeper into negative memories and feeling ever sorrier for myself.

I can see now that my early years were probably as average as those of any kid growing up in a white, middle-class neighborhood, but I felt cheated. It was obvious that my parents weren't in love with each other, that they were probably just playing the role of a married couple for the sake of their children. My father seldom came home nights; even now it seems he only showed up occasionally on weekends, though I suppose he must have been around more than that since I can recall my mother taking clothes to the cleaners for him all the time. Anyhow, to me this was our family and its normal routine. It was all I knew.

It came to an end when I was 12 years old.

Their divorce hit me hard. I remember my father taking us kids to the park to tell us the news. We all sat on a bench together and when my dad finished his little speech about their splitting up, my 13-year-old brother didn't say a thing, and my sister, 11 at the time, giggled.

On the other hand, I cried like a baby. I was devastated. I couldn't figure out what had gone so terribly wrong. I'd never heard them arguing about anything, so I couldn't understand why our "normal life" was being destroyed, and why my father—who'd never been around even fractionally as much as I'd wanted him to be—was now leaving us for good. I thought I'd done something to make him go. *It has to be my fault*, I thought. *Who else is to blame?*

Life continued, however. The sky didn't fall and soon thereafter my mother found a boyfriend named Ron. After knowing him for about six months, she let him move in with us. At first I thought he was all right, but then he started drinking—or maybe he just took the wraps off it. At any rate, booze turned him into a madman. After one or two snorts, for no reason at all, he'd start screaming and carrying on as if he were certifiably crazy.

My mother and Ron eventually made things official by getting married, but it didn't really seem to make any sort of impression on me. I mean, the guy was living with us anyhow, so no big deal.

What definitely made an impression was the fact that they fought constantly. I found it unbearable. At times, I thought I was the one who was going crazy. I couldn't sleep nights from the racket they made, and it wasn't just verbal. Lying there in bed, I could distinctly hear the sound of his fists hitting her. If she didn't cry out immediately, I'd hold my breath until she made some sound—I feared he had killed her. Some nights I was sure he had killed her and was on his way to my room to get me next. I took to sleeping with a butcher knife under my bed, so I'd be ready for him—13 years old, and I was going to kill the guy if I had to.

The craziness just went on and on. Once when my stepfather had been drinking, he didn't want my mother to leave for work so he rammed his car through the garage door into my mother's car. Another time, he trapped her halfway out of the house and then slammed the door against her repeatedly. Then he tore inside, ripped the phone out of the wall so we couldn't call the cops, and came back to beat her so thoroughly she wound up in the hospital.

I was terrified of him. He knew it and was always ready to push me to the limit. When I got a brand-new motorcycle, Ron immediately went out and kicked it over. Another time, I was watching TV and he came in and yanked the antenna cord right out of the wall, then turned to me with a smirk and said he needed it for something. I don't know why, of all things, that incident made me explode, but I lost control and yelled at him. Instantly, he was on me like a psychotic cannibal. He jerked me to my feet by the neck and then tried to strangle me. Instinct took over—I kicked him in the groin and ran. Since he was between me and the front door, I locked myself in the bathroom and screamed out the window for help. Then, when I heard him rummaging around in the bedroom, I made a run for it and got out of the house.

This was my daily pattern of life for two and a half years. When I was 15, I woke one night around 2 a.m. to the sound of my mother's bloody murder screams. It was by far the worst sound I had ever heard in my life—from her or anyone else—and I raced toward the kitchen totally out of my mind with fear. My mom was covered with blood, and everything else in her immediate vicinity seemed to be blood-splattered, too—walls, floor, counters, even the ceiling.

The phone had once again been torn from the wall, and my mother yelled at me to run to the neighbor's house to call the police. Staring at the scene in front of me, a flood of thoughts and emotions overwhelmed me. I was furious at my mother for letting Ron back in the house after she had kicked him out the night before. I was enraged at him for beating her. I was infuriated that she let him beat her that way, that they fought like this week after week, year after year, that I'd been awakened from a sound sleep once again.

This volcano of molten emotion was about to erupt on Ron—but I was terrified of what he would do, to her and me both. I felt sick to my stomach. My mind went blank. I could hear my mom yelling at me but it was like I'd been turned into a zombie. I walked back down the hall to my bedroom, and when I got to the door, I fell on my knees and sobbed.

I couldn't think; I couldn't act. She was still screaming and for all I knew, Ron actually could have been killing her, but I couldn't do a thing. Not because I didn't want to, but because I simply couldn't move. My focus turned entirely upon myself. *Why me? What had I done to deserve such a hellish existence? It's not fair!* It became a drum roll in my brain, forcing everything else out of my head, leaving me totally without the willpower to do anything but cry. I was all alone. Nobody loved me; there was nobody to comfort me.

It's amazing. I haven't thought of these things for a long time, but thinking of them now, all the old feelings become so vivid, so dreadfully real and alive again. Still, the incident I've just described wasn't an extraordinary occurrence, nor did it signify any change in our pattern of life.

As I later found out, when my mom began screaming at Ron, he grabbed her and clamped a hand over her mouth. She reacted by biting one of his fingers nearly to the bone. As he continued to slap her around, blood flew in all directions. That's what all the blood was from. Just your average little domestic squabble.

After that, everything settled back down again into its usual routine—Ron would drink; then he and Mom would get into it with each other. Every other month or so, I'd have to call the cops to come out and break up a fight. A couple of times I got lucky and they arrested my stepfather. It didn't really matter, though, because my mom always bailed him out the same night.

This insanity finally ended on August 14, 1974, after nearly six years.

Picture Covina in mid-August; the temperature stood at 109 degrees and the smog was lying over everything in half a dozen different colors. I was visiting friends six or seven houses down the street when our mailman, looking scared to death, suddenly appeared at their door. Gasping and quite hysterical, he told me that just as he started to put our mail in the box, he heard my mother scream for help. Then she yelled out that my stepfather had a gun on her, that he was going to kill her.

"I didn't know what to do," the mailman kept saying. "I just didn't know what to do. I was afraid that guy was going to open the door and either blow me away or take me hostage. I just said a quick prayer, then I turned and walked away as slowly as I could, acting like I hadn't heard a thing." Fortunately, once he got to the sidewalk, he saw my pickup down the street and came running. "Call the police," he begged, but I was already doing it, praying this wasn't going to be the time they just laughed and hung up.

Up the block, my mother was finding out that whatever hell my

164

stepfather had put her through before, it wasn't even a hint of his potential. Despite the outside temperature, every window in the house was closed and there was smoke pouring from the chimney. In the living room, her stark-raving mad, 42-year-old husband was pacing back and forth, holding a .22 rifle in one hand, trying to decide what to do next. She lay sprawled on the couch, horribly battered. Her arms were swollen and her face was bluish-black with bruises. Her clothes were in shreds and what remained of them was blood-stained.

Ron broke up a lot of the furniture, which was what he was burning in the fireplace, and he began throwing in clothing, all the pictures of us kids he could find, our birth certificates, papers for the house, and whatever other important documents came to hand. He had held a gun on her for nearly four hours up to that point, but when my mother saw him destroy these things, she tried to stop him. He shoved the rifle into her stomach and said he was going to kill her.

The cops not only responded to my call, but sent seven cars with two officers apiece. They arrived within five minutes, lights flashing and sirens screaming. At the end of our street, I met an officer with a shotgun. He seemed to be in charge and asked me what my stepfather looked like, how tall he was, what he was wearing, and whether he had any noticeable scars or other identifying marks. After he relayed this information to the others, they set off up the street. Having heard all the sirens, Ron decided to come outside. With police converging on the house, both on foot and by patrol car, he emerged holding my mother at gun point.

Like a drill team, two cops went to the left and two more peeled right into neighboring yards. The ones in cars jumped out to brace their weapons across the hoods, taking aim on him. Sizing up the situation, Ron suddenly threw my mother to the ground and fled back into the house.

Two more patrol cars screeched up the street while my mother crawled to safety under the car in our driveway. The newcomers hit the ground running, and with shotguns pointed skyward, they flattened themselves against both sides of the house and began side-stepping their way toward the back and front doors, ducking under the windows.

All of a sudden a single gunshot rang out and echoed in the air. The cops stormed the house and a moment later one stepped out the front door shouting at someone to radio for the paramedics. Without thinking—and without being stopped—I ran inside where I found my stepfather lying face up on the living room floor with the rifle still in his hands, blood and life draining away from him into the carpet. He shot himself.

Amazing story, huh? It seemed like those last 15 minutes had dragged by in slow-motion, but the next few hours flew past at double-time. More police arrived, with the fire department and paramedics soon after. An ambulance appeared and then departed with an empty stretcher. Some guys from homicide introduced themselves and asked me a million questions. Finally, the coroner showed up to take Ron's body to the morgue. It was like I was watching the whole thing on television. I simply couldn't comprehend that this sort of thing could actually happen to real people. It does, though—and it had happened to me.

Just prior to my stepfather's death I was actually beginning to feel somewhat better about myself. I had a girlfriend and was earning enough money to buy myself a brand-new car on credit, and that alone made me feel good. At last, I felt like I was somebody who was going places in the world—I was finally starting to get a handle on life.

Then once again my parade got rained on, and I, of course, had no umbrella.

On my way to work one afternoon, intending to park as far away as possible from all the congestion, I pulled into the parking lot and headed for the opposite side. Suddenly everything came to a grinding halt in utter darkness. I rammed into a three-foot high, eight-inch wide pole. Since I hadn't seen it, I was caught completely off guard and was thrown into the windshield which knocked me out cold. Of course, I would've gone right through the thing if it hadn't been for the steering wheel; as it was, however, the steering wheel not only interrupted my trajectory but broke some jaw bones and knocked out seven of my perfectly straight teeth.

I now had the wonderful opportunity to face the reality that life was nothing but a cruel joke. My body was messed up, my car was totaled, and my father wouldn't let me file a claim with the insurance company—he had a bad record and was afraid they'd cancel our policy. I had nothing to look forward to except six months of oral surgery and three years of payments on a brand-new, totally demolished car.

Believe me, I definitely felt sorry for myself then. I wasn't interested in struggling to live a life that kept stabbing me in the back. Having no close friends to turn to for comfort, I felt even more singled out for punishment, even more isolated and tormented. I wanted to scream out for help but no one was there to listen. *Why? I kept asking myself. Why me? What have I done to deserve the life I've had?*

I thought back to my parents getting a divorce; to all the horrible, crazy things my stepfather had done; to my mother throwing us kids in her car when I was 14 and dropping us all off on my dad's front porch and leaving us there; to me staying with him for awhile, then back to my mom's, which didn't work; to me living with a neighbor for eight months, then back with my father, and finally back to my mother and now this latest turn of events. Having taken this inventory of my first 18 years, I had no desire to find out what the future held in store for me. Life had let me down. I wanted nothing more to do with it.

It held no meaning. Every day just brought new pain, sadness, loneliness, and more questions without any answers. It seemed to me that I was headed absolutely nowhere, that there really wasn't any place to head for. With hindsight I can now see quite readily why I felt that way, why I was extremely shy, had no self-confidence, was afraid of people, didn't trust anybody, and was always putting myself down.

There was a container of codeine tablets next to my bed. I swallowed the contents and knew I was finally running away for good. Wishing there had been another way out, I started crying. Maybe I didn't take enough pills, or perhaps the codeine wasn't sufficient to end a human life. Whatever the reason, I woke up the following afternoon. I was still alive, and life continued to drag on, oblivious to my little gesture of defiance.

Seventeen days after the accident a friend from work came by to see me. Larry Shelton was a very religious guy who always talked about how good Jesus was to him. He had already disproved my theory that religious people were always funny-looking weirdos. He seemed to have everything in the world going for him—a good-looking, 21-year-old, married college student—and he radiated happiness. He'd been after me to come to his house for dinner for quite a while, and I'd always managed to refuse politely.

My attitude was that once you got involved with Jesus freaks, they would never let you alone. On this particular evening, though, I accepted his invitation to dinner even though we both knew I couldn't eat as a result of my car accident. *He wants to tell me about Jesus*, I thought, *but what do I have to lose?*

I believed in Jesus already. I believed that He was the Son of God and all that stuff, but I wasn't as certain about my beliefs as Larry was about his. As I got ready to go, I prayed to God and hoped that whatever Larry had to say, it wouldn't be some weird doctrine or off-the-wall mumbo-jumbo, but that his Jesus would be the same Jesus I had learned about in Sunday school as a child.

One thing I knew for sure—whatever it was that Larry had, I wanted some of it—particularly, the happiness, contentment and peace. If he'd found the answers in his religion, I was willing to let him tell me about it, at least briefly.

Larry's wife, Faith, met me at the door and welcomed me into their home. After a bit of small talk, we sat down to dinner. Larry held his hands out to Faith and me—I didn't know what for—but we all joined hands and Larry said an impromptu grace. Right then a small revelation occurred to me. Every other time in my life that grace had been said at the table, everyone had dutifully chanted, "God is great, God is good. Thank you for our daily food. Amen." Now I was in the presence of someone who wasn't murmuring a singsong rhyme, but was actually conversing with God in the same manner he talked with everyone else!

After Larry and Faith had eaten dinner, and I had socked away the milkshake concocted for me, I began questioning them about their beliefs. Though I'd just met Faith and didn't really know Larry much better, I could feel, almost physically, the love and concern they had for me. I was quite aware that they possessed something priceless that could change my life, and that they wanted to share it with me. Yet they didn't preach at me or rattle off some mysterious dogma built upon endless provisos. Instead, from the depths of their hearts, they offered me a new life through Jesus Christ.

I came to see that what they had wasn't what I'd previously thought of as "religious," but was actually a deep, intimate, personal relationship with God through Jesus Christ. They enjoyed person-to-person talks with Him. God, Larry told me, was a most loving Spirit, but sin in my life (however small it might be) prevented me from experiencing the abundant life God wanted for me. Saying that God is just and fair, Larry likened Him to a judge whose duty it is to refrain from letting criminals go free without penalty, for this wouldn't serve justice. He further explained that God couldn't have anything to do with me unless the penalty for my sins was paid because God is holy and therefore can't be associated with sin.

Faith clarified something I'd heard all my life but never really understood. Jesus had died, she said, to take upon Himself the sins of the world. His death upon the cross had paid the penalty for my sins, as well as everyone else's. All I had to do was repent—turn *away from* my sin, turn *toward* God, and rely upon Him for my life. I needed to believe by sincere faith that Jesus was who He said He was—that He was my redemption, had paid for my sins—and I, too, would be brought into a personal relationship with the Almighty.

How, I asked, could I receive God's forgiveness? Larry said I needed to go to God in prayer and accept Jesus as my Savior from sin, invite Him into my life, ask Him to control my life, be baptized, and open myself up to receive all He wished me to have.

I really didn't know how to pray, so all three of us prayed together. Larry prayed I'd receive restoration in all my needs: my injuries, my emotions, my finances, my relationship with my parents—and whatever else came to mind.

When we had finished, I felt as if 1000 tons had been lifted from my shoulders. Great peace and contentment instantly enveloped me. I knew everything was going to be all right, and I cried—for the first time in my life—from overwhelming happiness. God loved me and cared for me! I can't describe the peace I knew at that moment. It passed all my understanding. I'm not sure this can be expressed through our feeble methods of communication.

I slept that night like I had never slept before. The next morning I was awakened by a phone call from my father who said he'd decided to take a chance and turn my accident claim in to the insurance company. Overnight, God had answered this one prayer!

From that point on, everything else worked out above and beyond my greatest desires, for the Lord met even the smallest of my needs—though not always in the way I wanted, but in the way He knew was best. God promises so much for us and requires only that we establish the right relationship with Him in order to ask of Him what we will—He does answer prayer. Slowly and ever-so-gently, He began transforming me into a new person. The more I learned of Him through His word, the Bible, the more I saw my life changing within me.

I know you don't want to hear this because you've said time and again not to bring it up to you, but the fact remains that we need God in our lives. We are incomplete and lost without Him. I know you probably think that God hates you because of your homosexuality, but He doesn't. God hates the sin, not the sinner. He loves you, Mike, and wants to help you. He's not going to punish you. He wants to transform you.

Jesus came that we might live, buddy. He said He came to give us life, that we might have it abundantly. We're mixed up and broken people on this earth. Each of us suffers in some way or another, striving to achieve whatever it is we're looking for from life. God wants to heal and restore us. He knows how to truly satisfy us, for He knows better than anyone else our true makeup.

Think of it like this. When you buy something that's defective, what do you do with it? You return it to the manufacturer because they made it and know how to repair it. The same is true with God. If you're hurting, if things aren't going right for you, go to your Maker and let Him fix you. He's the only one who can repair you properly. Give Him the opportunity to do so, Mike. You have nothing to lose and everything to gain: joy, peace that surpasses understanding, hope, love, self-control, and much, much more, including eternal life with Him.

I'm praying for you, and I believe God will show you the way out of your despair. He's faithful and trustworthy, and I know that once you give Him the chance, He'll prove to you that He's God and that He still performs miracles today. Let Him perform one in your life.

I love you more than you can know and it really hurts me to see you so down. Yet, on the other hand, I'm also glad that you're searching for more out of life. I feel like I have a million things to say, but it would take me years to gather all these thoughts and write them out. Maybe by making a stab at it, though, my perspective will change. You know—one step at a time.

God bless you, my friend. I love you, Mike, so very much, and if I love you this much, I can't even imagine how much more God loves you. Write soon.

Love,

Bud

P.S.

From what I've said earlier you might be wondering how I could have been so burnt out on Christians and the Church, and now be "tooting Christ's horn." Well, I've learned that what God intends and what His people do aren't always the same thing. Unfortunately, many Christians—me included—can act out of ignorance rather than out of compassion. I'll write more about this later.

Aloha!

Dear Mike,

After putting my last letter to you in the mail, I realized I probably wouldn't hear from you until after Christmas. I've got to work until 3 p.m. on the 24th, so I'm going to be staying here for the holidays. What a variation on the "White Christmas" of popular sentiment! Not, of course, that Southern California offers many of them, either, but you know what I mean.

We've got about 20 people scheduled to get together with us at the house on Christmas Eve to spend the night, help decorate the tree, sing carols, and so forth. Everyone's bringing a gift to exchange on Christmas morning, and then we're all going to go to church. After services, we'll come back and get busy whipping up a traditional turkey dinner. Sounds like fun, doesn't it? I'm really looking forward to it as much as if I were a child anticipating the imminent arrival of Santa Claus.

What have you got planned? I was thinking that perhaps you might be persuaded to come over for a visit. It took some doing, but we've managed to get Daniel a flight on the 27th, so why not you, too? I'm sure you've heard by now that Daniel is alone again. Roger leaving him for some other guy has just devastated him—he called twice yesterday crying hysterically—so I'm glad he's going to be among friends for at least a week. Normally, I would've asked him to stay here at the house, but when Robert offered the use of his place because he's going to be in L.A. for two weeks, it seemed like a much better idea. I don't want any scenes going down in front of Ray, and you know that with Daniel anything at all can happen.

Hope you don't mind, but I've given Robert your phone number. No, he doesn't need a place to stay. I thought maybe you'd decide to go to Desert Stream with him (around January 4th or 5th, I think). Maybe you could just sorta keep those days open??? (Me, manipulative? Never! Ha.) Just trying to help in anyway I can…because I care. If I become too pushy let me know.

173

Again, kiddo, if you're not doing anything for Christmas, you'd be welcomed with open arms here, and naturally, I mean here at the house. Don't worry, I'll think of something to tell Daniel. Actually, I think it was his idea first to stay at Robert's, so it really isn't a problem. Please, try to come if you can.

If I don't hear from you before then, have a wonderful Christmas—I'll be thinking of you and wishing you the best there is. Love ya a bunch, Mike.

Your buddy,

Bud

Dear Mike,

Hi, buddy. How was your Christmas? Tried to call you yesterday morning around 9 a.m. your time, but no answer. Since I couldn't wish it to you on the proper day, I'll wish it to you now: Merry Christmas! I hope whatever you did, you were happy. We had a great time here—a final count of noses showed we numbered 29 instead of 20! Our next "scheduled event" is Daniel's arrival tomorrow. I'll keep you informed on how things go once he gets here.

The main reason I'm writing, besides the fact that I wanted to say hello, is to let you know I'm praying for you, Mike. This is such a difficult and painful time for you, so I thought maybe it might help a bit to know someone's thinking of you. Have you heard from Robert yet? He told me before he left that he would try to get in touch with you, and I really hope you two connect.

I also wanted to elaborate on what I was saying in a letter I wrote you earlier this month. God can and will help you through this time if you let Him. Go to Him in prayer, Mike. Give Him your life and let Him change it for the best. He truly loves you and desires only the best for you.

You've got to get a clear picture here, buddy. You wrote that you thought the Bible was just a bunch of do's and don'ts, and that you didn't want to "practice a lot of religious self-denial to find God." Well, to find God, there's two things we have to be willing to do.

The first is to turn from sin—sin being anything that puts our will above God's. Although we only see the short-term pleasure of sin, God sees it as long-term destruction. That's why He hates sin so much—because of the damage it does to us, the ones He loves.

The second thing, in view of this, is that we must embrace *His* method of dealing with sin. God let Jesus' death replace the death that was due us because of the sin in our lives. In the Bible, it explains that "the wages of sin is death, but the gift of God is eternal life in Christ Jesus our Lord." If we accept *His* way of dealing with sin and follow

175

Jesus Christ as Lord and Savior, then He accepts us as people with clean slates and gives us His eternal life.

He wants you to come to Him and find rest. He wants to replace your pain with comfort, love and peace.

Don't worry about things farther down the road. For now, just take it one step at a time. The first thing you need is hope and deliverance from your suicidal thoughts. God offers abundant hope. Give Him the chance to prove He's your Creator—ask Him to help you with a particular problem—and allow Him to transform you.

As for the Bible being a bunch of do's and don'ts, remember a while back when I said that the Word of God was like an owner's manual for mankind? Well, the Bible is also your personal owner's manual from God. Look at it this way: when you buy a brand-new car, you put a lot of money into purchasing it. The price includes an owner's manual that you're supposed to take home and read thoroughly before you go out and start driving. The manual tells you what things you must do to get maximum performance out of the car to keep it running properly. You're told what oil to use, when to change it, the proper kind of gas and measure of octane needed, specifications for braking distance and such. If you want your car to last a reasonably long time, to run well and be dependable, you've got to follow the directions given in the manual.

This same principle applies to you and the Bible. Just as an owner's manual advises you on the maintenance of you car, the Bible instructs us to do certain things and refrain from doing others because God knows the *ultimate outcome* of all our actions. He knows what's best.

Just as you might be able to operate your car for quite a while without an oil change and not discern any appreciable difference in its performance, your neglect will reveal itself in the internal damage. The same is true with us. You might not understand at the time why God says this or that, but in the long haul His wisdom becomes apparent.

We are God's creation. To find out how we'll work best, we must refer to the owner's manual He gave us. The Bible gives us directions for living life properly, abundantly, more fulfillingly. If you view the Bible in this light, doesn't it make sense to obey His instructions?

Doesn't that provide a more positive outlook toward any changes we might be asked to make? The "do's and don'ts" in the Bible are there to guide us toward a fulfilling, satisfying and challenging life. We'll enjoy our relationship with God when we're "well tuned" by the Master Mechanic.

When you first accepted your gay identity, it felt great to experience the new sense of freedom you gained. Life seemed more natural and there was hope for the future. Society's restraints no longer affected you because you wouldn't allow those things to prevent you from being the person you thought you really were. You obviously encountered some hard times, but so did everybody else. Since you were satisfied in doing what you thought was right, you continued with your course of action. All the while, however, you were just depriving yourself of satisfying the unmet needs which were spurring your behavior. You, of course, didn't know this; all you knew was how you felt and what you thought you desired.

Look where you are now. Look at your gay friends. Are they anywhere close to where you want to be? Just like a car eventually falls apart when the buyer neglects the owner's manual, so will the person who neglects the wisdom in the Word of God.

Earlier this month I shared with you how I was introduced to Jesus, the *true* Master/Mechanic, the Great Physician of the soul. Jesus said He was the Way, the Truth, and the Life, and that no man could come to God except through Him (Gospel of John 14: 6). What an extremely bold statement! If you think about it, other "deities," like Buddha, claimed only to be a way, not "The Way." Interestingly, Buddha isn't essential to the teachings of Buddhism, nor is Mohammed to Islam, whereas everything about Christianity is determined by the person and works of Jesus Christ. In every detail Christianity owes its life and character to Christ; its teachings are concerned with Him.

The other day I was talking with some friends of Ray's about my faith. At first they were sincerely interested in hearing what I had to say about Jesus. There was some good, thought- provoking dialogue going on. After a while, however, they became quarrelsome, asking questions they really didn't want answered and making statements to indicate how ridiculous they thought my faith was. I don't mind talking about my faith, in fact, I enjoy sharing about who Jesus is and what He has done for me. But when it starts to turn into an argument, I have better things to do with my time.

The really sad thing is these guys rejected Christ without having any factual basis for doing so. To them His claim to be God was absurd. Yet they hadn't done any research, examined what Jesus said, or even read the Bible in an effort to understand His claims. They rejected Him solely out of ignorance.

Ironically, however, they all agreed He was a good and moral person, a belief about which C.S. Lewis had this to say in his book, *Mere Christianity*:

> I am trying here to prevent anyone saying the really foolish thing that people often say about Him: "I'm ready to accept Jesus as a great moral teacher, but I don't accept His claim to be God." A man who was merely a man and said the sort of things Jesus said would not be a great moral teacher. He would either be a lunatic—on a level with the man who says he is a poached egg—or else he would be the Devil of Hell. You must make your choice. Either this man was, and is, the Son of God, or else a madman or something worse.

The good and moral teachings of Jesus conflicted with Ray's friends' lifestyles. It is so much easier for them to reject Him than to deal with their lifestyles and sin. Everyone should read the New Testament to see who Jesus was and learn what He said, and then judge for himself what's right and wrong. I mean, of all things, how could this not be worth checking out instead of summarily rejecting it? In *Evidence That Demands A Verdict*, Josh McDowell writes:

> Jesus claimed to be God. He did not leave any other options. His claim to be God must be either true or false and is something that should be given serious consideration. Jesus' question to His disciples, "But who do you say that I am?" (Mark 8:29) is also asked of us today.
>
> Jesus' claim to be God must be either true or false. If

Jesus' claims are true, then He is the Lord and we must either accept or reject His Lordship. We are without excuse.

If, when Jesus made His claims, He knew that He was not God, then He was lying. But, if He was a liar, then He was also a hypocrite because He told others to be honest, whatever the cost, while Himself teaching and living a colossal lie.

And more than that, He was a demon, because He told others to trust Him for their eternal destiny. If He could not back up His claims and knew it, then He was unspeakably evil.

Lastly, he would also be a fool because it was his claims to being God that led to His crucifixion.

Jesus claims to be God. If His claims were **False**, you have two alternatives:

(1) He *knew* His claims were false, therefore—>He made a deliberate misrepresentation—>He was a liar—> He was a hypocrite—>He was a demon—>and He was a fool, for He died for it.

(2) He *did not know* His claims were false,

therefore—>He was sincerely deluded—>He was a lunatic.

If His claims were **True**, that He is Lord, you also have two alternatives:

(1) You can *accept* Him.

(2) You can *reject* Him.

There must come a point in man's life when he knows there's got to be more to it than mere existence. A time when he realizes that neither he nor anything else could exist without a creator, that his creator is God, and that God is real. And just as surely as man exists because he was created, so there's a reason behind our existence.

God is the only one who can provide the answers, although the world has never lacked for those willing to put forth ideological explanations and precepts. Look at the various "consciousness-expanding" movements that have sprung up within the past decade or so, ones that purport to show you how to be content with the world and your lot in life by teaching you how to reach deep within yourself for "the truth." I've never found anyone who went through a program of this sort without emerging self-centered.

Before becoming a Christian, I used to go to the beach, enjoy its beauty, and find it gave me peace, but I also wondered what it was all about. Life? Death? Like at Christmas, when you see everyone rushing madly about—why? What is life all about? I know now. I have peace in my soul.

I can't do more than lead you to the door. It's up to you to open it, and I'm praying for you to do just that. You know, Mike, I'm not spending all this time for any purpose other than to help you; I don't get extra Brownie points for telling you about God. Since I know it's the only thing that *truly* works, why should I pretend otherwise? Jesus is alive and wants to help you.

Call if you've got any questions. I love you with all my heart. What more can I say?

Your friend always,

Bud

Dear Mike,

Between you and Daniel, I don't know what to do. Daniel is threatening suicide everyday, and you're so bummed, you're sounding suicidal, too. I can't believe this is happening with both of you at the same time. I know I'm supposed to be working here in Hawaii, but I really wonder if I should pack it in and go back to California. Maybe if I were closer to you guys, I could be of more help.

Later…

Just got back from a walk to clear my head. As I was walking, I realized something. Mike, I love you unconditionally, without any strings. I'd do almost anything for you, but my love isn't sufficient to do what must be done by you. The decision to change must be yours. You have to be willing to do whatever it takes. I can't do that for you.

I understand the agony and doubts you're experiencing. I empathize with you. Yet, I have to tell you, your pain may just be the thing that saves your life.

To be honest with you, I've been praying to God to do whatever is necessary to make you come to Him for salvation and guidance. I haven't been praying for things to get easier because that wouldn't help you. I've actually prayed for things to get so bad you'd finally see you have no other choice. Some people—like me—are so stubborn that they refuse to see the truth until they're at the end of their rope, until they've been pushed up against the wall and have nowhere else to go.

I'm looking at the pain and anguish you're suffering as something good because it can cause you to act, to move from where you are into something new. I had to get that desperate before I was willing to seek out some real alternatives. I had wanted them before, but I certainly wasn't willing to expend any of the effort necessary to change, nor was I open to experiencing any of the pain that might accompany such metamorphosis.

Yes, the unknown isn't very appealing when it's so frightening. It's extremely hard to give up everything familiar for something about which you haven't any personal knowledge at all, but where else can you go? You're up against the wall now, Mike, and death isn't the answer.

One of the positive things I learned from my attempt at suicide was that I had a choice—to live or die. To die meant giving up, which I was very willing to do. To live meant finding alternatives in my life. I tried to choose the easy way out. I was tired, fed up, aching with despair.

Luckily for me, I lived through it. For what? By dying I thought I'd escape the pain of living and at last discover the rest I so badly needed. If I succeeded, however, I would have been in for a big surprise. I now see that in dying without Jesus Christ as my Savior, I would have gone to hell where there's eternal pain and suffering.

I believe it was C.S. Lewis who claimed that hell begins here on earth for those who reject Christ; likewise, heaven begins on earth for those who trust in Him. It's an appropriate observation when I look at the situation in light of choosing Christ over suicide and sexual freedom over bondage. Heaven or hell begins here—it's our choice.

Just think how close I came to missing out on life as it's meant to be experienced! I can't begin to tell you the joy I have in living now, Mike. I'm experiencing a whole wealth of feelings I never thought possible.

The only way for you to understand what I mean is to experience it yourself. Yes, it's going to be painful to break off old associations and to change your most basic habits, but you're the only one who can give yourself the opportunity to experience the pure joy that results from getting your true needs met.

By nature we're inclined to avoid things that might produce pain, even if we know that in the long run we'll benefit from them. Unfortunately, there are those instances in life that require us to experience pain in order to gain our goals, whether it's working out at the gym to get a better body or denying confused and misdirected sexual feelings to obtain healthy, legitimate sexual desires.

A lot of gays have heard all the things I've been trying to tell you, but they're not willing to do anything about the state they're in. In the past, for instance, I've frequently asked gay friends the following question: If I had a "miracle pill" that would instantly transform you into a complete heterosexual, would you take it? The answer was always yes. But when I ask if they'd be willing to invest some time and energy into the transformation process, the answer was usually no.

Incredible? Not really. One of the biggest roadblocks to recovery is a lack of motivation. Though they freely admit they're not happy with their lives as they're living them, the familiarity of their lives makes them comfortable. They're not hurting enough to care about getting out of the mess they're in, so they remain in their homosexual identity, even though it leaves them feeling empty, lonely, dissatisfied and longing. These people are miserable in the lifestyle they've chosen, but it's a misery they're accustomed to. They deceive themselves into thinking that the lifestyle is somehow "safe" and that change is "risky."

What's your choice, Mike? You do have one. Sure, you could kill yourself, but it won't end your suffering. You could also continue to live your life the same way as in the past, but you already know where that takes you. How about a decision that'll produce what you've always wanted from life?

It's your decision to make. The whole future—your whole future—depends on what you decide to do with yourself right now. You've been saying that you never had a choice. The fact is that you never knew you had a choice, but now you know you do. You know you don't have to be gay; you know you can change.

You also know it's hard to live life without help. Let God help you, Mike. With Him all things are possible. Just look at me, I'm living proof of it. If I could make it, then anyone can.

I can't say it enough; I love you, buddy. I'd be deeply saddened and hurt if you took your life. Even if no one else in the world cares a bit—which isn't true—I care. God cares. Write soon.

Your friend,

Bud.

Dear Mike,

Just got your letter—what wonderful, welcome news! To answer your first question, no, I wasn't surprised to hear you became a Christian. Robert called me that same night. He knew what I had been trying to tell you and wanted me to know how much better you felt. I'm so happy for you, Mike. My prayers are being answered.

Accepting Jesus Christ as your Savior opens the door. And now comes the exciting part. You'll be learning a lot, so just remember to take each day as it comes. Robert said he told you about the importance of going to a Bible-teaching church. You're really blessed—there are some good churches quite nearby.

Last month you asked me why, if God is so powerful, He didn't heal my homosexuality, by which I assume you mean why didn't He heal me right away. I used to wonder the same thing because in the New Testament it says, "With God, all things are possible" (Matthew 19:26 KJV). It took me ages to comprehend the fallacy of waiting for God to "do something" in my life.

Seriously, I prayed at least five years for God to magically "heal" me. I prayed, I fasted, I begged…I even promised God that I would become a pastor or missionary if He would only cure me. I thought my healing would be, or should be, instantaneous. I had this vision of God coming down and zapping me, transforming me into a heterosexual within a split-second. Shazzam! Instant healing!

I wanted to be delivered from my homosexual thoughts and feelings because I saw them as a curse. You know what, though? Homosexual thoughts and feelings weren't my problem, and that's why I didn't receive His healing touch. My perception of what needed healing was wrong.

Remember a long time ago when I mentioned that homosexual feelings are actually homo-emotional feelings? The feelings themselves aren't bad or wrong; it's our response to them that's off the mark.

185

Maybe I ought to briefly run it by you again. Your "homosexual" (homo-emotional) drive is an innate, proper urge to correct your deficiencies, a reparative thing, built within the human mechanism so it can set itself right. It pulls you toward other guys so you can meet homo-emotional needs—but not on a sexual level. By misinterpreting homo-emotional needs as sexual desires, however, you go right off the track. Instead of meeting your needs in a legitimate, non-erotic, non-sexual way, you act upon your desires through sexual expression. So my prayers to be "healed" or "cured" of my homosexual feelings weren't valid—that's why God never "zapped" me.

Dr. Elizabeth Moberly, in her book *Homosexuality: A New Christian Ethic*, says:

> One should not try to cure, or ask God to cure, something for which cure is not necessary. God does not "cure" people of legitimate needs. Rather, the Christian faith indicates the proper, as distinct from inappropriate, means of fulfilling such needs. It is not merely ironic, but tragic, that people have attempted to "cure" what should rightly be *fulfilled*.
>
> God does not cure people of legitimate needs. To block the homosexual urge, as distinct from its sexual expression, is to block the very process of healing. In this sense, it is quite improper to speak of homosexuals as "individuals trapped by forces beyond their control," or as "in bondage to their habit." It is not a matter of bondage to be subject to normal and legitimate developmental needs, and it is only the fulfillment of such needs that may justifiably be regarded as healing. Similarly, it may be misleading to speak of deliverance from homosexual temptation. Deliverance from the sexual expression of homosexual needs is right and proper. But it must be clear that such deliverance applies to inappropriate means of meeting such needs, not to the needs themselves. Otherwise, to speak of deliverance from homosexual temptation is tantamount to saying that a child should be "delivered" from its normal love-need for the parent of the same sex.
>
> To stop being a homosexual means to stop being a person

186

with same-sex psychological deficits. This can only happen through the fulfillment of such needs and the resolution of any barriers to such fulfillment.

In short, through healthy, non-sexual, same-sex friendships, we fulfill our God-given needs. What barriers do you see preventing you from fulfilling your same-sex needs, Mike? Look at the roots of your homosexuality. (Have you ever drawn up that list of your own roots I asked you to compile?)

The obvious barriers I found in my life included feeling unlovable, inadequate, uncoordinated, insecure, and inhibited. My self-image and self-esteem were on the negative side of zero, plus I was lazy, lacking in motivation, and afraid to try...and those were just a few of the obstacles I needed to overcome.

What caused these feelings? All the things I've cited in previous letters. However, through prayerful introspection I pinpointed the roots of these problems and dealt with them individually, one at a time. By bringing them to the surface, I worked through the past hurts, misconceptions, misinterpretations, and my wrong responses. Finally, I was able to take responsibility for my actions. I no longer felt a victim of circumstances beyond my control.

In *How To Say NO To A Stubborn Habit*, Erwin Lutzer lays it on the line to people who try to find excuses instead of solutions:

> The schools of modern psychiatry based on...unbiblical principle have fared poorly in helping with emotional problems. Such psychiatrists have become professional excuse-finders, sifting through the rubble of the past, the pressures of the present, and the anxieties of the future, searching for a doorstep where the blame can be placed.
>
> How contrary to the Scriptures! The Bible calls each individual a sinner. We are fully responsible for our choices. Although that's a tough pill to swallow, it is basic to our hope that God can change us. After all, if we are responsible, we are in control of our choices. We can change. And we can choose to let God change us!
>
> Let's take the serious problem of homosexuality as an

example. A man told me that his abnormal desires began at puberty, but not through association with a practicing homosexual. Rather, there were unhealthy factors in his home that were so conducive to perverted thinking and behavior that this young man grew up believing that he had been born a homosexual. In his words, "predestined to be weird."

Can he change to heterosexual feeling and behavior? Not if he blames his environment or his genes for his actions. This man did change. Listen to his words: "For years I believed that I could never change because I was a homosexual by constitution, not by choice. I took no responsibility for my behavior. But as I began to read the Scriptures, I began to believe God could change me. The first step in that direction was when I took full responsibility for my homosexual behavior. No excuses, no alibis."

Every mature person needs to stop blaming and begin taking full responsibility for what he is—past, present, and future.

You need to find the roots we've been talking about, Mike—not to place blame, but to bring them out in the open and resolve these character deficiencies. I realize that many of the things that happened to you when you were a child were beyond your control, but your response to them was of your own choosing. Although it stemmed from ignorance, you still responded to your feelings in the wrong way, and this was sinful.

What is sin? Actually, sin means "missing the mark." Just as in archery, when you shoot an arrow toward the bull's-eye but miss the mark, sin is missing God's target for your life. The Word of God gives us certain guidelines to follow, certain restrictions to respect, so we can grow and mature as godly men. When we fall short of following His instructions, we've sinned. Sin is not obeying your owner's manual; it is anything contrary to God and His Word, and there's always a price to pay for it.

A wrong response here, a wrong response there, missing the mark—it all adds up to a distorted image of yourself that God didn't intend. God knows our makeup and the consequences of unmet same-sex needs, just as He knows how the environment can affect identity. God wanted to make it perfectly clear that sexual encounters with our same sex wouldn't fulfill the deficiencies of same-sex needs. Thus, He called it sin (Romans 1, 1 Corinthians 6), and warned His people to avoid such behavior because He knows its harmful effects.

Homosexuality misses the mark of the abundant life God has for us. In light of this, we can see the wisdom of our Father. By calling homosexual behavior sinful, there's no doubt about it being our choice because God doesn't hold us accountable where there is no choice. Actually, Mike, that's good news—if God didn't call it sinful, and therefore a matter of choice, then it truly would be a matter of constitution, and therefore unchangeable.

In *Competent To Counsel*, Jay Adams puts it this way:

> The picture is somewhat as follows: Early in his life…Frank became involved in homosexual activities. Before reaching his teens he began to engage in homosexuality with some regularity. Homosexual sin may first have begun out of curiosity or in order to act "smart." Frank's sin had a typical beginning when a group of young boys gathered together in a hideout on a vacant lot to form a club. All was innocent enough until someone got the idea that admission to membership in the club should be restricted to those who were willing to take off their clothes. However details of any particular story may go, homosexual sin does not appear to have been the result of genetic factors, but is, as in Frank's case, a learned activity.

> Before long a fixed pattern develops, and once having become a habit, homosexuality becomes a way of life. The habit may become so firmly established that homosexuality at first appears to be a genetic problem. But there is no reason for viewing homosexuality as a genetic condition in the light of the Scriptures which declare that the homosexual act is sin.

Notice that Adams carefully denoted the "act" of homosexuality as sin. The feelings at the root of gay behavior aren't sinful; it's what we do with them that can become sin. If we pervert these feelings and turn them into lustful thoughts, if we act upon these feelings in sexual ways, then we've missed the mark and sinned. Homo-emotional feelings exist to draw us toward the fulfillment of same-sex needs—honest, legitimate requirements for maturity.

In my case, I needed to follow His instructions because His word brings life and healing. Although I realized that the Bible is full of great wisdom, I remained blind to much. Why? Because I was consumed with receiving "the miracle healing" from God before I would apply the rest of God's Word to my life. I was confused, you see, and thought that in order to change my homosexual feelings it was a prerequisite that God perform the miracle I so desired. I wasn't seeing God's Word for what it is. I didn't recognize the transforming power obtained through obedience to God—doing the things He required of me.

When I first became a Christian, everything was new and exciting. I was so overwhelmed by the love in the church that for quite a while, I was less concerned about my homosexual thoughts because they weren't as strong. However, the longer I was a Christian and the longer that part of me seemed unchanged (though in fact, I was changing for the good), the more I began to feel hopeless.

Eventually, I got mad at God. I knew He was real and what He said was real, but this knowledge wasn't working for me, at least not in the area I needed it most—my homosexual feelings were still with me. I wanted to deny God because He hadn't "fixed" me. But I couldn't deny Him. Once I experienced a real relationship with God, rather than simply holding Him as part of some vague religious beliefs, I could never deny His existence.

So, although I continued to believe in Him, I began to think no hope existed for homosexuals and, therefore, no hope existed for me. It wasn't until I started doing some research on my own that things finally began to click. I began reading books from such authors as Moberly and Hurst, and though I eventually started to understand the scheme of things, initially I found myself more confused than before.

What was it that perplexed me? Well, I knew that these studies on homosexuality had only been done in the past 30 years or so. And

I knew that studies about the effects of environment on our gender development had only been done in the past 100 years or so. That left me with the big question: What about all the homosexuals that lived before the age of modern psychology? Was God's power there for them, too? Since they didn't have access to the knowledge we have today, did that mean they were without hope? Were the answers I was discovering only for us today? What could have helped the homosexuals of olden days?

Then one day I realized that if God is "the same yesterday, today, and forever" (Hebrews 13:8 KJV), then His word *must* have the same healing attributes for those who existed centuries ago. The answers were right in front of me! All the things I had learned and all the things I needed to do to be transformed were simply *applied Christianity.* They'd been in my owner's manual all the time; I just needed to apply them 100 percent.

Initially I thought there was no hope because the Bible didn't specifically state how the homosexual could be delivered from his consuming behavior. The only thing the Bible said, to my knowledge, was that homosexual behavior was sinful and homosexuals were bound for hell. I'd been trying to suppress my feelings in the hopes they'd vanish if I was a good Christian, whereas if I had simply been applying the wisdom in the Word of God to my life, transformation would have automatically taken place...slowly but surely.

Now I know there is hope because I've discovered homosexuals of the past *did* change—the Bible even says so:

> Do you not know that the wicked will not inherit the kingdom of God? Do not be deceived: Neither...male prostitutes nor homosexual offenders...will inherit the kingdom of God. *And that is what some of you were.* But you were washed, you were sanctfied, you were justified in the name of the Lord Jesus Christ and by the Spirit of our God (1 Corinthians 6:9-11, NIV, emphasis added).

If an individual simply follows God's teachings, he will be transformed, no matter what his problem may be. By the same token, suppressing feelings (or attempting to suppress them as I had been doing) only blocks transformation and consequently creates more problems. Emotional suppression is quite harmful.

I was a good Christian, and God's power was working in my life. He was changing me from a shy little kid into an outgoing, loving person. He was doing His part; I just didn't see my part about taking Him at His Word. You have to understand that I had a problem letting go of the identity I thought was mine.

A Bible verse, 2 Corinthians 5:17, gives some insight into this problem: "If any man be in Christ, he is a new creature: old things are passed away; behold, all things are become new" (KJV). At first glance this passage seems to be saying that there's an instantaneous miracle, that everything will be rosy, and that we'll live "happily ever after" in this new life—no more old life, no more old desires. But it doesn't work that way.

This verse, I believe, describes things from GOD'S viewpoint, not ours. From His perspective—now that we're His children—the former person is gone. The "all things are become new" portion refers to the potential we have to live life according to His hopes and dreams for us. I had to remember that He doesn't set limits on our growth—we do.

I needed to see myself as God saw me—whole and hetero-sexual—then think of myself that way. My thinking was holding me in bondage to a homosexual mindset and identity, "for as he thinketh in his heart, so is he" (Proverbs 23:7 KJV). I was being controlled—or rather, I allowed myself to be controlled—by my thinking. I wasn't living as I should have, which prevented the healing agent of God's Word from working in my life and also prevented me from receiving and living the new identity I had in Christ.

Again, God was doing His part, but I didn't see it. He put me into all sorts of situations where proper identification and affirmation could have taken place, but I wasn't open to them. I was certain that I had to be "healed" before I could leave the gay scene. All that time, of course, healing was available, but I just wasn't open to receiving it.

God now wants us to recognize that the former man is dead—and to live accordingly. I'm not supposed to see myself for the person I always thought I was, but for who I am—for who I can become in Christ through His power and wisdom.

Once you see by faith that the former man is dead and gone, you can go forth with boldness to start anew. How? Follow the Word of God. Start with the New Testament. Read the Gospels and get to know Jesus and the things He taught. His words are powerful and transforming.

Don't just *read* the Word of God, though, Mike. You have to *apply* the things you learn, for they're useless if they don't become a part of you. The Bible says:

> Do not merely listen to the Word, and so deceive yourselves. Do what it says. Anyone who listens to the Word but does not do what it says is like a man who looks at his face in a mirror and, after looking at himself, goes away and immediately forgets what he looks like. But the man who looks intently into the perfect law that gives freedom, and continues to do this, not forgetting what he has heard, *but doing it—he will be blessed in what he does* (James 1:22-25 NIV, emphasis added).

Incorporate the Word of God in your daily life. Walk in His light, and you'll no longer walk in darkness. He'll guide you forever if you'll let Him.

Each day I ask God to bring opportunities for love and affirmation into my life—and not just for me, but through me to others as well. When we give of ourselves, we receive. For instance, someone could love you immensely, but if you didn't love them in return, you wouldn't necessarily receive the love they offer.

Think about it. When have you felt love the most? There are times you feel it when someone's doing something nice for you, of course, but when do you feel it the most? I'll bet it's when you're giving love, when you're doing something special for someone else. My healing process gained momentum once I recognized this principle of God, once I (by faith) stepped out of my shell and became willing to reach out to others instead of waiting for someone to reach out to me.

193

We both want people to love us, Mike, to reach out and say "hi," to be kind, etc. Also, I'm sure we've both heard of God's command for us to treat others as we would have them treat us, yet we're all inclined to draw lines as to whom we'll treat well and whom we won't. God's instruction, however, was that we must love our neighbor as ourselves.

Do you see His wisdom? Put into practice, His love comes back to us in countless ways from countless sources. Just as our behavior toward others has the potential to set them free, following God's instructions in these matters brings freedom into our lives, immediately changing things for the better. People are hungry for love and kindness, and will respond in kind.

As you follow Christ's teachings, the inner healing you need—and that He wants you to have—will have to take place. It can't be stopped. The more you get to know Him through His word and through communicating with Him, the more faith you'll have in Him. He'll then give you the boldness and confidence to approach all new situations.

Go to it, Mike. I'm praying for you all the way, and I'm excited by the prospect of seeing what God has planned for your life. Do you realize we're now brothers in Christ? You always said you wanted a brother. Now you've got one! I love you.

Your bro,

Bud

Dear Mike,

Sounds like Southern California is enjoying more Hawaiian-type weather than the islands themselves at the moment. I sure don't remember any January with temperatures hovering in the mid-80s when I lived there—you must be loving it. I couldn't believe the tan Robert came back with!

You would have to ask me about Daniel. What can I say? He left Saturday afternoon. Beyond that, it's a long story that I'll try to reduce down to its essentials. Daniel was definitely a basket case when he first arrived. The *only* thing he talked about was killing himself—for hours on end, day after day. I listened, and tried to share some of the things you and I have been talking about, but he didn't want to hear it, didn't want to know, didn't want to try. He was so into his misery it seemed it was his whole reason for being. It even appeared he was actively pursuing that misery at times, and for sure, he wasn't willing at all to help himself out. As bad as things were initially, they managed to get worse on a daily basis until I was convinced he was going to kill himself.

Then, all of a sudden, he seemed to be feeling much better. He got out and about, took in a bunch of the local sights, and looked like he was enjoying himself as much, or more, than a tourist in a TV commercial promoting Hawaiian travel. After a few days of this, he haughtily announced that he'd met three guys from Florida and was having sex with them. I couldn't believe it. They left for home last Thursday morning and Daniel instantly fell right back into the basement of all-out depression.

I went over to Robert's to see Daniel that night and we actually had a pretty good talk. He let me tell him how I had felt after breaking up with Brian, how things had improved tremendously for me within just a few months, and he truly listened for the first time to what I was saying. He said that he now saw the way he always tried to avoid dealing with his feelings, and even tied it in to suppressing his feelings toward Roger while his "friends" from Florida had kept him entertained.

I spent the night there and the following morning we went to the beach and talked all day. Sometime in the middle of the afternoon Daniel suddenly said he'd come to the decision that he wanted to get out of the mess he was in, that it was stupid to throw his life away. He became just as up as he'd previously been down and I felt like cheering for him because he was so revitalized.

We went back to Robert's to make dinner, still talking a mile a minute, and then the phone rang. Guess who? Roger. He told Daniel he wanted him back, apologized, said he'd been wrong, and that he would never cheat on him again. Yeah, sure. Anyhow, Daniel immediately forgot everything we'd discussed, booked the first flight home he could get, and that's where things stand.

You know, I honestly feel sorry for Daniel. I'm not the most patient guy in the world and he sure knows how to annoy me at times, but I just can't be mad at him. Not for very long, at any rate, and then only because he's so self-destructive. This thing isn't going to work out any better now than it did before. Still, I understand how lost he feels and why he keeps grasping at straws. He's looking for answers, just not in the right places.

So, anyway, what about you? How are you handling your feelings for Reed? Fill me in on the latest. I'm stoked to learn you've enrolled at Orange Coast. It's an excellent school and I know you're going to enjoy yourself there. Why are you worried about declaring a major now? Almost everybody changes their major at least once before graduation. You've got time. Wait and see what interests you.

For now, just concentrate on getting the most out of what you're doing. Set some goals, and take some chances. Reach out and be willing to make the first move toward getting acquainted with someone. Be open to what God wants to do in your life to produce healing and transformation. *Don't let the fear of rejection keep you from experiencing the joy of acceptance!*

You're a new person, Mike, with a past that God has forgiven and forgotten. You can be anybody you want to be now, so try not to place the same restrictions that plagued your old identity on your new one. Look at yourself as a newborn baby with all possibilities in life open to you. Your opportunities are limitless now that you've placed your life in God's hands. Remember to go to Him daily and ask Him to guide your steps. Ask Him to show you what you need to be doing, and to give you the courage and strength to carry through.

Though it may seem strange, I think we often forget we can call upon Him at any time and ask His help with little things just as much as for matters of greater importance. He sets no limits on His grace, you know.

You asked what you should be doing to grow and resolve your unmet needs, and, at the risk of sounding simplistic, this is my best answer—everything. You need to do everything possible to help promote your desired transformation.

Let's briefly outline the problem again. First, the cause of homosexuality is weak gender identity based on feelings of inadequacy as a male, lack of gender affirmation, and an absence of love and acceptance from the same sex—whether truly absent or simply unreceived. Only you know which specific events and/or circumstances contributed to these things, so you must look at the list of roots to your homosexuality and begin working your way through them. I highly recommend the book I mentioned in my last letter, *How To Say NO To A Stubborn Habit*, by Erwin Lutzer. For anyone trying to break loose from ingrained behaviors that have caused them grief and trouble in the past, it's an absolute must-read.

In my case, I went to God and asked Him to show me how to demolish the barriers that had prevented fulfillment of my same-sex needs. What was it that had kept me from experiencing life as God intended? The answer was me. I limited myself from growing by clinging to my homosexual identity and allowing insecurities and inhibitions to rule me.

Through prayerful introspection I was able to see my homosexual feelings for what they were. At least 90 percent of my attraction toward other guys was based on envy. My self-image was so poor that almost every guy caught my eye, and since I didn't recognize these feelings as envy, I interpreted them as homosexual temptation. Once I realized this was what was happening, I was able to start dealing with it by stopping to dissect the attraction whenever I found myself being pulled toward another male.

That's why it's so important to get in touch with your true feelings, Mike. Get beyond the surface and break down the things going on underneath. If you're walking across campus and some guy grabs your attention, analyze what you're actually feeling. Your initial reaction is a learned sexual response, but you must determine the essence of that attraction. Nine times out of ten it'll prove to be simple misguided envy. Perhaps it's his haircut that caught your eye or his features. Maybe it's his build or the way he's dressed. When I discovered my attraction was so heavily based on envy, it became clear that I needed to see myself as God saw me, not as I saw myself. I had to say "no" to the child inside who held me back, and say "yes" to God and the things He held out to me.

It's God's business to take broken, shattered people and turn them into something beautiful. Therefore, becoming the person you want to be requires obedience to Him. Your owner's manual, the Bible, contains His instructions and tells you what He asks of you. Again, start with the New Testament and as you follow His directions, remember you're no longer to identify yourself as a homosexual. You're a new man. The former person is dead. If you don't like something about yourself, go to God in prayer and ask for His assistance in changing the things you can and accepting the things you can't. He won't let you down.

I want to give you an idea of how pervasive—and ridiculous—this matter of envy can be. Having grown up in Orange County, I was primarily attracted to (envious of) surfers. The "surf & beach look" of Southern California was something I'd always wanted for myself, but due to my poor self-image and low self-esteem, I prevented myself from experiencing that lifestyle and even from dressing the part.

Instead, I stayed on the sidelines, filled with unconscious envy, and eventually twisted these feelings into sexual desires. Looking from afar, I lusted after that life and the people who lived it. It seemed such a carefree lifestyle—the leisure look of freedom—and a far cry from the walls of restraint I had placed upon myself.

I was afraid to be the person I wanted to be—afraid of looking like a fag dressed in surf clothes. I didn't have any confidence in my ability to carry it off. Other people could, but not me. What a waste!

198

To think of all those years I permitted that type of thinking, unaware it was preventing me from living.

Surfer guys that you wouldn't think were attractive, I would, simply because everything about a surfer had magnetic appeal for me. That certain way of talking, dressing, walking—everything. At the time, I thought the attraction was based on individuals, but now I can see it was also a matter of lifestyle.

Of course, I should have done what any emotionally healthy boy would have done—learn to surf and become a surfer. Lousy self-image had kept me from doing that and had prevented me from identifying with that group, so it became my goal to have that image. I stopped denying myself permission to live and look like a typical Southern California beach dweller. I jumped in with both feet. Once I began living and dressing the part, I started liking myself much better, and I also found my old envy-attraction disappearing. God allowed me to become who I wanted to be by opening my eyes to my envy and giving me the courage to put past fears behind me.

You're now free to become the guy you've always wanted to be, but you must first search within yourself to see what prevented you from doing it before. Determine the roots to your character deficiencies. Zero in on those things that have kept you from getting your same-sex needs for love, affirmation and identification met. Orange Coast is a perfect spot to let the interaction you need begin taking place. You couldn't ask for a better opportunity to meet new guys and start identifying with them. It won't be easy at first, but you must not take the easy way out. Stick with it and reach your goals.

Identifying your roots is only the beginning, Mike, not the solution. You'll start altering your concept of yourself with each proper decision, which will bring you closer to the man you want to be. You'll experience life instead of being a bystander to it because you are freeing yourself from those negative emotions that had a grip on you in the past.

Go for it, Mike! I love you and I'm very proud of you.

Your bro,

Bud

Dear Mike,

Thanks for the letter. It was great to finally hear from you. I tend to get a little antsy when the weeks between your letters add up to more than a month.

I feel the same way as you about last Tuesday. Ray and I had flown over to the "big island" because we had a couple of days off from work. When the news started coming in about the space shuttle we were completely stunned. I felt as if I'd been caught away from home when war broke out or something. Just like the day Kennedy was shot, I don't think I'll ever forget where I was and what I was doing. Even now, after seeing endless replays of the explosion, it still somehow seems unbelievable. Did you know one of the astronauts was from Hawaii?

I want to respond to your last letter but bear with me if I'm a little out of it. In your letter you asked what things you should be doing to speed your healing—and I have a couple of additional suggestions to make. One, I urge you to get Moberly's book, *Homosexuality: A New Christian Ethic*, and two, how are you doing at keeping your journal? It's really important to be consistent with this.

I'm really glad to hear that you've made some friends but I'm a little concerned about some of the things you said regarding those new relationships. Remember that stopping or suppressing homosexual behavior alone doesn't resolve the homosexual dilemma. All you're doing is temporarily avoiding dealing with it. You need to treat the hidden emotional problems underlying that behavior, otherwise you're not even attacking the "symptoms," let alone the illness. (Remember my analogy of the common cold?)

You've got to dig out those roots, Mike, because those are the barriers that have prevented you from fulfilling your same-sex needs. Once you begin to understand yourself better by seeing why you respond to certain things the way you do, you'll be able to effect permanent change, to develop and mature as you were meant to do.

It's the fulfillment of same-sex needs that produces transformation of identity—and there isn't any shortcut. Suppressing your feelings only hinders your progress by stopping you dead in your tracks.

I remember when I first began making a lot of new friends. It felt great and I thought I was on the verge of total healing. For the most part I didn't have any desire to be sleeping with anybody, and the rest of my homosexual tendencies seemed to be fading away, too. The key word, however, is "seemed." In a sense these feelings were merely falling back to regroup themselves, although I didn't know that at the time. I was meeting people, having fun, and staying so busy I hardly ever thought about my "problem." It only surfaced every now and then, and compared to where I'd been before, this struck me as a great accomplishment.

Similarly, what you've told me thus far indicates that you think your homosexual feelings will miraculously go away over a period of time as long as you stop all homosexual conduct. That's not how it works, buddy. This is a big misconception of the healing process. Right now you feel you've made great strides in all areas, but in fact your progress on this one level is non-existent as long as you continue to just "live around" the root causes. Your new friends and busy schedule will only temporarily keep your mind occupied and off old thought patterns, but in terms of producing lifelong personal change, forget it.

In no way does stopping homosexual behavior signify recovery. Recovery ultimately must occur from within. Sure, stopping homosexual behavior is necessary, in fact vital, but your whole identity needs to be restructured and set upon a godly path through the renewal of your mind. Don't you see your whole self-perceived identity needs to undergo radical transformation, Mike? By suppressing your desires, you unconsciously attempt to avoid the pain of changing, but sooner or later you've got to face these growing pains.

It's essential that you deal with your homosexual identity on a daily basis, that you be willing to do whatever is necessary to quicken the process of healing. Presently, you're only postponing it, which means you're at a standstill.

Don't get me wrong. The problem isn't that you're so busy; it's that you're not using your new social life to your real benefit.

Spending time with people and having fun is great, but not at the expense you've described. Going out and having a few beers, and then a few more, and sometimes more yet, just isn't a healthy way to go about developing interpersonal relationships. Instead of learning to relate to people and building communication skills and self-confidence, you're leaning on beer to temporarily loosen your inhibitions and relieve you of tension and anxiety. This isn't helping you progress, except possibly into one more critical arena—that of alcohol dependency.

I'm not passing judgment. I fell into the same trap at the beginning. I started hanging around some guys at school, joined their ski club, and got really wound up about our first trip of the year, which was set for four days over the Thanksgiving weekend. We packed two buses to the gills and headed off toward Snow Bird—what a disaster. There were two kegs on my bus and in no time flat everybody was tweeked out of their gourds. Guys were urinating on the floor and throwing up on themselves, and everyone was doing his level best to be the greatest "gross-out" ever seen.

It was the absolute pits. I'd had such high hopes of meeting new guys and experiencing affirmation and identification, but the last thing I wanted to do was to identify with those clowns. I felt severely depressed, like I was caught in some black comedy. I made all this effort to meet same-sex needs in a positive, healthy way, but I was stuck with a bunch of jerks. I decided to fly home early.

When I returned, I told a friend about the whole scenario. I explained to him how much I needed to fulfill my same-sex needs in order to become the man I wanted to be. He smiled, pulled a book out of his bookcase entitled *Learning To Be A Man*, by Kenneth Smith, and read me a passage:

> A man becomes a man when he becomes what God wants him to be.

What a slap in the face—and a much needed one, at that. I'd been trying to receive legitimate identification from other lost people! It was like the blind leading the blind. What I needed to do was identify with godly people, with Christ Himself. I needed to find my identity as a Christian, to discover who I was in Christ. That's why I've been harping on you to read the New Testament—I want you to know the person of Jesus Christ because He's the supreme example of manhood.

Before you became a Christian I urged you to return to school because it seemed like the next best thing for you. However, now that you've made the big step, you need to involve yourself in church groups. I know that sounds dull, but it's not. Get involved in the college group at your church and you'll find they do a lot of fun things.

My church, for instance, holds picnics, goes on outings everywhere from the mountains to the beach, organizes ski trips, and offers a whole bunch of sports activities. The environment is extremely conducive to learning and growing because it offers endless encouragement to everyone, no matter what his level of accomplishment.

You'll build some of the best friendships you've ever dreamed of having because Christian men who desire to be like Christ are much more open to expressing love. Most of my friends and I hug each other freely, and nobody feels restrained from verbalizing love and affection for one another.

I'm not saying these guys are perfect. Christians have faults just like everyone else. They are different because they're seeking victory over their problems through Christ and His wisdom. So give yourself the chance to experience the affirmation and identification of Christian fellowship.

I've gotta fly—Ray's waiting for me to run an errand with him. I love you very much and I hope to hear from you soon.

Your big brother,

Bud

Little Bro,

I'm really glad you called last night—and I appreciate your honesty. Just one more time, for the record, let me assure you I'm not going to judge you or give up on you if you blow it. I don't expect you to be Super Christian or anything, you know. You're only a "baby" Christian at the moment, Mike, and you need to be taught proper, godly ways to handle your life.

I understand how strong your homosexual desires can be, but fighting them, dwelling upon them, or attempting to suppress them isn't the answer. In *How To Say NO To A Stubborn Habit*, the book I recommended by Lutzer, he gives some insight I trust will help you in this area:

> None of us can overcome evil by simply renouncing it. Rather, we can only do so by substituting the good in its place. Sinful habits cannot be broken without replacing them with righteous ones.
>
> Try this simple experiment. Think of the number eight. Have you visualized it? If so, exercise your willpower and stop thinking of the number eight right now.
>
> Were you able to do it? Of course not. At least, I'm still thinking about that number. Can we, by sheer willpower, stop thinking about the number eight? By no means. Trying to push it out of our minds actually causes us to focus our attention upon it.
>
> Can we really be free? Yes, we can control these thoughts, but not by trying to stop thinking about them! To simply resist evil is to make it grow stronger. Our determination not to think lustful thoughts only reinforces them in our thought patterns.
>
> How, then, can we be free? Let's return to our experiment once more and think of the number eight. Although we

can't stop thinking about it by sheer resistance, we can push that number out of our minds quite easily. Here's how: Think of the number one thousand. Then divide it by five. Concentrate on this new information and you'll stop thinking of the number eight.

You can handle sinful thought patterns in the same way. Fear, lust, covetousness—all of these can be squeezed out of your mind by turning your thoughts to the Scriptures. Freedom comes by filling your mind with God's thoughts.

As I told you last week, stopping homosexual behavior doesn't in itself mean recovery because recovery must ultimately occur from within. The very nature of your identity must be restructured and set upon a godly path through the renewal of your mind.

Now, remember our discussions about homosexuality being a learned behavior? First, your environment influenced the way you think, and then your response to your environment programmed your subsequent behavior.

Let me share with you something Og Mandino says, writing in *The Greatest Miracle In The World:*

> For countless centuries man compared his mind to a garden. Seneca said that soil, no matter how rich, could not be productive without cultivation and neither could our minds. Sir Joshua Reynolds wrote that our mind was only barren soil, soon exhausted and unproductive unless it was continually fertilized with new ideas. And James Allen...wrote that a man's mind was like a garden which may be intelligently cultivated or allowed to run wild, but whether cultivated or neglected, it would produce. If no useful seeds were planted, then an abundance of useless weed-seeds would fall into the land, and the results would be wrong, useless, harmful, and impure plants. In other words, whatever we allow to enter our minds will always bear fruit.
>
> The computer people have a phrase, actually an acronym, "GIGO"..."garbage in, garbage out." If one puts faulty information into a computer, out will come faulty answers.

So it is with our minds...put negative material in...and that's what you'll reap. On the other hand, if you program in, or plant, beautiful, positive, correct thoughts and ideas, that's what you'll harvest.

The Bible teaches the same principle, Mike:

> Do not be deceived, God cannot be mocked. A man reaps what he sows. The one who sows to please his sinful nature, from that nature will reap destruction: the one who sows to please the Spirit, from the Spirit will reap eternal life. Let us not become weary in doing good, for at the proper time we will reap a harvest if we do not give up (Galatians 6:7-9 NIV).

Now, let's go back to Lutzer:

> The adage puts it succinctly: You aren't what you think you are; but what you think, you are!
>
> Let us suppose you could flash all the thoughts you had last week on a giant screen. Within minutes you would know how you are doing spiritually. Your thoughts not only shape your life, they are your life.
>
> A man recently released from prison was having difficulty adjusting to his freedom. He tried this experiment: He took a glass bottle with a distinct shape and crammed it full of wires, some small and some large. After some time had passed he smashed the bottle with a hammer. The result? Most of the wires retained the shape of the bottle. Those wires had to be straightened out, one by one.
>
> The man had established his point: It is possible to be technically free and still retain the traits of bondage. Even though a man is liberated, he must adjust to his freedom and carefully dismantle the habits of the past.
>
> As a believer, you are legally free in Christ, but you can still be enslaved by the fantasies of the flesh and the vices of the world. You can yield, surrender, and "pray through," but your mind will revert to familiar territory as soon as your

experience wears thin. To leave this self-defeating cycle, you need to outline a specific strategy for experiencing the freedom you have in Christ, and accept the victory that is legally yours.

Sound familiar? Don't waste any more of your precious time. Write out your goals and establish what tasks you must undertake to accomplish them. Take positive action, Mike. Start making proper decisions that carry you toward recovery, regardless of your desires. As you begin consistently applying these principles, you'll find those desires changing. Handling your emotions in a constructive manner brings resolution instead of destruction. You can't suppress feelings, so replace the former man with a new means of identification. The new will drive out the old. Fulfillment of same-sex needs will stop your homosexual desires.

Take care, my friend. I love you and I pray for you daily.

Yours,

Bud

Dear Mike,

Tomorrow marks my nine-month anniversary as a resident of Kauai and would you believe, I finally got a P.O. box in Hanalei—no more hour-long drives to Kapaa for my mail!

Nine months…and to think I was only planning to be here for the summer. I get homesick once in a while, but most of the time I'm having too much fun to even think about it.

Life is a lot slower out here, but I seem to be in complete accord with the pace on Kauai. There certainly isn't much to keep one entertained. Gathering with friends and doing whatever comes along is it, but it's so pleasant compared to the endless hassles of trying to achieve some quality of life in southern California. Everything here is centered around people and nature. If you're not surfing, you're hiking, sunbathing, exploring a freshwater stream, swimming, playing volleyball, softball, or backgammon. Oh, yeah, we also work—some of the time.

Most of all, we talk, really talk, about things that matter. Nobody gets caught up in trivia. We always seem to be digging into each other's beliefs, not to put them down, but to learn what we can. The prevailing viewpoint among this crowd is that life's a great adventure and we have a free choice of which path we want to take through it. My friends here all want more out of their existence than a five-bedroom house with a BMW in the driveway, 2.3 kids, and a membership at the club. They want to experience life to the fullest. It's not that any of us think a BMW and such things are bad, it's just that if that's someone's highest aspiration, it's pretty sad…especially if the primary motivation behind it is a desire to impress the family down the street.

I feel fortunate in having found people here who share the same goals in life, people who want to live for themselves (not the Joneses), and realize that it can only be done through living for one another. We motivate and inspire each other to such an extent that after spending time together, we go home challenged to be better, to do something positive with our lives.

Although they all know I'm working on a book, I haven't told any of them, including Ray, what it's about. Wonderfully, my privacy has been respected, and in addition I've received a whole lot of support and encouragement. (If that's not giving, I don't know what is.) I chose not to tell anyone about either the book's subject matter or my past because I want to be accepted for me, the real me. I don't want to be known as an ex-gay, but as Bud, the Bud I am today.

I like the person I am now and I hope to like myself even better as I continue to grow. I think the neatest thing that came out of changing my life is the realization that I can do anything—that I was the only one who ever placed restrictions on what I could do or be. Over the last couple of years I feel that God has granted me a chance to live and enjoy the happy life I didn't have during childhood. I'm doing things I would have thought impossible in the past. I'm living a life I would have envied terribly.

This morning I went with Ray to watch him play in a volleyball tournament. When we got there, we learned that one of his team-mates was a no-show, so I was asked to fill in. Just a few years ago, I would have refused by making up some stupid story as to why I couldn't play. Today, though, having grown considerably since then, I jumped at the opportunity. To understand the full impact of just how much growth has taken place, you'd have to have seen these guys— every single one was an all-out gonzo jock. In the past, I would have been intimidated by them, but today I was one of them and it felt terrific!

This brings up a good point. In her book, *Crisis In Masculinity*, Leanne Payne says:

> An automatic and serious consequence of a man's failure to be affirmed in his masculine side is that he will suffer from low self-esteem. He will be unable to accept himself.

She could have been writing that about the old me. The description certainly fits. A defeatist by nature, I never felt good enough, strong enough, or man enough. I wanted to do so many things, but I always "knew" it was impossible, so I gave up before even trying. I kept this attitude alive by constantly feeding my mind negative thoughts about myself.

Negative thoughts flooded my childhood—I felt very uncoordinated as a kid. The most dreaded part of my life was having to attend physical education classes. I was always one of the last to be picked when teams were chosen, and I was sure even the girls probably wouldn't have taken me. I couldn't catch or throw a baseball, and just looking at a football terrified me. I felt horribly inadequate, physically ill-equipped, the clumsiest of klutzes.

It wasn't until I became a Christian that I began feeling different about myself, allowing the image I had of myself to be transformed. Instead of saying, "I can't do this" and "I can't do that," I started taking God at His word—and He freed me of the countless restrictions I'd placed upon my life. God tells us that all things are possible to those who believe. He declares us free from our former selves, from that child within who keeps telling us we're no good, that we're awkward and lousy at sports.

There's clear evidence that most boys have the same abilities to achieve and excel in sports. What sets some apart from the rest is their measure of self-confidence. What builds confidence? Improving through instruction. The more confidence you gain, the more your skills become sharpened and your performance improves.

Most homosexuals, however, grow up lacking confidence in themselves. Like the old me, they avoid sports because of the possibilities for failure and humiliation. They never develop those skills or recognize the opportunities before them. Instead, they reinforce their negative self-image by telling themselves,"I can't."

The boy who can't catch a baseball is usually the boy who closes his eyes at its approach because he's sure that he can't catch it and almost just as sure it's going to hit him. The boy who's full of confidence, however, has an aggressive attitude. He runs toward the ball as it approaches in the hopes of catching it. If he misses it, he just keeps on playing, determined to do better the next time. For the boy without this sense of confidence, missing the ball confirms his belief that he just can't play baseball. He railroads himself into a vicious cycle, robbing himself of good self-image and a healthy, confident masculine identity.

In *Overcoming Homosexuality*, Dr. Kronemeyer writes:

> Telling themselves they are "frail" and have no coordination, many homosexuals manage to bring about the self-fulfilling condemnation that they are "lousy" at sports. By and large, they are just as healthy as the rest of us, and no clumsier, but they are convinced that they can't catch or hit a baseball, clear a hurdle, or shoot baskets. Feeling inadequate is merely the fruition of negative programming about one's "maleness" and ability to compete.

Similarly, you're afraid of trying, afraid of rejection, and afraid of failure. But trying unsuccessfully isn't failure, Mike. *Failure means not trying at all.* You'll be amazed at what you can accomplish if you give yourself the chance. You want a complete transformation, don't you? Well, that means all areas of your life, not just one or two.

Remember my motto, "Run toward the things that frighten you"? Don't avoid your inhibitions and don't accept them. Free yourself of them once and for all by facing them head-on with God's wisdom. Don't let anything—especially yourself—prevent you from experiencing the fullness of life.

Once I placed my trust in God, I tried everything I'd previously denied myself. I learned to ski, swim laps, play tennis, softball, volleyball, and other sports. I went water-skiing and got up on my first try! Strangely, I was almost dismayed to find out that not only could I do all these things, but I could do them reasonably well.

The realization that I'd ignorantly wasted so much of my life and lost so many opportunities was pretty uncomfortable. That's why I'm pushing you to get involved, now, both in this time at school and through church functions. Team activities are ideal for providing affirmation and acceptance—for canceling out same-sex deficits. Equally important are the interaction and friendships you develop while regularly attending a Bible study group. I'm positive that if I allowed myself at a younger age to belong to—and feel a part of—

a group of guys, it would have eliminated my gender confusion. I would have received fulfillment of same-sex needs without even consciously realizing it, and never would have acquired a homosexual identity.

Of course, not all gays fit this general pattern. Some who take up individualized activities (such as diving), actually shy away from sports that require team interaction. Then there are those few homosexuals who actually get involved in contact sports such as football. Why didn't this interaction among team members satisfy their same-sex needs and move them on in their development as heterosexual males? Haven't I been telling you that this is a way to bring about affirmation and identification?

I wonder if you happened to read an article entitled "One Family's Struggle," in *Newsweek* magazine last month. The piece centered around a guy named Kelly, first-string tackle on his high school football team and an excellent student, and how his family dealt with their discovery that he's also gay. According to the article, "Kelly saw his perfectionism as a way of hiding from himself and from others. By always being the teacher's pet, by being a hustler in football practice, and by being the fringe member of many social groups but the leader of none, Kelly managed to mask his insecurities. Despite his achievements, he had long felt himself an outsider, separate from his peers."

If you get a chance, dig up the magazine and read the article for yourself. In the meantime, the point I want to illustrate is Kelly's view of himself. Growing up he considered himself "an outsider, separate from his peers."

Now I don't know this guy, but my opinion is that by perceiving himself as different he let his insecurities block fulfillment of his same-sex needs for acceptance and proper identification. He probably didn't allow affirmation to take root but based his identity on misunderstood feelings. My opinion is, although affirmation and identification were available, he wouldn't allow himself to *receive* them. I believe Kelly was in a healthy setting, but more than likely things in his early childhood caused him to suffer massive self-doubts that kept him from bonding healthily and wholesomely with his same-sex peers.

Newsweek pointed out that "he had been named after K.O. Kelly, Brenda Starr's rough-and-tough comic strip boyfriend because his father wanted him to be 'tough as hell.'" The article said Kelly's father "... was proud of his own aggressive instincts in business but thought them lacking in his son. 'If we could just get him to be a little meaner,' Paul [Kelly's father] would say, 'he could go as far as he wanted to go.'"

I don't know about you, but I'd have to guess that Kelly played football just to please his old man. While it's only a guess, I think it's likely that his insecurities stemmed from his awareness that he couldn't match his father's expectations that he be "tough as hell."

I have a friend named Gary whose dad wanted him to be the best all-around athlete in school and forced him to participate in activities he didn't like and wasn't interested in. Gary said he always felt he was letting his father down, that no matter how hard he tried he just wasn't good enough. Consciously, he wanted his father's love and approval, but subconsciously he couldn't—or wouldn't—identify with someone who seemed to relate to him only as chattel on the order of a show dog. When Gary didn't measure up to his father's rugged standards of masculine performance he began feeling an ever increasing sense of inadequacy. Based upon the way he responded to his father, one negative reaction led to another which contributed to his confused gender identity and, consequently, his unfortunate identification as a homosexual.

As children, we're woefully ignorant of the ramifications of misinterpreting our feelings. That's why we need healthy role models to guide us through our identification process and help us receive fulfillment of our same-sex needs for affirmation and acceptance, love and approval, and a sense of belonging with other males.

Frank Worthen is founder of Love in Action, a counseling center for men and women struggling with homosexuality in San Rafael, California. He says in his book, *Steps Out Of Homosexuality*:

> During our more than ten years of ministry, having counseled with thousands of former homosexuals, we have learned much about the homosexual condition. We feel that the deepest root of homosexuality is a lack of a SENSE OF

BELONGING. Due to a variety of circumstances, a bonding has not taken place principally with the father figure.... This lack of bonding sends the child out into the world searching for affirmation, many times from a person of the same sex.

The roots of homosexuality, therefore, are nonsexual roots. The desire for sexual interaction comes long after the simple desires for love, attention, and someone who will say, "You're OK!"

Search out your own feelings and see for yourself how true this is, Mike. See what you felt as a kid and what your real needs were. The insight will help you grasp everything I've been saying for the past nine months. Don't get stuck in seeing only your homosexual feelings. Explore your feelings, attractions and desires, and you'll discover they have nonsexual roots based on legitimate unmet needs.

My fingers are sore from all this typing, so I'm going to call it a night. Write soon.

Your bro,

Bud

Dear Mike,

Although I'm fairly sure there have been times when what I've said has appeared to be no more than theory, I know that there have been other times when something inside you responded to what I was saying. Something clicked and you knew it was true. Remember, however, that insight into the roots of your problem isn't enough to produce healing and transformation. Significant change won't occur until you get involved in, and begin experiencing, healthy male relationships.

One of the greatest things about establishing such relationships is that you'll discover how very much you're like every other guy. Things you thought were exclusively homosexual doubts, feelings, insecurities, etc., will prove to be the same as those experienced by a lot of males, as I've found out from many of my new friends who never struggled with homosexual feelings. A surprising majority of them have even felt similar inadequacies. The differences that I thought existed between me and the average guy were self-imposed. It was how I interpreted my feelings, and how I then responded to my interpretations that caused my problems. Only by relating to other guys in healthy, nonsexual ways, did I make the wonderful discovery of how much we have in common, including ordinary emotions.

This is part of the healing process, Mike. Let yourself find out what feelings are mutual among straight guys. Relate to them, listen to them, learn from them, and receive affirmation from them. In short, identify with them. I don't think you could ask for a better payoff than the realization that you're more like them than you ever thought possible.

After Brian and I broke up, he attended classes at USC and made new friends. One in particular, Mike, was an especially healthy relationship for him. I was jealous—I wanted someone like that in my life! So I asked God to send me a "Mike" and He sent me Greg. The pleasure I derived from even the simplest things Greg and I did

217

together was unbelievable, whether it was walking to the market, going to movies, or having in-depth conversations. He liked me and valued my opinions. Knowing nothing of my past, Greg talked to me just as if I were heterosexual, too, which I was; I just didn't know it. Slowly, I began identifying with him, and through him I formed several other friendships.

I had past acquaintances with straight guys, of course. However, I blocked identification with them because I gave in to the doubts regarding my sexuality. Since I viewed myself as "different," I didn't let myself see the fact that I was more like the straight guys than I thought. But with Greg and my new friends, I let myself receive their affirmation, which allowed my gender identification to develop.

Of course, having straight male friends doesn't in itself bring about recovery any more than understanding the nature and root causes of your homosexuality. If you're still clinging to your gay identity, you're blocking the healing properties of identification from working. You've got to see yourself for who you truly are, not who you think you are—or were. You're a man, Mike—a heterosexual man deceived into believing you are homosexual. There are no homosexuals except for those who believe the lie that they are gay—you are what you think you are. Give yourself a break and stop denying your inner self the opportunity to grow and mature. Nurture the real man inside. Stop being so hard on yourself and allow your new identity to take over.

As important as male bonding is, it's necessary to keep things in perspective. Everything you do must be in submission to God's wisdom for your life. Your ultimate goal isn't to become heterosexually-minded, but Christ-minded. Healthy lateral relationships with men begin with a healthy vertical relationship with God. Our main desire should be to become as Christ-like as we can and to identify with Him. Identity with Christ truly instructs us how to identify with men.

God bless you, my friend. Let Him perform wonders in your life by keeping faith in Him.

Love,

Bud

Dear Mike,

Just received your letter, and wanting to respond immediately, I tried calling—only to once again be frustrated because you weren't home. I would try calling you later tonight, but Ray and I are leaving this afternoon to go sailing with friends for a few days. I guess I'll just have to make do with the old-fashioned way of communicating.

I don't know why you think I'll hate you for having sex with Reed. You're a friend, Mike, a very special friend. I empathize with how you're feeling and what you're going through. I know how rough it can be in the beginning, and I assure you that your progress hasn't "gone right down the drain." I'm not trying to minimize the consequences of what happened, but it's only a temporary setback, so don't let it defeat you. All is NOT lost, buddy. Just get right back up on your feet again with new resolve.

Right now, you feel you're a failure because you gave in to your desires. You said you felt like, "I might as well give up, it won't work." You're not a failure, though—you merely slipped up. Don't focus on the fact that you messed up. Concentrate instead on the progress that's taken place.

Reread your journal and see how long it's been since the last time you gave in. Notice the change in your heart, and the changes in your desires from all that you now know to be true. If you look at your recent growth you'll see you've made tremendous strides. You've become more confident and self-assured. You've made new friends and experienced acceptance from them. These are the things to keep your eye on. It's going to take time to transform your old ways, buddy. There aren't any overnight shortcuts.

This may sound like a stupid illustration, but suppose Fat Joe had been dieting diligently for three months and lost 20 pounds. One day when out with friends, someone suggests getting an ice cream cone. On the spur of the moment, Joe decides to get one, too. It's terrific.

After he finishes it, though, he feels horribly guilty. He's given in to temptation. He's failed.

Although he goofed up, he has a new choice to make. Either he can immediately resume his diet, or he can fall into the self-defeating trap of allowing his guilt to send him on more binges. *Oh, well, I've already blown it today, so I may as well live it up.*

Say that he takes the latter route and eats all sorts of junk, and that it carries over into the following days. Before he knows it, he's regained ten pounds. Now the added weight so discourages him that he doesn't even think about resuming his diet. He continues to eat, gains all his weight back (and then some), and is miserably unhappy. He feels he has no hope of losing weight—the diet didn't work.

Notice what Joe's done. He's blamed the diet for not working, but the diet was working just fine. It was the way Joe responded to his initial setback that caused his defeat. By allowing guilt to drag him down, Joe prevented himself from achieving his desired weight loss.

You've got the same choice before you as Joe, Mike. Are you going to let this one incident cause you to lose all you've thus far attained? Or are you going to bounce back and press on toward further healing? The only way to respond to setbacks is *positively*, by taking note of what you've already accomplished and letting it encourage you to resume your efforts. Don't let guilt defeat you, buddy.

When you sin, go immediately to God and repent (which literally means to stop where you are, and go in the opposite direction). Seek God and His wisdom. Ask His forgiveness, then get right back on the track. The more common response is to avoid Him because of guilt, but if guilt actually drives you away from God, it can only come from Satan himself. Conviction, the way God uses guilt, is meant to draw us to God for forgiveness. Responding right to God's conviction restores our fellowship with Him so we can continue to walk in His wisdom and grace.

God loves you at all times, and His forgiveness is available 24 hours a day, just for the asking. His love is limitless, as well as timeless. He loves you when you're doing well, and He still loves you when you're doing badly. The Bible says:

220

Therefore, since we have been justified [made "OK" in God's sight] through faith, we have peace with God through our Lord Jesus Christ, through whom we have gained access by faith into this grace in which we now stand. And we rejoice in the hope of the glory of God....

And hope does not disappoint us, because God has poured out His love into our hearts by the Holy Spirit, whom He has given us. You see, at just the right time, when we were still powerless, Christ died for the ungodly. Very rarely will anyone die for a righteous man, though for a good man someone might possibly dare to die. But God demonstrates His own love for us in this: While we were still sinners, Christ died for us (Romans 5:1-2, 5-8 NIV).

Christ died for you when you were still a sinner. You didn't have to get your act together first. He's there to help you get it together. The important thing is to repent, and immediately reestablish your fellowship with Him. By faith, you may (and must) believe He's forgiven you. "If we confess our sins, He is faithful and just and will forgive us our sins and purify us from all unrighteousness" (1 John 1:9 NIV).

The Word of God also states that, "As far as the east is from the west, so far has He removed our transgressions from us" (Psalm 103:12 NIV). The pastor of my church once pointed out the special meaning of this. Notice God has deliberately specified east and west, instead of north and south. Why? Assume you're traveling around the globe in a southerly direction; eventually you'll reach the South Pole and then start heading north because this is one point where north and south meet. However, if you're traveling east around the globe, you'll never meet with west but will continually move in an easterly direction. We are meant to understand from His Word that when God forgives, He forgets. So accept His forgiveness, Mike, and let go of the guilt.

Believe me, the pain you're experiencing is normal—and perhaps necessary. You'll continue to have "growing pains" as you work through the emotional conflicts which have habitually occupied your thoughts for so many years.

I went through a lot of rough times on the road to recovery, too, buddy. I know what you're going through because many times after mutually deciding to break up, Brian and I temporarily got back together for sex.

Unfortunately, deeply set patterns aren't easily broken, and the effort it takes to overcome them isn't without cost. However, all your emotional turmoil will eventually resolve itself as you continue your progress into your new identity. God's loving power will see you through even the most unbearable days, so turn to Him and allow His strength to carry you.

You will mature out of this destructive behavior that dominates your life, Mike, when there is growth and healing of the hurt child within you. This child of the past is strong enough to impede your thinking as he seeks instant gratification without regard for costs. Don't let the excessive or misdirected desires of this inner child rob you of what can be yours. Healing comes as that little boy within starts to mature.

Maturity also implies responsibility. Growth begins with your resistance to the fleeting desires of the inner child, the one who identifies himself as gay. Start doing whatever is necessary to mature and develop as you should. I realize I sound like a broken record, but this is a message that's got to be repeated until it finally sinks in. Healing will occur as prior unmet needs are satisfied, and as you receive and accept your new identity.

By doing everything necessary to end this compulsive inner child's domination, you'll begin to develop full emotional independence. Don't allow your desires to control you. Instead, be in control of your desires. Restrain the inner child, and stop him from doing what you've unconsciously taught him to do for the past 23 years. Start teaching him proper ways of responding to things.

One of the greatest impediments to recovery is feeling defeated by the growing pains of personal change, but if *you hang in there*, you'll soon see things in perspective. Temptations will become less enticing and dwindle in number. You'll achieve greater mastery of your desires and start seeing their origin. You can and will change, Mike.

What helped me most in overcoming my sexual desires for Brian was analyzing my wants. At first, I almost always gave in to my desires. Although I tried not to, and prayed for the strength to resist, I rarely was able to say "no" to these desires. Needless to say, I grew terribly discouraged, and thought I'd never succeed in changing. Then, as I'd done before in order to find the roots to my homosexuality, I began analyzing my sexual desires. The key question I had to ask myself was this: how was I feeling when I wanted Brian sexually? What was I really longing for?

The resulting insight brought me the freedom I was seeking. I had to learn to deal with the source of my sexual drive, not with my behavior. I discovered that most of my feelings weren't sexually based at all. I just interpreted them that way, keeping to my old established pattern.

Simple loneliness was one of the hardest things for me to overcome, and it would drive me to do things I'd ordinarily never think of doing. In the past, I responded to loneliness and boredom through homosexual pursuits, learned behavior that had become so ingrained that they seemed perfectly natural. When I tried to discontinue the habit and stop reinforcing old behavior, I was left with a dreadful void. It was imperative to learn new ways of handling my loneliness.

After praying for guidance, I was blessed with the God-sent realization that my worst periods of loneliness—the times I was most tempted to give in—occurred at night. I decided to get a nighttime job, and stayed with it until I was strong enough to handle being by myself. I also got involved in different activities through my church and I met some fantastic people who soon became my friends.

As these friendships developed more fully, and I allowed love, affirmation, and acceptance to take root in my life, I discovered I was becoming a better person. My loneliness and my dislike of being by myself seemed to indicate how little I liked myself. I needed to stay busy, constantly entertained in order to keep my mind off my problems.

Other times, I slipped up when thinking about how Brian was making new friends and no longer needed me to bring happiness into his life. This would bum me into calling him and frequently we'd get together solely for quick sex.

223

When I ferreted out the root of this urge, I discovered that I wanted him to need me. It hurt to think he could go ahead and live his life without me, even though I was trying to do the same thing in my life and it's what we both wanted. His desire for me, even if it was just temporarily for sex, made me feel loved, or at least made me feel I still had a place in his life.

Once I knew what was behind my feelings, I was better able to say no to them. By asking God to help me fill that void in my life through righteous means, I soon found my path intersecting with people who needed me in godly, healthy ways. If we allow Him, God always brings us victory where we once stood alone and defeated.

Occasionally, when hanging around straight guys, I'd find myself subject to a profound sense of inadequacy. Though it felt good to associate with them, initially it seemed impossible I could ever become one of them. Often, when feeling inadequate to the challenge they represented, I would seek a "shot of masculinity" by having sex with Brian. This provided me with a momentary boost of maleness, but it was always followed by total self-hatred and a sense of being robbed of the very thing I'd been hunting—masculinity.

I experienced healthy identification with my new acquaintances only to turn upon myself and follow it up with an interlude of disidentification through sex with Brian. Even though I kept stumbling off the path, I knew the things I needed to be doing and I didn't give up. I allowed room in my life for the legitimate fulfillment of same-sex needs. Eventually, the joy I found in their actualization so far exceeded the momentary pleasure of homosexual gratification that it no longer tempted me.

Of course, before I reached that point, there were also those times when I wanted to be with Brian just to love and be loved, when I just wanted to be intimate with another human being. Those are normal, valid needs, but I tried to satisfy them in a homosexual way. Since I'd learned to respond to my natural sex drive in a homosexual way, I wanted Brian to satisfy this need. It was a learned behavioral response. Because my only experiences with these feelings were with Brian, I longed for him whenever I felt the desire for intimacy, and I reinforced my gay identity every time we had a homosexual encounter.

I remember when we first met. Just the thought of kissing him made me sick, and I wouldn't do it. It seemed so "gay." My need in those days was to identify with another guy who felt the same way I did. Unconsciously, in search of my own identity, I was drawn to other gay guys, people like me, unaware that my real problem was an identity crisis—not my homosexual tendencies. What happened? I finally capitulated to the doubts that were fertilizing those tendencies, and responded to my feelings through homosexual means. I learned to enjoy kissing Brian—a member of my own sex. (Wow...just as I wrote that, I felt a tremendous sense of alienation from those feelings. How wonderful to see what God's done in my life—and to be able to promise that He'll do the same for you!)

The ambivalence you feel toward your relationship with Reed is to be expected. Living with him—no matter on what rocky ground— has been a form of security. It was home for the last couple of years. But now you're in a new environment, trying to navigate a stormy mix of old and new feelings while learning fresh and proper responses to them.

It's really no wonder you're not always clear on where you stand. There's a real battle taking place. However, no matter how often you think the relationship might work ("if only...") the stone-cold fact is that it won't. A homosexual relationship, by its very nature, will not—cannot—satisfy its participants.

About nine months into my liaison with Brian, I felt like I was on top of the world. He was everything I'd ever wanted and it truly seemed we'd been made for each other. We talked a lot about being the perfect gay couple, and thought we had proved that homosexuals can maintain a lasting relationship. We experienced the usual ups and downs, and weren't fazed by them, but then the insane jealousy crept in.

I've seen an incredible number of gay relationships break up over jealousy and the insecurities it masks. The rest always seem to end with one of the guys deciding to move on because his "needs" are no longer being met. The dilemma is that the homosexual is trying to fulfill needs within himself through relationships with other men suffering the same deficiencies. Regarding this problem, Dr. Moberly says:

225

Both partners in a homosexual relationship have similar psychological needs, varying only in degree, and thus each partner's needs and deficits render him...less able to meet the other person's needs.

You have needs which must be met, Mike, and you need to realize that Reed can't fulfill them for you. The problem exists because you think that by having a relationship with him, you'll be content. However, contentment comes from fulfillment of the deficits in your same-sex identification process, not from a dependent relationship with another man.

Remember my earlier statement about the joy to be found in fulfilling old same-sex needs? I wish I could describe that sensation well enough to provide you with just an inkling of how it feels, but I can't. It's something you just have to experience for yourself. When it happens in your life, you'll know—once and for all—that the things I've been telling you are absolutely right on.

I know the feeling of hopelessness you have now, but it'll pass, and believe it or not, you can survive without sex during this time. Start dissecting your feelings and desires. By exposing many of their nonsexual roots, you'll find that the fulfillment of same-sex needs and proper handling of these nonsexual roots will eliminate most of what you currently perceive as sexual feelings.

In reading your letters, I'm very much reminded of myself not so long ago. I missed Brian tremendously, and whenever I thought about never sexually loving him again, I'd be blitzed with doubt and depression. Basing all future possibilities on how I was feeling at the moment, it depressed me horribly to think about never again being intimate with Brian. I couldn't cope with it. The only way to preserve my sanity was to develop an attitude that I was to just live for today, taking each new day as it came. I was fine as long as I didn't think in the absolute terms of *never* and *always*.

Today, right now, this minute, you can cope with not having Reed. It's only when you turn your focus to tomorrow that you draw that black cloud over yourself, so don't do it. Take each day by itself as it comes. When you're preoccupied with tomorrow, you miss out on the meaningful experiences of today. Concentrate on the present and you'll see that the future takes care of itself. That's a promise from God: "And we know that all things work together for good to them that love God, to them who are the called according to His purpose" (Romans 8:28 KJV). Claim this mighty promise from Him; He means for you to have it.

I love you, little brother. I pray for you daily and I believe in you. I know you'll climb this mountain to stand high atop it as a free man. Write soon.

Love always,

Bud

Dear Mike,

I'm really sorry to hear you're feeling down. Believe me, buddy, I understand your sense of hopelessness. How could I not, having stood in your shoes looking at the same situation? I've got news, though, that ought to make you feel a lot better.

One of your problems is that you're reckoning your progress on the basis of how you feel toward women. That's not a valid yardstick, though it's certainly a common misconception, even among psychologists. That's why traditional psychiatry has such a poor track record in changing the homosexual condition—the general thinking has been that all you needed was to learn to enjoy sex with women. Of course, as you know from firsthand experience, having sex with women doesn't solve a thing. The reason it doesn't is that the essential needs of your identity still haven't been met.

Some time ago in one of my letters, I made passing mention of the fact that homosexuality in men isn't a problem of relating to women, but of relating to other men. You need to remember that, and judge your progress accordingly. In other words, how are you doing in relation to other guys? You can't advance to the stage of being sexually attracted to women until you've succeeded at identifying with other males in a nonsexual way. Remember, maturity comes only through a step-by-step progression from one level of development to the next. You've got to master the one you're at now before you can proceed.

Let's take the average boy as an example. When he was very young, he played with both boys and girls and thought nothing of it. Girls were okay as friends in the same manner that boys were. Then he got a little older, and through peer pressure and same-sex identification, our average boy quit playing with girls and began associating exclusively with other boys (at least in public). Girls at this stage in his life had somehow acquired a strange thing called "cooties."

Now, our boy doesn't just wake up one morning and decide that

229

girls no longer have cooties. It's a process of development, and it takes him a few years to get there. Then, once again through peer interaction and identity, he learns to view girls as the hot ticket. This usually happens before full-blown adolescence and thus before sexual impulses begin dictating forms of behavior.

Just as our identity is a product of our environment, so is our sexual development. Sexual behavior and feelings are learned—not inborn. We are taught to respond as we do, whether someone teaches us or we teach ourselves. We're influenced by environment, experience, and observation, and ultimately our patterns of sexual behavior reflect cultural and social expectations. Some portion of our sexual nature is naturally affected by biological changes at puberty, but environment usually plays the biggest role.

Consider the fact that at the turn of the century, plump, voluptuous women were the ideal; thinness was undesirable. Because the style of that era mandated long dresses, men were turned on by the sight of a woman's ankle. Just a mere glimpse was sufficient to cause physical arousal. Why the difference between then and now? Because we're taught to respond to certain things through the influence of our peers, the media, society as a whole. Back then, male beachgoers hoped to catch a little ankle action; today they're looking to see a whole lot more and hoping the women will be wearing a whole lot less!

Even before puberty, girls become a topic of conversation that's endlessly fascinating to boys. The older boys knowledgeably hold forth on the allure of the female body and all the rest of the boys display great interest, even the ones who actually haven't the slightest interest in that particular subject yet. It's all part of identifying and being one of the guys.

Peer pressure is a big factor among adolescents. Each boy is searching for his own identity as a male, as one of the gang, as someone independent from his parents, etc. He wants to belong and fit in—to be accepted.

When dating begins, boys often feel compelled to talk up their "conquests" in lurid detail. Again, it's a learned behavior. Aside from sex, dating offers the adolescent male an enhanced reputation. He's a cool dude, possibly even a real stud if he's dating a girl who's widely considered to be desirable. Particularly in the early stages of dating, a boy's selection of female company may be entirely based on the desire to show her off to his peers.

Most gays missed this identification process by maintaining a certain distance from other boys during their formative years or by their inability to effectively relate due to earlier detachment between themselves and their fathers. The boy who will later identify himself as being gay is attracted to other males by his same-sex deficits and a need for identification.

When adolescence arrives and his attraction to other males persists, he interprets this attraction as a confirmation of his homo-sexuality. Unfortunately, he remains stuck in this stage of develop-ment. His body continues to mature and develop, but his emotional/sexual growth has stopped.

What I'm saying, Mike, is that on the physical level you're an adult, but on the emotional/sexual level you're still a child. For anyone to expect you to have heterosexual desires at this point in your healing process is as ridiculous as expecting a six-year-old boy to be sexually/emotionally attracted to an adult woman. It's just as ridicu-lous to think you should all of a sudden be able to advance from A to Z, without regard to the basics in between, simply because you know Z is there.

I've already told you about my first romance, back in junior high. Though it was quite enjoyable, it was really nothing more than puppy love. I mean, we did kiss a couple of times, but considering she was my girlfriend for nearly an entire school year, that's not saying much.

Three years after that relationship ended, when I was a junior in high school, I met Fran. I really loved her, but I didn't know how to show it because I was so uncomfortable with anything even vaguely bordering on physical familiarity. While my insides were screaming out for love and physical affection, I didn't know how to respond when I received it. So instead of learning how to touch, how to hold and be held, I pushed her—and love—away. This only added to my confusion.

I read that homosexual tendencies were common among young boys, and I was very aware of my attraction to other guys, but I hoped I'd outgrow it. As time went on and the attraction failed to fade away, my doubts about my masculinity edged their way across the border into certainty.

It's all so obvious now. If only I'd had someone to talk to, someone who would have guided me onto the right path, such little things might have made all the difference in the world. Knowing that fathers have the ability to sway their kids one way or the other, I think people should have to take a test to determine their parenting skills before being allowed to procreate. (You've gotta admit, it would certainly have a drastic effect on the population figures!)

Sometime back you told me that you had tried to be normal by dating girls and going to bed with some of them in the hopes that you would acquire heterosexual desires. This scheme didn't work for reasons already discussed—chiefly, fulfillment of legitimate same-sex needs must precede advancement into heterosexuality.

Remember, Mike, homosexuality is an emotional problem, not a sexual one. Many of your emotional needs are still that of a young boy, and great conflict arises when this emotional child tries to fulfill your otherwise-adult sexual desires. Think of yourself in that light. See the little boy in you who missed part of his development and must now attend to what was previously neglected.

It's like Andy Comiskey said in one of his Desert Stream seminars:

> To develop a healthy sexual identity means to grow—to move from one stage of development to the next, equipped to embrace the challenges of each succeeding stage. For example, the major transition in a child's moral development involves moving from an absolute self-centeredness to the increasing capacity to recognize the needs of others. Sexually, we progress from the task of recognizing and affirming our uniqueness as either male or female. As sufficiently resolved members of our own sex, we then proceed on to explore opposite-sex relating as adolescents. Developing heterosexually, then, involves securing through interaction with others a healthy sense of who we are as boys and girls.

As far as dating is concerned, forget it for the moment. I know that friends can be well-meaning but demanding busybodies. I also had my share of this pressure in the beginning from friends who wanted me to get out there and start hustling women. Whenever I heard from one guy who knew about my past, he'd always make a point of asking how the dating scene was going for me. Each time, I had to explain all over again how that wasn't where I was just then. I first needed to take care of the way I related to guys. It was frustrating—he never did get a handle on it.

The priority in your life right now should be attempting to satisfy your unmet same-sex needs, which can only be accomplished through spending time with other straight guys. Women can't resolve your same-sex deficits, so don't be pushed into dating or trying to establish a heterosexual relationship. Your sexual desire for women will come in its own good time.

I'll end with some pertinent words from Elizabeth Moberly:

> The homosexual cannot just "turn heterosexual," bypassing the normal route to heterosexuality. The goal of development may not be attained without passing through the process towards the goal. Same-sex needs are to be fulfilled—according to the natural, God-given laws for human growth—before relating to the opposite sex as heterosexual. Much advice to the homosexual has, by implication, tried to bypass this process of growth. The healing process of growth is to be promoted, and not blocked, short-circuited, or bypassed. Thus, it is important not to pray about heterosexuality directly, but about the fulfilling of homosexual needs, which, if truly accomplished, will lead to heterosexuality, and without which heterosexuality cannot be truly obtained.

Stay with it, buddy. I love ya lots.
Your bro,

Bud

Dear Mike,

WHERE HAVE YOU BEEN??? I've tried calling all day and now I guess I'm going to have to take Federal Express at its word to get this to you by tomorrow morning. It's bad news, buddy—Daniel killed himself last night.

Jimmy called early this morning to tell me. Apparently, Daniel called him sometime yesterday, really depressed, and asked if he'd come by after work. When Jimmy got there he found a note taped to the door, saying Daniel intended to drive his car off a cliff in the canyon. He called the police, but it was too late. They found Daniel somewhere off Mulholland, about 900 feet down, and it looked like he died instantly.

I can't believe he did it. I don't want to believe he did it. I talked to him Saturday night and he sounded terrible—talking about his loneliness and how tired he was of being used—but when I talked to him Monday he seemed much better. Why did he give up?! I'm so upset! I feel like my insides are being torn out. Why didn't he call if he was feeling that bad? I mean, Saturday he was really terribly bummed, but there was absolutely no hint of suicide in anything he said. Mike, I haven't cried this much in years. I feel so terrible—hurt and angry both. Why, why, why didn't he call someone for help? I wish he would have called me. He knew that I knew how he was feeling and that I wanted to help, and now it's just too late.

If I haven't managed to get through to you by the time you get this, please call. The funeral is going to be Saturday at 1 p.m., and I'd like to go together. In fact, I can't do this by myself. It's going to be tough. Will you go with me? I'll be getting into LAX Friday afternoon and will give you the flight info when we talk. Since I could only get three days off from work, I'll have to fly out again Sunday morning. Talk with you soon.

Bud

Dear Mike,

I spent most of the day at work thinking about this weekend, wishing we'd seen each other under different circumstances. But you know what? I have never felt closer to you, Mike. The emotional bond and level of intimacy we shared at the funeral and even more during dinner Saturday evening gave me strength. I needed a friend. Thank you for being there, Mike. I cherish our friendship so very much. I want you to know that, buddy!

I've got to plunge on with what you and I are doing. It's the only way I can keep my mind off Daniel, and maybe it's a good memorial to him. I just keep thinking "There, but for the grace of God go I." If you're not quite in the mood to receive this, don't worry about it. Just set it aside for a few days, and then come back to it. Hopefully, it'll be just as therapeutic for you whenever you read it, as I'm praying it will be for me today.

I'm sure I've mentioned this before, but it's worth repeating because I don't want you to make the same mistake as some others I've known. These were guys who came to the group one or both nights regularly each week, and then slowly, one by one, began fading away. At first, I thought that they'd gotten so much better they didn't need to attend any longer, but then reports started trickling in that some of them had gone back into the gay lifestyle. The first few times I heard this I couldn't understand why. Eventually, though, I realized they had never fully committed themselves to changing. They wanted the miracle cure with no effort required on their part.

Kevin's a pretty good example of what I'm talking about. He came to the group twice a week, and willingly shared all his turmoil, struggles, and downfalls. However, after a whole year had gone by, he was still saying exactly the same things he had said at the beginning. Things were actually getting worse for him. He expressed doubt he could ever be healed of his gay identity and said he'd begun to wonder about God's power and love in his life. Finally, he began to doubt God altogether. Clearly, he was getting worse by the day, not better, and it just didn't add up.

I started meeting with him outside of the group to see if I could find out what was going on. Although he told me how hard he had tried to change to rid himself of the old desires, it was his answer to my question about how he was going about this that provided the first clue.

"Hey, look, I'm going to the group twice a week, you know," he said. When I asked him what else he was doing, it turned out that was it—he was going to the group and attempting to suppress his feelings the rest of the time. He felt that was a sufficient investment of effort on his part, even though it obviously wasn't.

Kevin was listening, but not acting on what he heard. (Remember that passage about the man in the mirror and being a doer of the Word, James 1:22-25.) Because of his daily struggles, he believed he was doing something yet all he was really doing was wrestling with his desires in an effort to suppress them rather than trying to work through them. He wanted more than anything to be out of the hell he was in, but he still wasn't willing to do all he could to achieve this goal. He was too lazy to move forward, almost as if he was on a level he was comfortable with, even though he was miserable there. Kind of like Daniel.

The leaders gave everybody at the group a list of books to read. Kevin didn't even bother to read one of them. He worked hard at his job, he explained, 10-12 hours a day just to keep occupied, and consequently didn't feel like reading when he was home—he was too tired. It seemed to me that if he had any expectations at all from life, it was that the passing of time itself would change him. Ten years will pass and he'll still be in the same place he is today, except he'll be ten years older and those ten years will have gone down the drain. Yet there's nothing anyone can do for him. No one else can change him. He has to do it himself.

Lutzer illuminates why people like Kevin will always miss the boat:

> One reason why these people reverted back to their old
> behavior patterns is that *they misunderstood the full extent of*

their problem. True, they wanted victory, but they didn't understand how or why God would bring it about. They, like most of us, wanted to overcome a specific habit—for their own benefit. They wanted to be free of the symptoms of their problem, but did not want a thorough examination that would reveal deeper problems in their lives which they were unwilling to face. The habits themselves were like the tip of an iceberg.

I found this such a fascinating insight that I couldn't resist developing my own illustration on the following page to bring it into full perspective for you, Mike.

HOMOSEXUAL BEHAVIOR
(*Symptom* of underlying deficiencies)

•Envy
•*Misinterpretation* and eroticization of
homo-emotional needs into homosexual desires

•Feelings of masculine inadequacy
•Gender confusion
•Need for recognition of masculinity,
identification, same-sex approval

Other *unfulfilled* homo-emotional needs:
•Sufficient male bonding with peers
•Male gender identification and affirmation of gender role
•Same-sex acceptance and approval
•Same-sex nonsexual love

•Insecurity in gender role
•Isolation/separation from male peers
(physically and/or emotionally)

•Defensive detachment from father-figure who may be
inefficient, hostile, or even absent
•Lack of proper male role model
•In most cases, insufficient bonding with the father and
unfulfilled same-sex love need

•Feelings of being hurt, unloved and/or rejected:
even if love is offered,
the boy has unconsciously blocked it from being received

•*Overly-sensitive disposition*
•Incident(s) boy *interprets* as intentionally hurtful
•Absent, inefficient, or hostile father/father-figure:
Not necessarily how the father was, but more importantly,
how the boy *perceived* his father's behavior as signifying a lack of love

The roots of the real problem (unresolved conflicts of the past) are represented by the iceberg as a whole under the waterline, while the manifestation of such conflicts (homosexual behavior) is just the tip of it. In order to eliminate homosexuality, it's necessary to stop dwelling only on one's homosexual behavior because that's simply an indication of hidden conflicts. As Lutzer explains:

> Sinful habits are usually indicative of unresolved conflicts. We must always seek underlying causes rather than treating the symptoms. God uses our struggles with sin to diagnose our true condition. Temptation is His x-ray machine, discovering the hidden conflicts that need attention.

Kevin didn't want to do a thorough self-examination and house-cleaning. He didn't want to deal with the roots of his attitudes, thoughts, pride, selfishness, fears, insecurities, and overall self-image. He only wanted to be rid of his homosexuality. Since he determinedly refused to research the causes of his problem, he doomed himself to disappointment and finally reverted back to his old habits and behavior.

A mutual friend asked him one day why he was no longer trying to change his homosexual identity and Kevin replied, "It doesn't work." (Remember Fat Joe and his diet?)

The friend then said, "What about Jeff? He's changed."

To which Kevin answered, "Well, I can't do all that stuff," referring to all the ways I actively pursued my transformation. Of course, Kevin was once again missing the point. He completely overlooked the fact that I had done my house-cleaning.

Seeking freedom in every aspect of my life, I'd given up pursuing a career for the time being. For my own good I decided to live at the beach, be a waiter at night, and the rest of the time lie in the sun, sail, cycle, swim, learn to surf, and simply enjoy life in general. This was vitally important to me because I wanted to overcome certain inhibitions and rid myself of the crippling envy I felt toward everyone who lived that life. I also wanted to get in shape, so I joined a health club. Hating my lifelong feelings of being awkward and incompetent at sports while other guys seemed to have been born on

241

the playing field, I learned how to play softball and then volleyball by taking morning classes at Orange Coast College. I was determined to overcome anything that I allowed in the past to restrain me. Every root I could find to my negative self-image and homosexual behavior was regarded as a challenge.

Kevin makes about five times as much money as I do in a year but what good is it to him? He thinks I've made some sort of sacrifice—I know better. I've just begun living and that's hardly a sacrifice. When Kevin said he *couldn't* do what I was doing, he meant he *wasn't willing*.

I'm certainly not expecting you to do the exact same things I've done. It would be stupid to assume we share all the same needs and wants out of life. What I'm saying is that after you have dug up the roots to *your* homosexual identity and negative self-image, you've got to do whatever it takes to reach *your* set goals.

Self-image is an incredibly powerful force for ill or good, depending on whether it's negative or positive. If the image you have of yourself is that of a homosexual—homosexual behavior will most likely follow. Those guys I told you about who left the group and returned to the gay lifestyle didn't comprehend the power of their self-image at all. They began going to the group in order to get help but they did nothing for themselves to change their identity and self-image. They merely drifted along from week to week, hoping something would happen for them.

In his book, *Psycho-Cybernetics*, Maxwell Maltz talks about the power of self-image:

> The "self image" is the key to human personality and human behavior. Change the self image and you change the personality and the behavior.
>
> But more than this. The "self image" sets the boundaries of individual accomplishment. It defines what you can and cannot do. Expand the self image and you expand the "area of the possible." The development of an adequate, realistic self image will seem to imbue the individual with new capabilities, new talents, and literally turn failure into success.

The self image is changed, for better or worse, not by intellect alone, nor by intellectual knowledge alone, but by "experiencing." Wittingly or unwittingly you developed your self image by your creative experiencing in the past. You can change it by the same method.

It is not the child who is taught about love but the child who has experienced love that grows into a healthy, happy, well-adjusted adult. Our present state of self-confidence and poise is the result of what we have "experienced" rather than what we have learned intellectually.

The Power Of A Positive Self-Image, by Dr. Clifford Baird, is a book I would highly recommend to you because of its intelligent and practical insights. In it, Baird states:

I believe that all your behavior—everything you do, everything you attempt, everything you say, everything you dream, everything you like, everything you dislike, everything—is subordinate to your self-image. When this self-image is formed, it becomes resistant to change. Self-image is not permanent; it can be changed, but there is a definite resistance. If you believe you can't do something, you avoid it or do it badly and so prove to yourself what you believe. Believing you can do something, you give it a good try and prove yourself. What you do every day is a product of how you see yourself and also of the situation you are in. While your situation may change from day to day or from place to place, the things you believe about yourself are always-present factors in determining your behavior.

This is what Baird has to say about realistically appraising yourself:

We can always correct those things which God leaves to us as choices. But about some things we have no choice; and we should make the best of them, especially physical characteristics we can do absolutely nothing about. In my seminars, I suggest that people memorize "The Serenity Prayer."

> God grant me the serenity
> to accept the things I cannot change,
> courage to change the things I can,
> and the wisdom to know the difference.

That passage is especially meaningful to me. After I had analyzed things sufficiently to see that envy was a predominant negative factor in my life, one of the things I most wanted to improve (change) was my appearance. I probably looked okay from anyone else's point of view, but in my eyes I needed to shape up.

A little further thought on the matter revealed the physical traits that aroused the most envy in me—flat stomach, no love handles, firm muscles. These were qualities I also could have by simply working out and sticking with it. By the same token, several of the guys who left the group were a little overweight or sort of flabby—and every one of them had talked about the difficulties they had in handling their attraction to men with good bodies. On the other hand, I've always wished I were a little taller but that's just an occasional wish. I can accept my height.

Mike, you need to alter the way you think of yourself. See who you are in Christ, as a child of the living God, and move toward this new identity. It doesn't matter how numerous or great the flaws are in the image you hold of yourself at this moment. You can change that image to one you like, one that enhances your sense of confidence.

The secret is to start moving and stop allowing your negative self-image to hinder all the work that needs to take place in your life. Feeling better about yourself makes it that much easier to relate in a positive manner to other guys, cleansing you of envy and helping to eliminate your sense of inadequacy. Boiling it down to its simplest equation, every positive experience you step up to spawns further hope and motivation.

I'm praying for you, buddy. Keep up the good work.

Bud

Dear Mike,

Yesterday's letter was meant to encourage you to do everything you can to improve your self-image because it's so fundamental to improving your whole life. Hopefully, it didn't appear to be some sort of heavy-handed lecture.

Unfortunately, I can't really recommend any specific actions, for only you know the things you need to do to accomplish that objective. I can, however, elaborate on the importance I placed on getting myself in shape, and maybe that'll make the way clearer for you.

First, if you look better, you feel better. Second, it's been proven that people who exercise sleep better, are healthier and happier, and are more motivated to seek proper nutrition and avoid substance abuse. The discipline of regular exercise also brings a certain amount of order into your life, as well as improves self-esteem, even if you only work out three times a week. It makes you feel more in charge of your life to be actively involved in making yourself look and feel better.

Some Christians play down the importance of one's outward appearance, and in some respects, rightly so. Vanity, for instance, isn't a desirable trait in anyone. Most of the condemnation, however, comes from those who are too spiritually lazy to do anything about improving themselves—physically or spiritually. They're fat or sloppy, afraid to try, lack discipline, and are totally defeated by their own problems.

I'm not saying we should get caught up in the latest fashion or try to always appear "in style," or even that a good body is the end result we're after. Indeed, its not. Sure, we should care about how we look. But remember, and I don't say this lightly, getting into shape *only complements the work being done inside—inner growth is where the focus should be placed.*

Nonetheless, a positive self-image is vital to growth and to loving yourself. So change all you can and accept all you can't—but don't cop out. Turn to God for help. Rely on His wisdom to direct you. That's the key, Mike, relying on God's wisdom to guide you and to change you. The older I get the more I realize the necessity of relying on God in all areas of my life—and this even includes your self-image. Because ultimately, as Baird states in *The Power Of A Positive Self-Image*, the cure for a negative self-image is found in the Lord:

> The cure for a negative self-image lies in understanding God's will for your life. God expects you to employ those skills and talents He has given you. Do not neglect God's word or faithfulness in prayer. There are many imitation cures available today, but they will not last. A negative self-image will be cured permanently only through spiritual growth.

God's wisdom is intended to create whole, healthy human beings, full of peace and joy, with love to give, as well as the capacity to receive it. Christ came to give us all an abundant life, Mike, so turn to God and allow His wisdom to guide you.

Your friend,

Bud

Dear Mike,

You'll never believe what happened last week! I went to a party in Koloa, near Jeff's place in Poipu, and while I was talking with some guys, in walked the most beautiful gal I've ever seen in my life. I asked Jeff who she was and instead of telling me, he led me over to her, Cindi, and introduced us.

We talked for most of the night. Cindi is 24 years old, a transfer student from San Diego. She moved here in January to get out of the rat race in southern California and lives on the other side of the island in Puhi, near the junior college.

There were definitely vibes between us. When I asked her out for the next day, she said yes. So after work the following day I drove to her place, picked her up, and we went out for a drive. We talked, went for a walk along the beach, talked some more, went back to her place for dinner, and then talked on into the wee hours of morning.

Mike, we enjoy all the same things in life. I found that absolutely incredible. So, last night I popped the question. Yes, I asked her to marry me! Can you fly over for the wedding next weekend? I sure hope so, because it would be great to have you here sharing in the celebration. Before going any further, though, I've got to say one more thing: "April Fool! "

All that aside now, happy birthday, bro. I hope you got the package I sent. The folks at the post office assured me it would arrive in time, but ever since that business with my car (Remember when it got on the slow boat to China instead of the fast boat to Kauai?), I've reserved a healthy skepticism for this sort of promise.

Things are going pretty well here; basically, the same old stuff. One exception, though. Daniel sent me a letter the day he killed himself, but because it went to my old P.O. box in Kapaa, it didn't arrive in Hanalei until last week. I cried…it's so hard to accept that he's gone.

To answer one of your questions, most of your homosexual

desires can be traced back to unmet same-sex needs, although they sometimes mask themselves in other forms. The bottom line, though, remains your confused gender identity. Since you say you've tried to analyze your feelings to get to their roots and haven't been successful, let's see if I can help.

Take your attraction to the male body, for example. On the surface, it appears you're simply attracted to the male physique. But a closer look will reveal the roots you're looking for. As I've mentioned before, most of this attraction is based on envy. You're drawn to certain characteristics you wish you possessed, or that you feel inadequately supplied with: body hair, stature, appearance, whatever.

Another thing causing this attraction goes hand-in-glove with envy, and likewise springs from unmet same-sex needs: an inadequate sense of masculinity. Those unmet needs caused gender confusion and deprived you of confidence in your masculinity, thus you unconsciously seek to acquire it from other men sexually.

Remember the "cannibal compulsion?" Perhaps this seems a bit farfetched, but go back in memory and recall your behavior at times when you've felt insecure or inadequate. Be honest, what did you do? You went searching for quick sex as a fix.

Identity is a subtle thing and can be elusive to anyone. In your case, as in mine and that of so many others, the need for identification has been misinterpreted as a sexual need. You're drawn toward other guys because of your incomplete sense of male identification; unfortunately, however, your learned behavior causes you to regard this attraction only in sexual terms.

Masculinity isn't a physical attribute, despite our cultural conditioning to the contrary. It isn't "tall, dark, and handsome." It isn't a large penis, or a hairy or well-built body. If we stop to think about it for a moment, we're bound to agree that these things not only don't make a man, they don't even make him any more of a man.

If I were a married heterosexual man who in some freak accident had my penis cut off, wouldn't I still be a man? Of course I would be. If a woman loses a breast—or even both breasts—to cancer, isn't she still a woman? She certainly is! I realize there are some ignorant, sexist jerks who feel otherwise, but that's their problem. A woman is a woman and a man is a man not just because of their respective sexual organs, but biological makeup as well.

Masculinity is something you *experience* through properly fulfilling same-sex identification needs—it's a process of being, not knowing. We identify ourselves as males by becoming familiar with our own gender; through same-sex interaction, conversation, and imitation—in normal circumstances without even knowing it.

The homosexual is unaffirmed in his masculinity, has unmet same-sex needs, and hasn't experienced proper identification. Because of these deficiencies, he's unable to fully see or accept his own identity as a male. He therefore sees these needs as something physical, and searches for them in a physical sense. That's why the homosexual hunt, with ever increasing perversion and decadence, continues from one partner to the next...and the next...and the next....

Instead of meeting the same-sex needs underlying the search, the homosexual habitually reacts with wrong responses. Not only do these responses reinforce his homosexual behavior, they further distance him from fulfillment of his same-sex needs, and create a greater sense of alienation than before.

Because he constantly compares himself to other males, he's always left feeling shortchanged. Comparison causes envy, which leads to low self-esteem and poor self-image, and ultimately leads to further comparison. It's a wretchedly destructive cycle.

Masculinity isn't what we look like; it's something we are. If you haven't lived a masculine identity from within, accepting your own maleness and the intrinsic maleness of others, then you're left with identifying it through external factors. That's something very few men can live up to. You need to see beyond the outward signs of what our culture deems masculine, Mike, and begin to live it internally. Once you identify with other males, you'll see they're no different from you on the inside. Get the male body off that pedestal; stop worshiping maleness and masculinity as some tangible that can be observed. It's not a physical manifestation.

Take good care of yourself, buddy. I hope to hear from you soon.

Bud

Dear Mike,

I don't have much time to write tonight because I'm supposed to go to Kapaa with some friends to see a surfing flick, but I wanted to comment on your friend Eric. How did you happen to meet him, anyway? He sounds like a really nice guy, but he also sounds terribly vulnerable at the moment. That's why I'm trying to collect my thoughts on the run here.

Please either let Eric read this for himself, or pass on to him what I'm about to say. I fully identify with what he's feeling, but it's got to be kept in perspective. Here he is, a very good-looking 21-year-old, who for most of his life has experienced the same feelings (inadequacy, insecurity, alienation, etc.) as you and I did.

Fortunately, he's managed to stay clear of homosexual activity up to this point, but now for the first time he's met some other guys who share the same feelings—and attractions. Meeting homosexuals is actually a treat for him.

Imagine it—he's found some guys his own age he can relate to because they've experienced the same struggles. He no longer feels alone. He's finally getting attention and acceptance from other males, and since he's good-looking, he's certainly being sought after, which boosts his ego. He probably feels like a whole new world has just been opened up to him.

Eric's needs are the same as yours, Mike. His unmet same-sex needs can be temporarily gratified, and as sexual desire intermingles with these needs, he'll eventually seek out sexual gratification through homosexual means. Since this comfort is doomed to be short-lived, he may continue his pursuit of homosexuality even further. Yet, the farther he goes in this direction, the farther he removes himself from truly satisfying and fulfilling his deepest emotional needs and desires.

My heart really goes out to him because he's at a place in his life where positive change can occur rapidly. If he only knew how close he is to actually fulfilling his real desires, he wouldn't be considering homosexual behavior. Since he hasn't acquired any memories to deal with or taught himself to respond as a homosexual, why don't you give him the truth about all the garbage that really goes on? Tell him about the pain and loneliness, about the irrational jealousies and bottomless depression—tell him about Daniel.

I understand his desire to try homosexuality. His feelings appear to be very strong and he might think he can't control them. However, the minute he starts to act upon them in a homosexual way, they'll start to grow just like a prairie fire. You know as well as I do that telling yourself, "Just this once and that will satisfy the urge," doesn't work. Giving in and acting out simply empowers those desires and makes them even harder to control.

This is what Andy Comiskey had to say at one of his seminars:

> When we give in to the sexual urge we become mastered by a pretty powerful force. There is no denying it, there's no minimizing it; sexual sin does exact a great cost. In other words, when we commit a sexual sin it's not a neutral act. We become more vulnerable to that happening again. We are in a sense satisfied for a brief moment, and in that sense we are rewarded; and in a sense, longing for more—longing for another fix at another point in time.... We become mastered to that which dictates our course, even beyond what we know to be true or right.

When I first started college I had really strong "homosexual" desires. If someone had told me that they would actually get stronger, it would have been hard to believe. Yet, as I look back to how I felt then, those feelings seem insignificant compared to how I felt four years later. If I'd known then the things I know now about the causes of homosexuality, I could have fulfilled my needs quickly and had more years to live as a healthy male.

At that point, I was like Eric and had no real homosexual background. Without all the acquired homosexual responses—the learned ways of interpreting my needs and acting upon them—I would have been able to easily fulfill my same-sex needs. However, after having acted upon my desires, not only did I ultimately have to take care of my same-sex needs, but also had to endure the pains of letting go of old memories and of learning to respond in new ways while refraining from following my old patterns.

Currently, Eric doesn't have much reprogramming to do. His transformation into a whole, emotionally healthy person would be much easier than what you and I have experienced. All he needs to do, basically, is see his desires for what they really are, and set about fulfilling them in the proper ways.

Talk to him. Tell it like it really is. It will undoubtedly be hard for him to comprehend at first because of the new excitement he's experiencing. But as you or any other honest person who is, or was, gay knows only too well, the gay life is anything but. Help him, Mike, by showing him the ugliness under the veneer, and then by showing him the alternative—what he should be doing.

Gotta go—my friends just drove up. If I get a chance, I'll write more tomorrow.

Later,

Bud

Dear Mike,

Well, the fact that Eric's asking so many questions makes me feel better. At least he's examining the issue instead of barreling straight over the edge. How long is he going to be in town? I was thinking maybe you could take him by Desert Stream before he goes back to Chicago.

You know, you didn't do so badly in the question department, either. I'm not sure I've got time to answer all of them tonight, but I'll do my best. The one I want to tackle first is about a mother's influence on the male homosexual.

Until very recently, psychology focused on these ladies as *the* cause of homosexuality. I'm sure you've heard the standard description that's meant to place blame and provide an excuse, "... an over-protective, domineering, manipulative mother, she turned her boy into a 'girl'." Baloney. I think mothers got the rap because society views homosexuals as guys who want to be girls, a perception that is obviously light years from the truth. Of course, it shows us one more reason why homosexuals never receive any valid help or have not been given any hope in the past. They have been provided the wrong solutions to the wrong problem.

My mother did everything in her power to encourage us kids to get involved in different activities. She prompted me to go out for Little League, but after my first year, I felt like such a failure that I quit. My brother, on the other hand, played Pop Warner football, joined the Cub Scouts and played baseball through Pony League. My sister was in the Girl Scouts, took tap dancing lessons, etc. Mom did her part to see we were affirmed in our respective roles. I was the one who just didn't try.

Looking back, I guess you could say I was a "mommy's boy." I mean, I would have done anything for her and that's why, when I first read about the mother's role in developing a homosexual son, I believed it. My mother, though, wasn't over-protective, manipulative, or domineering. She was just your average mom.

If I were to fault her on anything, it would only be her inability to show the physical affection I so desperately wanted and needed. That, however, was merely the result of her not receiving it during her own childhood. She simply didn't know how, having never experienced it herself. I think she did a good job of rearing three kids on her own.

Moberly sees the "mother fixation" as an effect rather than a cause:

> To be attached to one's mother is in itself entirely normal. However, if there is a defensive detachment from the father, the only remaining channel for attachment is that to the mother. What is normal when complemented by a father-attachment becomes abnormal when isolated from this. But it is only the fact of this isolation that is abnormal, not the attachment as such. Thus, the so-called "mother-fixation" in the male implies, not an abnormal attachment to the opposite sex, but an abnormal detachment from the same sex.

I became a mommy's boy as a result of my detachment from my father. Normal attachment to him just wasn't available as an option, so I clung to my mother. That's your cause-and-effect.

Do you by any chance have my previous letters? You might want to let Eric read some of them, and that way we won't have to repeat ourselves unnecessarily. I think once he reads some of the things we've covered, he'll know unmet same-sex needs are the roots of his problem, and not this bogus stuff he's picked up here and there.

In fact, let me ask you this—how many times in the past have you heard "mother fixation" blamed for homosexuality? What was your response? Something inside you didn't click, did it? You knew it wasn't the answer you were looking for. If it was, you'd still feel helplessly bound to your homosexual orientation because that analysis offers absolutely no hope of ever changing.

Once you heard the good news, though—in other words, the truth—something inside told you it was right, even if you didn't want to believe it. Eventually, you were able to see what your real needs were as a kid, and how your misinterpretation of those needs and your subsequent responses got you off-track. You didn't have someone to help you fulfill those needs at the time. You didn't have the necessary attachment with your dad and didn't receive affirmation from him or your male peers. When the picture takes this much shape, you *know* what's lacking inside you: the sense of belonging, of love and acceptance from other males.

Now don't get me wrong, Mike. As I have mentioned before, homosexuality is multi-faceted, deeply rooted, and quite complex. Many things lead to a homosexual orientation. And while I don't believe "mother fixation" is *the* cause of homosexuality (which many say it is), I do believe a mother *can contribute* to her son's homosexual identity. What I have shared thus far are some of the *core* roots to a homosexual orientation. There are other factors which influence a person toward homosexuality, and the mother can be one of them.

The best way to convince Eric that the "mother fixation" isn't the cause of homosexuality is to ask him questions that make him ponder these ideas further. Make him think. Let him examine himself to see what really makes him tick. Sooner or later, he's bound to see the pieces that are missing in his puzzle.

Somewhere in one of the letters I've written you, I talked about how a child is more apt to acquire a good gender identity and solid gender role if he has a strong father-figure who's supportive, nurturing, and actively involved in his son's life. The child is least likely to develop a healthy gender identity when the father is ineffective and passive, and the mother is dominant.

We've heard it a thousand times: "The Passive Father and Domineering Mother Syndrome." Studies have shown this to be true in the majority of cases. Some mothers overindulge their sons which can cause their sons to have a damaged view of femininity. So when a homosexual has an aversion to intimacy with a woman, it isn't because he hates women. In fact, I haven't met a homosexual yet who hates women. They might have had an overdose of "femaleness" and, therefore, they don't desire to bond intimately with women

257

because they've had too much already. It might also be that the boy had too much of the mother and not enough of the father.

In a lot of cases, the fact that the mother is domineering is a direct result of the husband-father being ineffective or passive. Someone has to carry the weight in the family. Obviously, this isn't true of every weak father/strong mother situation. There are those mothers who like being the boss, although I don't believe that's the way God intended us to live. I think the father's role in the household should be that of the one who "wears the pants" and is in charge—not in a male chauvinistic way, but in a godly, sensitive, loving way as shaped by the father role itself. He should be the leader of his family.

There are certainly cases where the mother is indeed very domineering and unduly influences her son. Some mothers are emotionally needy. She may have her own unmet needs leftover from childhood. Or perhaps her present needs aren't being met by her husband, who may be absent, ineffective, or hostile. So the mother unconsciously may attempt to meet her emotional needs through her son. The mother may look toward the son to respond as an adult to meet her physical and emotional needs, to meet her needs that her husband cannot or will not meet.

There are a couple of good terms floating around these days which describe this situation well: *emotional incest, surrogate spouse,* and *adultified child.* That says it all in a nutshell. The boy grows up equating most women with his mother—especially women who appear to be needy in any way. Hence, the boy avoids intimacy with women.

But even then, the father has the responsibility to exercise veto power over the overindulgent mother. God designed man in his role as father and family leader, giving him the power to override negative effects the mother may cause. If he chooses to abdicate his responsibilities, he's guilty of great moral wrongdoing.

Daniel's early life is a prime example of this sort of paternal negligence. When he was born his mother was terribly disappointed at having a son instead of a daughter. For the first four years of his life, she kept him in dresses during the day and only put him in boys' clothing just before his father got home from work. I'd have to say that Daniel's mother definitely played a major role in his homosexual identity. Daniel wasn't receiving the love and attention he needed from his father, so he was willing to do what it took to get love and acceptance from his mother.

The first time his father happened to see him dressed as a girl, he didn't affirm Daniel's masculinity or encourage him to assume his rightful gender role. Instead, he started calling him "little girl" and "little princess," and persisted in cutting him down all the time. Up went more walls between them, further blocking Daniel from receiving any love this poor excuse-for-a-man may have been willing to offer. Even after the dressing-up had stopped, Daniel still identified more with his mother and he unconsciously picked up typically feminine characteristics and mannerisms through this identification.

I firmly believe that if Daniel's father had been more loving and sensitive Daniel's homosexual orientation wouldn't have occurred. If his father had encouraged him to be like other boys and simply affirmed the little boy Daniel was, Daniel's life would have been much different. His father had the power to override the mother's effects, but didn't exercise it. Remember, the roots of homosexuality lie in unmet same-sex needs—and that's where Daniel's father failed him. If he had affirmed Daniel's masculinity and allowed Daniel to identify with him, the confusion created by his mother could have been wiped out and replaced with a wholesome, proper sense of who and what Daniel was.

A friend who works at a preschool told me about one of her three-year-olds whom she thought might grow up to become homosexual. The parents were divorced and the mother had custody. The child was allowed to watch his mother get dressed every morning, putting on pantyhose and makeup, etc. Because the father wasn't around, the boy identified solely with his mother.

Since it's a natural part of the developmental process for children to imitate those around them, especially their parents, it shouldn't surprise you that while "playing house" at preschool, this child identified with the mother-figure and wanted to play only the mother role. He wanted to be the one who put on nylons and lipstick. When asked to play the father or son, he'd staunchly refuse. Even when highly encouraged, he wouldn't play any typical male role.

This isn't a child who wants to be a woman; he's just a boy who's over-identified with his mother out of a total lack of identification with his father. If his mother doesn't encourage his masculine behavior and make sure that there is a man who plays a father-figure role model in his life, he's stuck with identifying only with her.

The more he identifies with female behavior, the more inadequate he'll feel as a male. He'll start to feel more comfortable identifying with girls instead of with other boys. When he's given the opportunity to play with other boys, he may well choose to play with girls instead, further hindering his identification as a boy and preventing him from fulfilling his same-sex needs. If this process continues, it's almost a given that he'll grow into homosexuality.

My friend decided to inform the child's parents of her observations. The mother had been oblivious to what was going on, and merely thought the child's behavior was cute. Her response, therefore, encouraged his behavior. The father, on the other hand, seemed surprised that a three-year-old would need a father for anything other than paying the bills.

What incredible ignorance—but at least they didn't hesitate to ask my friend's advice. She suggested that when the mother was getting dressed, the child be given something to do—a diversionary task in another room. For the average child with a source of male affirmation, observing his opposite-sex parent going through these routines wouldn't pose a problem. In this case, however, the child needed to be separated from unwittingly over-identifying with the wrong parent. He should be praised for undertaking whatever task his mother sets for him as a diversion, and encouraged and rewarded for participating in typically masculine activities and roles.

The father was advised to become involved in his son's life, and to have the child stay with him as often as the parents could work it out. In the father's home setting, the boy could begin to become acquainted with his male parent, and by observation be provided with a new and appropriate role model to imitate. My friend likewise advised the father to encourage the child in boyish activities. But, most critical of all, he should work as hard as possible to develop a warm, loving relationship with his son. At last report, the father seemed to be making a sincere effort in that direction.

As cases like this show, heterosexuality isn't black or white. No one is 100 percent homosexual or heterosexual. I think the following statement from James Vander Zanden's book, *Human Development*, puts it very well:

> Most of the general public assumes that there are two kinds of people, heterosexuals and homosexuals. In reality, however, it is more accurate to view heterosexuality and homosexuality as poles on a continuum. Individuals show various degrees of preference, including bisexuality, in which both opposite and same-sex objects are about equally preferred.

Everything that comes our way has either a positive or negative influence. If a kid is reared in a warm, supportive environment, the odds are he'll grow up well-adjusted. If he's deprived of affection and emotional stability, his personality and identity will be adversely affected. In other words, the healthier your gender identity—the more your same-sex needs are fulfilled—the more heterosexual you are, and vice versa.

The strength of your attraction toward men *indicates how much you're lacking in homo-emotional fulfillment*. Homosexuality is only one emotional dysfunction that can arise from a weak masculine identity and needs left unmet from childhood. The behavior of rapists, child molesters, and wife beaters is also attributable to a deficit in same-sex needs and improper growth.

Wow, somehow it's gotten to be 3 a.m. and I have to be at work early, so I've gotta head for bed. Hope to hear from you soon.

Your bro,

Bud

Dear Mike,

Sorry I haven't written for so long—the last couple of weeks have been incredibly hectic. I've suddenly been presented with some new opportunities and making the decisions is requiring a lot of my time. The major one is that Ray's going to work for his dad in Hong Kong this summer and has asked me along! I'm sure I don't need to tell you that it's an awfully tempting offer. If it weren't for my book, I'd already be packed and waiting by the front door with my passport in hand.

Unfortunately, though, between one thing and another, the book project hasn't been shaping up as fast as I'd hoped. I have a ton of notes and Robert has been quite helpful at providing direction, but I haven't started writing yet. If I go away for the summer, I'm afraid I'll lose sight of the whole thing, so I'm praying about it.

Either way, if you want to see Hawaii while I'm here, you'd better get it together soon. Ray's parents have rented out the house for a year starting July 1, which means I've got to move regardless of whether I go to Hong Kong. Maybe I'll just return to southern California.

What a shame Eric has to go back to Chicago. No, I don't know of any ministries for homosexuals there, but he could write to: Exodus International, Box 2121, San Rafael, CA 94912, and request its nationwide list of recommended ministries. Since it is a nonprofit organization that survives on donations (just like Desert Stream), please suggest he include a couple of dollars to help cover expenses.

As to Eric's question about how and why I acquired a homosexual orientation and my brother didn't—even though we grew up in a similar environment and have the same father—there are a couple of reasons: environment growing up, and individual differences between us.

My brother was the firstborn; I was born 18 months later. My parents' relationship had changed a lot by the time I arrived. Also, my dad's work situation wasn't the same; there were different pressures affecting the household. For instance, he wasn't home as much.

My parents' attitude about having kids also changed between their firstborn and their second. My brother may have been planned and wanted, while I wasn't. Maybe my parents wanted a daughter for their second child and were disappointed.

I could speculate endlessly, but to what purpose? I guess my point is that our environments weren't exactly the same as it might first appear. So my brother was certainly treated differently from me, and those differences really reflected changes that had overtaken the whole family. I'm sure my parents weren't aware of treating us differently, but the point is that my brother's early environment was different from mine.

As to differences between individuals, Dr. Moberly has this to say:

> There is no reason to expect that all the children of the same parents will be affected in the same way. What we are speaking of is not a general similarity of environment, but specific difficulties in individual relationships.

A friend of mine, Randy, assumed a gay identity and his brother didn't. While Randy is sensitive, his brother is thick-skinned. When they were kids, Randy told me if his dad yelled at him he would cry. His brother on the other hand would just shrug his shoulders and disregard the rebuke. Randy was also poor in sports, and you guessed it, his brother was outstanding in most of them.

In hindsight Randy has discovered that his brother excelled in order to achieve his father's love and approval. While Randy detached from his father as a result of feeling rejected, his brother did everything to please his dad in order to achieve his attention, approval, and love, and he may have gained a better sense of acceptance as a result. His brother also found alternative ways to learn the basic elements of masculine gender role through peers and other adults that perhaps enabled him to relate more adequately to his father.

You have to remember that kids are different from one another, totally unlike the old saying about "peas in a pod." *The pre-homosexual child usually is more sensitive.* Problems in the home tend to be more upsetting to him—the pain more intense—and because of this he would feel rejection, hurt and inadequacy to a greater magnitude than his sibling. Again, it is important to remember that it's not necessarily how the environment was, but more importantly, how the boy *perceived* this environment.

Perception can definitely cause an emotional conclusion. The way I received, interpreted, and responded to things bore no resemblance to the way my brother did. I think the main difference between us was how we individually reacted to having an absent father. My brother had enough self-esteem to seek affirmation and identification from others, while my sense of being unlovable prevented me from doing that.

This brings up another point. Although my brother didn't acquire a homosexual identity, he still suffered some detrimental effects from our childhood. It seems to me that the way he treats his wife reflects the lack of a proper role model and it also reveals certain feelings of inadequacy as a male. Perhaps he never experienced homosexual desires, but his early environment has adversely affected the way he interacts with others nonetheless. Leanne Payne's book, *Crisis In Masculinity*, covers this subject in some detail if Eric's interested in delving further.

Now, on to something else Eric brought up. I don't fault him for his views about Christians. In fact, I agree with most of his observations. I've worried about how some straight Christians would respond to the book I'm trying to write. A great many Christians need to repent for their attitudes toward homosexuals, specifically their thinking that homosexual sin is the worse sin of all.

Sin is sin, period. As the Bible says, we've all sinned and fallen short of the glory of God. The only difference is that some sins bear greater consequences than others. God also doesn't hate the homosexual, but loves him just as much as He loves any other individual. Again, the Scriptures tell us that God isn't a respecter of persons. God hates sin, yes, but not the sinner—and there's an appreciable difference between the two.

I certainly don't believe AIDS is God's curse, judgment—or

whatever—against homosexuals. I think AIDS, for the homosexual, is simply the consequence of their actions, not God's wrath or judgement upon them. God gave us His supreme wisdom in His Word, for He knows what's best for us. Because He created us, He knows what effects upon the body result from unnatural acts, abuse, and promiscuity. That's why He provided us with limitations and restraints, so we might live a rich, abundant life. If we follow the Bible as our owner's manual, we'll achieve such a life, but if we go against His laws, there are definite consequences.

Speaking of owner's manual, I've got to get going. Ray and I are attending a Bible study/potluck dinner tonight. Write when you can—and how about seeing if you can make it over here soon?

Love,

Bud

Dear Mike,

Sure is great to hear you sounding so upbeat. I'm really happy for you and proud of your progress.

I really don't know what my job responsibilities would be in Hong Kong. Something in sales, although I don't think I'm going to take the job. I know the opportunity sounds like a once in a lifetime chance, but I have a few other options I'm looking into, one of which is my book. I really want to finish it. I'll keep you posted as to the decisions I make.

Now on to some things I've been thinking about. Mike, I really feel that I've got to warn you about something. Here in the early stages of your transformation, you're beginning to experience the joy of being accepted by your male peers. For the first time, you're allowing identification and affirmation to take place.

Even so, part of you will still feel a sense of inadequacy for a while until enough time has gone by to heal your old emotional scars. Though you're more open to identification with other males, you still have a residual sense of alienation. This results in a tendency—quite unconscious—to seek out friends with the same insecurities as you, such as Eric.

Now, don't fly off the handle, buddy. I can see the progress you're making, especially in the relationships you've described with Paul and Todd. The common mistake we all make, though, is that of taking the easy way out. We tend to attract friends who are just like us, or worse, whose problems are greater than our own. Continue to challenge yourself, Mike. Seek friends you admire and want to be like.

Another thing, it's not a good idea to tell everyone about your homosexual past. I understand this need to "come clean," to weed out mere acquaintances from prospective friends by letting them see you, warts and all. I had the same compulsion myself at first. You want people to know the real you, the things you feel and are going through. You want them to reassure you that everything's going to be okay and that you, yourself, are okay in their book. There's also a not-insignificant need to elicit tales of similar experiences. I'm sure you have other reasons of your own, as well.

When I first told Vern about my homosexuality, I was suicidal and without hope. Later he asked me to take his roommate, Bob, also a friend of mine, into my confidence as well. At first I wouldn't, but Vern explained that he wanted Bob to know so that they could pray together about my situation. After a while I finally agreed, and as it turned out, I wouldn't have wanted it any other way. Bob wound up calling me everyday, just as Vern was doing, and together they got me through the darkest part of the storm.

You, too, need someone to confide in, someone you can trust and open up to, someone who'll provide honest feedback. But keep it to just one or two people. Any more than that can be detrimental by interfering with the growth that needs to take place. People relax in front of those who know all about them and tend not to move out of old habits and ways of identifying. Conversations tend to linger on the past instead of providing you with opportunities to learn new ways of thinking and responding.

Let me give you an example. Since Vern knew about my past, whenever we talked together we'd invariably discuss my problems and struggles. Vern would cite the things he saw in me that seemed to reflect progress, and as far as it went, that was very encouraging and made me feel better.

On the other hand, coming from my friend Greg, who knew nothing of my past, the same sort of compliments meant a great deal more. Not that what Vern said didn't matter—it mattered tremendously. It's just that I wasn't able to receive it in its full capacity as I could with Greg.

Even though I knew Vern was being honest with me, I suspected him of saying those things to make me feel better. Though my suspicions weren't at all true, they were enough to unconsciously block the full extent of this affirmation for me.

With Greg, though, I could role-play. It was a chance to be anybody I wanted to be and fit right in. It made me feel free to say things I would have never said before, things that helped me to fit in better. Do you see my point about using new friendships to grow out of your past?

It was quite a lesson to me when I thought it all out. It taught me the importance of not taking everyone into my confidence. With Vern and Bob, I held myself back and didn't allow my newly emerging identity the same free rein because I felt they knew too much about me. At the same time, I learned the importance of having trustworthy friends and the value of bouncing ideas off other guys. Vern and Bob helped me to understand myself better by giving me a clearer picture of things. Their feedback and support kept me alive.

Find someone you can talk to openly, a reliable person who'll keep your confidence—and choose someone who's straight. Resist the inclination to pick someone with whom you might be able to relate, like Eric, because he might be able to relate only too well. Ask God to bring a stand-up gut-buddy into your life, and in the meantime, until He provides a friend nearby, remember you've always got me, anytime, day or night. I realize I'm a little far away, but there's healing in sharing. You hold a lot back, my friend, but you need to be set free from memories of the past and forgive yourself, as well as forgive others.

Don't ever forget that I care. I honestly love you and I'm still praying for you. Keep up the good work.

Your bro,

Bud

Sunday
May 18, 1986

Dear Mike,

Just got home from the travel agency and I'm so excited I can barely sit still to write. Tried calling you a couple of times yesterday and today both—are you ever there to answer the phone? I wanted to hear your reaction. You won't believe what's happening.

I'm going to Europe! Ray and I are going to travel around over there for six weeks before he goes to Hong Kong. I've been able to save some money this past year, and since I decided not to go to Hong Kong I thought, *Why not Europe?*

This isn't nearly as impulsive as it sounds, it's just wonderfully exciting. The people who were planning to rent the house decided they wanted to buy it instead and made Ray's dad an offer he couldn't refuse. When they stipulated that they wanted to move in June 1, before escrow closed, he agreed, leaving Ray and me with less than two weeks to pack up and get out.

Bummer, right? Ray's dad let us dangle in the wind wondering what in the world we were going to do. That lasted all of ten minutes and then he sprang his big surprise. He has to go to Frankfurt, Germany, on business and asked us to go along! He felt bad about our short moving notice so he's paying our fare from Hawaii to LA, where we'll stop over for a day, then from LA to Frankfurt.

Isn't this incredible? We'll be staying with Ray's parents in Frankfurt and Paris for the first week before we set out to discover Europe on our own. We're leaving here Wednesday, the 28th.

Everything is happening so fast, my head is spinning. It seems so weird to be dropping names like Paris and Frankfurt as if I had been doing it all my life. Did you know that my flight over here was the first time I'd ever been on a plane?

I'm really going to miss Hawaii. It feels more like home to me than any other place I've ever been. I've made so many good friends here, but who knows, maybe I'll be back. We're having a huge going-away party at the house over Memorial Day weekend, which I should

271

point out will be your last chance to see me here, so what do you think about joining us? Yes, of course I'm serious—why not do it?

Hey, thanks for the idea, buddy. It just might make for a good book at that, so it's sure a good thing you saved my letters. I really don't remember all that I've said over the past year. Can you do me a big favor and save them for me until I get back from Europe?

I've got to get on with my packing, or at least try to figure out what should be packed. Please write soon—it might be the last letter I'll get from you while I'm here. I love you, Mike. Take care and thanks again for the book idea.

Your buddy,

Bud

P.S.

I meant what I said about winging it over for the party.

Dear Mike,

Well, this is it—my last night in Hawaii. I'm full of mixed emotions. On one hand, I'm sad about leaving. On the other, I'm even more excited than I was the last time I wrote. By the time you get this, I'll be in Germany, but I don't think I'll really believe it until I'm actually there. It all still seems too good to be true.

Of course, it almost wasn't, because I nearly didn't apply for my passport in time. Wouldn't that have been something?! I can't stand to even think about it. Anyhow, I've got a backpack now, so I'll be sure to be recognized as a tourist wherever I am. I've got my Eurail pass ordered. Traveler's checks are next. In other words, I'm ready to go—I think.

Mike, if you're serious about your healing, and I know you are, get the books I've recommended. They're a MUST, believe me. The things I've discussed with you are just the foundation for you to build further learning on. From here on out, it's up to you. The best advice I can give you is this: learn as much as you can, apply yourself, and put what you've learned into practice. To that end, I'm enclosing a list I compiled when I was packing up my books, with all the titles and publishers' addresses, just in case you're embarrassed about getting them at a bookstore. (I got embarrassed too, you know!) I've probably left one or two out, but you could double-check the list against my letters when you're copying them.

This is a good basic, working library to have, Mike, because it will tell you in detail how to handle a lot of the problems you've encountered: controlling your sex drive; managing your emotions; escaping the past; overcoming bad habits, feelings of rejection, and loneliness; avoiding emotional dependency and narcissism; etc.

The books might set you back as much as $150, but isn't your life worth it? We're talking about your entire future here, buddy. You don't have to get them all at once, you know, just don't put it off any longer. You can also request your local library to carry these books. By any chance, did you write Regeneration Books for a free catalog?

Also, try to always bear in mind that homo-emotional needs aren't found just among homosexuals. The need for love, physical contact, physical affection, affirmation, acceptance, and so on, are common to all mankind. It's how the individual interprets his needs that determines his behavior.

Homosexuality is just one element of the human dilemma, a symptom of the identity crisis affecting most of humanity. We're all dysfunctional people—to one degree or another—who try to find our way in life around the terrible void that exists in each of us until it's filled by the love of Jesus Christ. Although everyone tries to fill that void in their own way—with sex, power, money, possessions, whatever—it can't be done. No one can truly experience contentment and peace until he welcomes our Savior into his life. Man's identity needs to be based on truth, not on the mores—social norms—established by other men. Jesus is our supreme example of maleness, of humanness, of life. It is Him we must identify with and strive to be like.

The Holy Spirit strengthens us and provides a fixed, never-changing standard against which to measure our progress. He gives us the means to live as God intended. Read your owner's manual daily, Mike, and learn how God desires you to live. Submit to His instructions and wisdom. Seek out the fellowship of other Christians by attending church and developing healthy friendships there, for you'll be much encouraged to continue growing in your life with Christ.

Dear little brother, I'm so very proud of you and the things you've accomplished during this past year. You've come a long, long way and surmounted a great many disheartening obstacles. Though you still have a way to go, I know you'll make it if you stick to your goals and never stop trying to learn as much as you can.

I love you, Mike, and I'll always be thankful for the past year and the opportunity of getting to know you better. No matter where I am in the world, you can count on me to be praying for you every day, so know that God not only hears you, but hears about you!

Carry on with what you've started, and God bless you, my friend. Your buddy always,

Bud

P.S.
I'll drop you a postcard from Europe!

*   *   *

MIKE'S AFTERWORD

"A good man, out of the good treasure of the heart, bringeth forth good things." (Matthew 12:35 KJV). Did I say earlier that I "happened" to run into Bud (Jeff) that fateful spring day back in '85? I'm positive that God set our paths to cross then, even though at the time I'd never given Him more than a passing thought—and then only in bitter scorn of His followers. In my opinion, the best of them were "airheads" and the rest were hypocrites who said one thing and did another.

I was really shaken that day by Bud's simple statement that it was necessary to allow God to help me. After I saw the changes in Bud, hope briefly flared up in me that he had the answers. The moment he mentioned God, however, our conversation was over as far as I was concerned. Bud, however, being the embodiment of the "good man" Jesus upheld to the Pharisees, was undaunted by my sullen indifference.

I didn't doubt his sincerity, but I was dealing with real-life problems. I wasn't interested in hearing how wonderful life could be by simply adjusting my attitude toward it. When Bud asked me if I would read what he had to say about changing his homosexual identity, I agreed, mainly to hasten our parting. When he asked if I would respond, I agreed again, thinking that—at the most—I'd scrawl a couple of lines on a postcard, toss it in the mail, and be done with it.

Of course, I didn't make any allowances for the mysterious ways in which God works His wonders. By the time Bud finally supplied me his address, the letters he sent hooked my interest. Just the enthusiastic self-confidence he had about relocating himself in a place he had never before been fascinated me. The Bud I knew would no more have been able to take such a step than I could. I wanted to know how he achieved this remarkable transformation.

Perhaps if he had realized the enormity of the undertaking, Bud wouldn't have put as much effort as he did into making sure that I grasped the information he was giving me. Naturally, I wanted the bottom line immediately: what one thing would I have to do, what single fact did I need to possess, if I were to decide to "go straight"? I went out of my way to stress the "if," just as I went out of my way to argue every point raised, particularly those that indicated there wasn't any *instant* cure.

I didn't care why I had become gay—if I hadn't been born that way, then someone had forced me in that direction. I was willing to blame everyone I had ever known, but I was *not* willing to scrutinize myself for responsibility. I was not going to give up the role of victim—the perfect alibi for drifting along, avoiding all accountability for my behavior. Never!

It's easy now to see that I was like a passenger on a sinking ship, one who hysterically refuses to open his eyes and jump into the waiting lifeboat. I maintained a white-knuckle grasp on the handrail of the doomed vessel. How sorry I felt for myself! How unfair that Bud should be waiting in that lifeboat, urging me to leap to safety as he had, when I couldn't swim if I missed it, and he could.

One can even take the allegory a step further and see this same pitiful passenger let go of the guard rail with one hand so that he could reach into his pocket for the pistol he carries as the ultimate solution to everything. He won't jump into the lifeboat and save himself—nor even make the attempt—but he'll gladly "triumph" over the realities of his situation by putting a bullet through his head!

When Bud first let me know what part the love and acceptance of Jesus Christ as his Savior had played in his recovery, I just wanted to die. I was already deep in utter hopelessness over my seeming inability to take the first step toward healing and my unwillingness to cut loose from any of my homosexual ties. I was shamefully scared by the mountains I would have to climb if I wanted to be free, afraid to acknowledge in my heart that I couldn't have things both ways. Because of all of these things, I perceived Bud's faith as yet another unfair difference between us. I couldn't handle any more strictures on my life; I had a bellyful already. Rules, rules, everywhere I looked, more hateful rules! These rules, I thought, were driving me crazy. Now Bud was telling me I would have to adapt myself to a whole new set of rules. I hated him for expecting me to humble myself, and I hated myself for being so weak that things had come to this point.

The night I found myself moved to ask God for His eternal love and shelter wasn't long in coming. In this, too, I see God's hand at work. Bud hadn't discussed his faith with me until I was so far down I didn't have the strength left to refute him and turn away. The chip I had been wearing on my shoulder crumbled into sawdust, leaving me without any of the illusions that I was somehow superior to everyone else.

In the moment before I turned to God, and acknowledged my belief in Jesus Christ as my Redeemer, I experienced the coldest, most shattering loneliness imaginable—for I was alone, nothing at all in the universe except a wretched, aching emptiness. In the moment after asking God into my life, well, as Bud had said, I experienced a peace that surpassed all understanding and spoken language.

The road to recovery bore scant resemblance to the formidable obstacle course I had perceived before. The mountains I had to climb seemed more like hills, and the rock-strewn valleys in between were no longer quite as deep or quite as wide. Sure, *it was a major struggle*— I won't deny that. But it was a struggle I no longer had to accomplish on my own. I had strength from above.

Of course, Bud was right about my slothfulness in getting started on my "homework." When he left Hawaii for Europe I finally felt compelled to get off my rear end and look into the reading material he had recommended to me. It was informative reading, and opened my eyes to a number of things about other people's behavior—as well as my own. They were things that I'm much better off for knowing and never would have known otherwise.

Bud was equally right about the first new friendship I sought to form in the aftermath of severing my emotional ties to the gay life and the identity I had there. I thank God for the practical suggestions and wisdom in Bud's letters, which is why I was so delighted that he accepted my suggestion about the format of his book. What he saw as an "overview" is much more than that, I think. It's a dynamic road map to recovery that any man who's known the curse of homosexual behavior can successfully utilize to find wholeness for himself.

I can see so clearly now through hindsight the process that produced my homosexual identity. Lacking a proper role model, feeling insecure and inadequate, I pulled away and became detached from my peers. As a result, I experienced a deficit in same-sex relationships and became a boy consumed with envy. Not understanding my feelings, I misinterpreted this obsession to look at other boys as meaning I must be gay. At least that's what all the books were telling me.

This is a lie. A lie out of ignorance, but a lie all the same. I simply misunderstood common feelings and normal, legitimate needs. Misreading these feelings and desires, and believing that individuals who experience certain feelings must be gay, I twisted and sexualized these feelings into a sexual problem. I became a victim of this lie.

A victim. But aren't we all a victim of our environment to some degree or another? Sure, I didn't have someone in my childhood to teach me, to guide me, or to love me. I should have had someone there to instill in me a good sense of self-worth, to build my self-esteem and self-image. When I was a child it would have been fantastic to have an ideal father who could have guided me through life. The fact is, however, we don't live in an ideal world. Life is not always fair.

Although I was a victim in a lot of ways, it was time to make a choice. I have chosen not to remain a victim any longer. As Bud so often stressed, I had to take responsibility—for the choices I made, for learning what my true needs were, and for doing the proper things to fulfill them.

I guess the greatest obstacle for me in entering this process was a fear of being let down after investing my heart, soul, mind, and spirit into it. Sure, all the things Bud told me made sense, but could they really work for *me?* Would my desires for men really change? Could I really be satisfied and happy as a heterosexual male?

I have discovered over the past few years that desires can change! They have for me! I no longer struggle with homosexual desires or feelings. I am attracted to women and have a wonderful relationship with a marvelous gal. Now don't get me wrong, I don't lust for women as some men do; that is not healthy behavior, either.

I believe that I'll get married someday, but even if I never do, the freedom I now experience from my compulsive homosexual behavior is awesome. I am happier today than I ever dreamed possible. For the first time in my life I actually like myself. I now know the feeling to be loved, and to experience acceptance and affirmation from other men. I am no longer an outsider. I'm one of the guys.

There are two questions people frequently ask me to "prove" to them that I am truly over my homosexual identity: "Have you had sex with a woman?" and "Did you enjoy it?" These individuals need to understand my problem wasn't with women. My problem was with men. Before I got involved in the homosexual lifestyle I did have sex with women. And I did enjoy it, to a point—but it did not satisfy my deepest longing. Something was still missing. The attraction for men remained.

I now realize my problem was not a sexual problem. My problem was a relational one. The solution to my problem was also relational. It wasn't until I fulfilled my same-sex needs in appropriate ways that I found the satisfaction and healing I was looking for.

The difference now is how I view myself and other men. When I see an attractive man it no longer has the same effect on me. Where I once desired homosexual activity, I now recognize a man for his attractiveness without sexual implications. Sure, I feel envious at times, but I know the source of this feeling. Envy no longer has such a hold on my life. The wonderful thing is that as I grow and become more of the man I was meant to be, the more I like myself. And the more I like myself, the less envious I am of others. I am discovering that I'm OK. And it feels great!

I can't tell you what my life is like today in any way that would be meaningful to you as strangers, but for those who remain suspended in homosexuality's limbo, just knowing that I exited should be convincing testimony that this is the road home. The door stands open—I hope you'll join us. You don't have to be gay!

Michael G. 1989

AUTHOR'S FINAL WORD

Did this book help you? If so, please let me know. In addition, through the course of reading you may have discovered things you disagree with or question. While I have devoted great effort to present the truth about the root causes of homosexuality and how one overcomes a homosexual orientation, I don't presume to have written with complete clarity or without flaw. *Although I won't be able to respond, I would be deeply indebted to those who are kind enough to share their concerns and insights with me.* Comments may be sent to Jeff Konrad in care of Pacific Publishing House. If suited, I will include those corrections and suggestions in a subsequent revision.

Believe it or not, I did not want to write this book. I fought this project from the start, dragging my heels the whole way. If you look behind me, you'll see the skid marks…deep and thick. But some-thing deep within urged me to write—to press on—to offer the comfort, hope, and transformation I have received. So I wrote.

I didn't want my family harassed or bothered by people as a result of this work. Therefore, to protect the privacy of my family and friends, some names have been substituted, including my own. Dates and circumstances of a few individuals have been changed as well; however, my experiences are factual, told as they really happened.

As a result of my research on this subject I have read some excellent books about homosexuality. Unfortunately, the titles of some of these books are so obscure (no mention of homosexuality in the title) that the average person on the street wouldn't know that such books existed. I realize the title of my book is rather bold. As a reader once commented, "It's sort of difficult to carry around a book with GAY emblazoned across its front and still retain any sort of anonymity."

I understand the awkwardness in purchasing a book with a title like this, even more, your fear of taking it home and having it around the house. It was either having to deal with this problem and the possibility of a relative or roommate discovering the book, or perhaps miss the potential reader altogether. I wanted all who were looking for such a book to be able to find the answers they were looking for, a title that declares the truth about homosexuality. And the fact is people don't have to be homosexual.

You Don't Have To Be Gay is based on actual letters to one person. However, in order to adequately cover the topic of homosexuality, the character Mike actually comprises three different individuals. Some circumstances took place with one "Mike," while others with a second or third "Mike." This approach not only protected the original "Mike," who wished to remain anonymous, but it also enabled me to explore other aspects of homosexuality that do not relate specifically to him.

As of this writing, August 2000: Michael #1 was married and had three children. I am very sad to say he died of A.I.D.S. a few years ago. "Mike #2" returned to the gay lifestyle for a time before returning to the recovery process. His primary problem, as he willingly admits, was that he didn't invest himself into the healing process. He didn't read recommended reading, and didn't follow through on things he knew he should have been doing. He remained a victim, hoping that someone else would do the work for him. After experiencing major fluctuations, Mike finally made a full commitment to the recovery process in 1991 and started applying the knowledge he had gained over the years. He is happily married and has two children. "Mike #3" made tremendous strides and embraced all the truth he could find. Five years later, Mike married his lovely bride Angie. In December 1999, Angie gave birth to a baby boy, Bennett Michael.

Usually the first question I'm asked is, "How long does it take?" I can't promise total transformation for anyone in six months, one year, two years, or even ten years from now. Yes, sexual reorientation is indeed a reality; however, the time required varies from person to person.

So many factors come into play. For example, how motivated are you? What are you willing to do to obtain this desired transformation? How much are you willing to invest in the process? What are you willing to give up? Are you going to aggressively engage in and grasp hold of the *process* rather than passively wait for the desired end product—the goal of heterosexuality?

Personally speaking, it took me approximately two years to comprehend the root causes of homosexuality and to completely sever my sexual and emotional ties with Brian. Nearly another year and a half passed before I reached a plateau where I was no longer sexually attracted to men nor did I yet have any desire for women. And it was still another two years before I grew into my true heterosexual identity with its subsequent attractions and desires for the opposite sex.

The second question people frequently ask me is whether I'm married. That's a natural question—probably one I myself would have asked to judge whether a person truly has been transformed or not. I am not married—yet—although I'm looking forward to it. I typically inform people that marriage isn't the standard to measure degrees of heterosexuality. Many gay men are married to women. What determines transformation is what takes place *inside* an individual. I once was sexually attracted to men; I'm not any longer. A person's inner perspective is what should be examined—marriage doesn't prove a thing.

I have personally known several gay men who were married to women. They thought marriage would "cure" them, or set them straight; it doesn't. But on the other hand, I know other men, previously gay, who dealt with their same-sex issues, had these needs met in appropriate ways, and married. These men are the best husbands and fathers I have ever known. They were fulfilled first as men among men—men appropriately identified with men—and then as men with women. This process is the proper sequence of growth and development.

Another question I'm frequently asked is "Have you had sex with a woman?" No, I have never been sexually involved with a woman. Before dealing with my same-sex issues I was not in the least sexually attracted to the opposite sex. Just thinking of having sex with a woman was a total turn off.

Unfortunately, my views of women and femininity were damaged as a child by the pornography my father had in the house. What I heard from my dad and what I saw in pornographic magazines contributed to my negative interpretation of women—they were merely a man's property for him to use in sexually obscene ways. As a child, I saw women in various demeaning positions and I was appalled; it disgusted me. I didn't think of women as ordinary people, but as individuals who wanted degrading sex.

As I grew older, I thought of girls only as sexual objects. Because I already felt inadequate in my masculinity, these feelings frightened me. I then blocked and/or suppressed my sexual feelings for women because my need for men was so much greater.

Now, however, I see women for who they are as persons and their sexuality is beautiful. I am very interested in and attracted to women. Indeed, now I find intimacy with a woman arousing—holding hands, walking arm in arm, caressed hands over the dinner table while talking at a fancy restaurant, hugging, etc. That doesn't mean heterosexual fantasies run rampant, but this new feeling gives me the assurance that I will not have problems responding sexually with my future wife.

I never dreamed I could feel this way. I would have been happy just to be free from the homosexual struggle. But this radical change in my view of women and my feelings toward them is incredible!

Of course, this did not happen over night. It was a *process* of getting in touch with the things that distorted my concept of women and femininity. I had to learn (and am still learning) normal, healthy, and proper ways of perceiving and responding to them.

I have dated over the years. I had high hopes for a deeper level of commitment with one particular woman, but it didn't work out. Strange perhaps, but for the first time I was hurt in a relationship with a woman instead of the other way around. I learned from this experience and am a better man as a result.

I am indeed a new person. *I am the man I always wanted to be.* I never dreamed that I could be this free and at peace with myself, my fellow man, and with God. I no longer have the feelings, desires, temptations, orientation, or identity of the past. The Lord has truly performed a dynamic transformation in my life.

It's even hard for me to believe the man I once was. With the major insecurities and inhibitions of the past gone, I am living the way I only dreamed life could be—with the ability to love and be loved, to receive proper affirmation and identification from other men, and to give it in return.

A proverb states: "Hope deferred makes the heart sick." I want to instill hope in those who think their homosexuality is permanent and hopeless. Some people say I shouldn't tell anyone that I have been set free. They fear I'm giving false hope to those who will try to change but will give up after a period of time if transformation hasn't occurred. Quite the contrary.

I will not minimize the power of my testimony. It is real and it offers hope. This hope may be the very catalyst that helps you to stick with the process long enough to acquire your own desired change. Years may pass, but if you are applying the things I have shared, reading the books and applying the material I recommended, you will see such fantastic growth and transformation in your life that you will want to continue in the process to obtain even more growth and freedom. You will have experienced the rewards of fulfilling same-sex needs to such a degree that you will never want to return to homosexual behavior. The whole proverb that I quoted part of above says: "Hope deferred makes the heart sick, *but desire fulfilled is a tree of life* " (Proverbs 13:12).

Finally, some of you have asked, "What is Jeff up to these days?" My heart's desire was to be a schoolteacher or work with youth in some way. So after working with ex-gay ministries for a number of years years, I returned to university for my teaching credentials. I have been teaching 5th grade in southern California for the past five years.

I would much rather spend my time and energy building up boys and girls to be healthy individuals instead of repairing them later in life. Homosexuality in our society could decrease if more children were properly loved and affirmed, and taught about same-sex needs. This would present them the viable option of healthy relationships— they wouldn't have to give in to immature feelings and desires simply because they are unaware of any other alternative.

To help spread the truth concerning the root causes of homosexuality and how one can overcome a homosexual orientation, would you please give a copy of this book to someone in need and/or to a local church, youth organization, library or school. The information

I share in this book is what I wish I had known when I was younger. If this information had been available for me when I was in my teens, I'm convinced I would not have acquired a homosexual orientation. How many more can be helped?

If you learn anything from this work, please pass it on. Affirm and love someone else. Let's make this world a healthier place to live.

Jeff (Bud) Konrad

If you need help or know someone who does,
please contact:

Exodus International North America
P.O. Box 77652
Seattle, WA 98177
Call (206) 784-7799
Exodus International will direct you
to a referral agency in your area.

RECOMMENDED READING

Desires in Conflict
Joe Dallas, Harvest House Publishers

Reparative Therapy of Male Homosexuality
Dr. Joseph Nicolosi, Jason Aronson Inc.

Homosexuality: A New Christian Ethic
Dr. Elizabeth R. Moberly, James Clarke & Co., Ltd.

Homosexuality: Laying the Axe to the Roots
Ed Hurst, edited by Robbi Kenney

Steps out of Homosexuality
Frank Worthen

Emotional Dependency
Lori Thorkelson-Rentzel, IVP

The Rejection Syndrome
Charles R. Solomon, Tyndale House Publishers

How to Say NO to a Stubborn Habit
Erwin W. Lutzer, Victor Books

Friendship
Jim Conway, Zondervan

Putting Away Childish Things
David A. Seamands, Victor Books

Your Inner Child of the Past
W. Hugh Missildine, M.D., Pocket Books

The Power of a Positive Self-Image
Dr. Clifford G. Baird, Victor Books

Psychogenesis: The Early Development of Gender Identity
Dr. Elizabeth R. Moberly, Routledge & Kegan Paul Limited

Living With Your Passions
Erwin W. Lutzer, Victor Books

Managing Your Emotions
Erwin W. Lutzer, Victor Books

Jealousy, Envy, Lust, The Weeds of Greed
Richard P. Walters, Pyranee Books

Pursuing Sexual Wholeness
Andrew Comiskey, Creation House

The Broken Image
Leanne Payne, Crossway

Homosexuality & Hope
A Psychologist Talks About Treatment and Change
Gerard van den Aardweg, Servant Books

Counseling the Homosexual
Michael R. Saia, Bethany House

Counseling and Homosexuality
Dr. Earl Wilson, Word

A Step Further, Vol. 1 & 2
Frank Worthen

For Women:

Out of Egypt: Leaving Lesbianism Behind
Jeanette T. Howard, Monarch

Long Road To Love
Darlene Bogle, Revell

To purchase many of these books confidentially by mail, write for a free book catalog:

Regeneration Books
P.O. Box 9830-K
Baltimore, MD 21284-9830

BIBLIOGRAPHY

May 27, 1985

* Dr. Reuben Fine, *Psychoanalytic Theory, Male and Female Homosexuality: Psychological Approaches* (New York, 1987), p. 84.

* Dr. Edmund Bergler, *Homosexuality: Disease or Way of Life?* (New York: Collier Books, 1962), p. 227.

* Drs. Irving and Toby Bieber, *Homosexuality: A Psychoanalytic Study* (New York: Basic Books, 1962), pp. 318-319.

* Drs. Irving and Toby Bieber, "Male Homosexuality," *Canadian Journal of Psychiatry,* Vol. 24, No. 5 (1979), p. 416.

* Dr. Lawrence Hatterer, *Changing Homosexuality in the Male* (New York: McGraw-Hill, 1970), p. 138.

* Tim LaHaye, *What Everyone Should Know About Homosexuality* (Wheaton: Tyndale House Publishers, 1980), pp. 62-63.

* Dr. Charles W. Socarides, "Homosexuality." *American Handbook of Psychiatry,* 2nd Ed., Vol. 3 (New York: Basic Books, 1974).

* James Vander Zanden, *Human Development* (New York: Alfred A. Knofe, Inc., 1978), p. 331.

* Albert Bandura, *Psychological Modeling: Conflicting Theories* (Chicago: Aldine-Atherton, 1971).

* Albert Bandura, *Aggression: A Social Learning Analysis* (Eaglewood Cliffs, NJ: Prentice-Hall, 1973), p. 332.

* L. Kohlberg, In Maccoby, E.E. (ed.), *The Development of Sex Differences* (Stanford, CA: Stanford University Press, 1966).

* L. Kohlberg and D.E. Ullian, In R.L. Friedman, R.N. Richart, and R.L. Vande Wiele (eds), *Sex Differences in Behavior* (New York: Wiley, 1974), p. 327.

* J. Money and Tucker, *Sexual Signatures: On Being a Man or a Women* (Boston: Little, Brown, 1975).

* John W. Money, "Sexual Dimorphism and Homosexual Gender Identity." In *Perspectives in Human Sexuality,* ed. Nathaniel W. Wagner (New York: Behavioral Publications, 1974), p. 67.

May 29, 1985

* Norman A. Sprinthall and W. Andrew Collins, *Adolescent Psychology* (New York: Random House, Inc., 1984), p. 244.

* Ibid., p. 245.

* P. Mussen and L. Distler, "Masculinity, Identity and Father-son Relation-

ships." *Journal of Abnormal and Social Psychology* 59(1959):350-356; P. Mussen and L. Distler, "Child Rearing Antecedents of Masculine Identity and Kindergarten Boys." *Child Development* 31(1960): 89-100.

*   E.M. Hetherington, "The Effects of Familial Variable on Sex-typing, on Parent-child Similarity, and on Imitation in Children." in *Minnesota Symposia on Child Psychology,* Vol.1, ed. Hill (Minneapolis: University of Minnesota Press,1969), pp. 82-107.

*   Hetherington, "Effects of Familial Variables," M. Johnson, "Sex role learning in the nuclear family." *Child Development* (1963), pp. 319-333.

*   Leanne Payne, *Crisis in Masculinity* (Westchester, Illinois: Crossway Books, 1985), p. 13.

*   Vander Zanden, *Human Development*, p. 334.

*   Lynn, D.B. *The Father: His Role in Child Development*, (Monterey, CA: Brooks/Cole, 1974).

*   Lynn, D.B., 1976. "Fathers and Sex Role Development." *Family Coordinator*, 25: 403-409.

*   Block, J.H. 1974. "Conceptions of Sex Role: Some cross-cultural and longitudinal perspectives," in Winch, R.F., and Spanier, B.B. (eds). *Selected Studies in Marriage and the Family*, 4th ed. New York: Holt, Rinehart and Winston.

*   Johnson, M.M. 1975 "Fathers, Mothers, and Sex Typing." *Sociological Inquiry*, 45: 15-26.

*   Ibid., p. 335.

*   Mussen, P.H., and Rutherford, E. 1963. "Parent-child Relations and Parental Personality in Relation to Young Children's Sex-role Preferences." *Child Development*, 34: 589-607.

*   R. W., Burnstein, E. Liberty, P.G., Jr., and Altucher, N. 1966. "Patterning of Parental Affection and Disciplinary Dominance as a Determinant of Guilt and Sex Typing." *Journal of Personality and Social Psychology*, 4: 456-463.

*   Hoffman, L.W. 1961 "The Father's Role in the Family and the Child Peer-group Adjustment." *Merrill-Palmer Quarterly*, 7: 97-105.

*   Hetherington, E.M. 1956. "A Developmental Study of the Effects of Sex of the Dominant Parent on Sex Role Preference, Identification, and Imitation in Children." *Journal of Personality and Social Psychology*, 2: 188-194.

*   Hetherington, E.M., and Franke, G. 1967. "Effects of Parental Dominance, Warmth, and Conflict on Imitation in Children." *Journal of Personality and Social Psychology*, 6: 119-125.

*   Elizabeth R. Moberly, *Homosexuality: A New Christian Ethic* (Cambridge, England: James Clarke and Co Ltd, 1983), p. 2. Used with permission.

*   Sprinthall and Collins, *Adolescent Psychology*, pp. 245-246.

*   E.M. Hetherington, "Effects of Paternal Absence on Sex-typed Behaviors in Negro and White Preadolescent Males," *Journal of Personality and Social Psychology* 4(1966): 87-91.

* H. Biller and R. Bahm, "Father-absence, Perceived Maternal Behavior and Masculinity of Self-concept Among Junior High School Boys," *Developmental Psychology* 4(1971): 178-181; E.M. Hetherington and J. Devr, "The Effects of Father Absence on Child Development," *Young Children* 26(1971): 233-248.
* Moberly, *Homosexuality: A New Christian Ethic*, p. 2.

June 6, 1985
* Moberly, *Homosexuality: A New Christian Ethic* , p. 9.
* Ibid., p. 5.
* Desert Stream Tape Series #4, p. 3. Used with permission.

June 24, 1985
* Moberly, *Homosexuality: A New Christian Ethic*, p. 18.
* Maxwell Maltz M.D., *Psycho-Cybernetics* (Englewood Cliffs, NJ, Prentice-Hall, Inc., 1960), p. 2.
* Moberly, p. 40.

July 2, 1985
* Gerard van den Aardweg, *Homosexuality & Hope: A Psychologist Talks About Treatment and Change* (Ann Arbor, MI, Servant Books, 1985), p. 53.

July 3, 1985
* Ed Hurst, *Homosexuality: Laying the Axe to the Roots* (St. Paul, MN: OUTPOST, Inc., 1980), p. 20.
* Payne, *Crisis in Masculinity*, p. 28.
* Hurst, pp. 20-21.
* Payne, p. 28.

July 13, 1985
* Moberly, *Homosexuality: A New Christian Ethic*, p. 19.

August 12, 1985
* *Overcoming Homosexuality* by Dr. Robert Kronemeyer © Copyright 1980 by Jessica Julian and Dr. Robert Kronemeyer. For further information, Dr. Robert Kronemeyer, 9 East 67th St., NYC, NY 10021
* Sprinthall and Collins, *Adolescent Psychology*, p. 322.

August 17, 1985
* Charles R. Solomon, *The Rejection Syndrome* (Wheaton, Illinois: Tyndale House Publisher Inc., 1983), pp. 82-83.

September 26, 1985

* Alan P. Bell and Martin S. Weinberg, *Homosexualities: A Study in Diversity Among Men and Women* (New York, Simon and Schuster, 1978), p. 308.

October 3, 1985

* Kronemeyer, *Overcoming Homosexuality*, pp. 4, 27, 30, 31, 32, 38, 40, 41, 45, 46.

December 26, 1985

* Lewis, C.S., *Mere Christianity* (New York: The Macmillan Company, 1947), as quoted from Josh McDowell, p. 108:

* Josh McDowell, *Evidence That Demands A Verdict*, pp. 108-109, ©1972, 1979 Campus Crusade for Christ, published by Here's Life Publishers. Used with permission.

January 8, 1986

* Moberly, *Homosexuality: A New Christian Ethic*, p. 41.

* Ibid., p. 31.

* Ibid., p. 40.

* Erwin W. Lutzer, *How to Say NO to a Stubborn Habit* (Wheaton, Illinois: Victor Books, 1983), p. 27.

* Ibid., p. 26.

* Taken from *Competent to Counsel* by Jay E. Adams. Copyright ©1970 by Jay E. Adams. Used by permission of Zondervan Publishing House.

February 6, 1986

* Kenneth G. Smith, *Learning to be a Man* (Downers Grove, Illinois Intervarsity Press: 1970).

February 10, 1986

* Lutzer, *How To Say NO To A Stubborn Habit*, pp. 76-77.

* Og Mandino, *The Greatest Miracle in the World* (New York: Bantam Books, 1975), pp. 24-25.

* Lutzer, pg. 78-79.

February 11, 1986

* Payne, *Crisis in Masculinity*, p. 14.

* Kronemeyer, *Overcoming Homosexuality*, p. 64.

* Michael Reese and Pamela Abramson, "One Family's Struggle," *Newsweek*, 13 January 1986, Volume CVII, No. 2, pp. 55-58.

* Frank Worthen, *Steps Out Of Homsexualtiy* (San Rafael,CA: Frank Worthen, 1984), pp. 9-10.

March 4, 1986
* Moberly, *Homosexuality: A new Christian Ethic*, p. 19.

March 14, 1986
* Desert Stream Tape Series #4, p. 3. Used with permission.
* Moberly, *Homosexuality: A new Christian Ethic*, p. 40.

March 25, 1986
* Lutzer, *How To Say NO To A Stubborn Habit*, p. 45.
* Ibid., p. 48.
* Maltz, *Psycho-Cybernetics*, p. XIX.
* Ibid., p. XX.
* Clifford G. Baird Ph.D., *The Power of a Positive Self-Image* (Victor Books: Wheaton, Illinois,1983), pg. 10-11,36-37.

March 26, 1986
* Baird, *The Power Of A Positive Self-Image*, p. 56.

April 9, 1986
* Desert Stream Tape Series #2, side one. Used with permission.

April 17, 1986
* Vander Zanden, *Human Development*, p. 568.

May 3, 1986
* Moberly, *Homosexuality: A new Christian Ethic*, p. 5.

****

* Scripture references:

(NIV) Taken from the HOLY BIBLE: NEW INTERNATIONAL VER-SION © 1978 by the New York International Bible Society, used by permission of Zondervan Bible Publishers.

(KJV) HOLY BIBLE: KING JAMES VERSION.

LETTER INDEX

POSSIBLE PROJECTS IN THE WORKS

Jeff Konrad is considering selling video tapes of seminars he has conducted. He is also thinking about offering *You Don't Have To Be Gay* on audio cassettes. Mr. Konrad, furthermore, is in the process of writing a book on how to deal with your thoughts, another book on masturbation, and a book specifically designed for teenage boys struggling with homosexual feelings.

Questions? Jeff Konrad is compiling questions for an upcoming book, *Questions and Answers For Overcoming Homosexuality*. Although he will not be able to respond to your questions personally, your questions might be included in this book.

If you are interested in any of these projects would you kindly send us a note stating so. We will pass this information on to Mr. Konrad as an added incentive to work on them. If you would like to be informed about the availability and status of these undertakings, please enclose your name and address, and we will send you a brochure/order form upon their completion.

Thank you,

Pacific Publishing House

ORDER FORM

Mail to:
Pacific Publishing House
Post Office Box 5809
Newport Beach, CA 92662

Send _____copies of, *You Don't Have To Be Gay*, to:

Please Print:

Name _____

Address _____

City_____State_____Zip Code_____

$ _____ $14.95 per book

$ _____   + Shipping cost: $4.00 for first book and $2.00 for
                        each additional book

$ _____   + California sales tax of 7.75% for books shipped to
                        California addresses only ($1.16 per book)

$ _____   Total cost

Enclosed is my check/money order in the amount of $_____.
Check/money order in U.S. Funds only
(Make checks payable to Pacific Publishing House)

Credit Card Orders via the Internet:
pacificpublishinghouse.com

*For discretion books are mailed in plain, unassuming,
heat-sealed protected packages.*